DECONSTRUCTION
A STUDENT GUIDE

Coop Himmelblau, The 'Open House', Malibu, California

Peter Eisenman, Wexner Center for the Visual Arts, Columbus, Ohio

International Union of Architects

Journal of Architectural Theory and Criticism

1 : 2 : 91

EDITOR: Jorge Glusberg PUBLISHER: Andreas Papadakis

DECONSTRUCTION

A STUDENT GUIDE

Bernard Tschumi, Glass Video Gallery, Gröningen

ACADEMY EDITIONS · LONDON

Editorial Note

The Editor and Publisher are grateful to the architects who have supplied illustrative material for this issue. Photographic credits as follows: back cover: Nacasa & Partners Inc; p2: Dan Olshavsky ARTOG; pp5, 16, 62: Hélène Binet; p6: photo courtesy Vitra; pp10, 68, 69: Andreas Papadakis; pp14, 15, 87: Edward Woodman; p75: Dick Frank; p78: line drawing courtesy Vitra; p80: Robert Oerleman; p81: Gerald Zugmann; p86: Hans Werlemann; p90: Van der Vlugt & Claus.

We would like to thank *Architecture d'Aujourd 'hui* magazine for allowing us to reproduce the text on Frank Gehry (p78) and *UMRISS* magazine for the reproduction of an edited version of an interview with Coop Himmelblau (pp82-83). Translation from Spanish of the Foreword by Rosie Bartlett.

Front cover: Bernard Tschumi and Jean-François Erhel, 'Art et Publicité' installation, Centre Pompidou, Paris; Back cover: Zaha Hadid, Moonsoon Restaurant, Sapporo.

1 : 2 : 91

EDITOR: Jorge Glusberg PUBLISHER: Andreas Papadakis

Edited by Jorge Glusberg at the CAYC (Centre of Art and Communication)
Foundation, Elpidio González 4070, (1407) Buenos Aires, Argentina.
Published on behalf of the International Union of Architects by
The Academy Group Limited, 42 Leinster Gardens, London W2 3AN
ISSN: 0953 220X

First published in Great Britain 1991 by Academy Editions
an imprint of the
ACADEMY GROUP LTD, 7, HOLLAND STREET, LONDON W8 4NA
ISBN: 1 85490 035 8 (UK)

Published in the United States of America by
ST MARTIN'S PRESS, 175, FIFTH AVENUE, NEW YORK 10010
ISBN: 0-312-06229-X (US)

Printed and bound in Singapore

CONTENTS

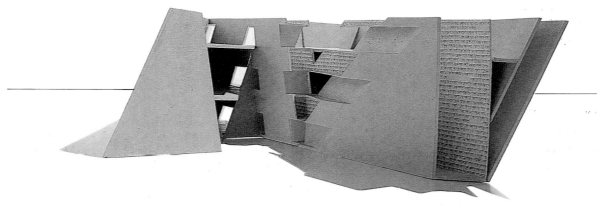

Daniel Libeskind, The Jewish Extension to the Berlin Museum

Geoffrey Broadbent
DECONSTRUCTION *A STUDENT GUIDE*

Frank Gehry, Vitra Design Museum, Weil am Rhein

FOREWORD
JORGE GLUSBERG

Deconstruction, if one can define it, is the substitute for this present-to-historic, anti-historic, and the essence of what is a transitory, fleeting contingent of a Post-Modern time and space.

Deconstruction (to denounce doctrines and to abolish standards), far from being a recipe or a standard, is usually seen as a scornful superficialisation of all fields of human creation and even of human life. It is neither a guide nor a puzzle, a school nor a code. It is a provocative method, aimed at discovery and discovering ourselves. Deconstruction has been theorised and exercised since 1967 by Jacques Derrida, its great exponent and practitioner, when he began to work out a way of representing it from its mimesis, which the same philosopher called *mimetology*. That is, the captivation of its representation through Logocentrism (metaphysics, which goes as far back as Plato to Heidegger and further still) according to what is written; and any type of inscription can only carry out secondary and subordinate functions as vehicles of speech, where meaning always precedes what is signified (precedence to what is purely intelligible with regard to what is merely tangible). It is the humbling of written words in the hands of speech which organises our symbols and concepts of meaning, thereby governing our notion of the truth.

Nevertheless, the general possibility of the written word lays the foundations for the possibilities of language itself. Derrida embarked (in *Of Grammatology*) upon reforming the concept of the written word, an archi-writing which logically precedes any opposition, destined to destroy – not to abolish but to surmount the written word by reintroducing it to its roots – all estimates of linguistics whose processes allowed it to evolve.

As a Post-Structuralist, Derrida believes that meaning and significance are not closely and identifiably related, but that, on the contrary, they continually separate themselves from each other and come together in other combinations. In the poetic, literary, artistic and architectural debate, no element may function as a sign without referring to another element which is not present. The result of this combination is that each element turns itself into a sign which combines other elements of the system. Each web is a text produced only by transforming one text from the others. Nothing, neither amongst the elements nor within the system, is now found to be either present or absent. Throughout, all that exist are *Différances*. (*Différance*: a neologism adopted by Derrida to describe both textual differentiation and its postponement and signs of signs of signs.)

The collage demonstrates these principles on the level of speech (Post-Modern speech). Its inherent heterogeneity (in poetry, literature, art and architecture) could neither be universal nor regular. Each quoted element breaks the continuity or linear pattern of speech and necessitates a second reading, that of the fragment perceived in relation to its original context and the same fragment incorporated into a new whole, a different entity.

Derrida insists that it is possible both to insert and to separate quotations as part of the whole structure of the sign. Any sign, linguistic or otherwise, may be quoted or placed between quotation marks; doing this may change the meaning of the given context completely, creating an infinity of new contexts in an unlimited manner. The insert ('writing means to insert') and the mimic (the text imitates the object studied) are two of the principal elements in Derrida's method of Deconstruction. Producers and consumers of texts (cultural objects), thus intervene to play a part in the elaboration of significance and meaning. This minimisation of the cultural producer's traditional hegemony creates opportunities for popular involvement and democratic decisions about cultural values at the cost, nevertheless, of a certain incoherence, or worse, of a certain vulnerability to massive manipulation. Anyway, the cultural producer creates primary materials (elements, fragments) and the consumer combines and recombines those fragments and elements. Thus, it is a question of breaking down the author's powers in order to impose meaning and to offer a continual narration; continuity, in the final instance is reduced to signs (signs of signs) that leave fragments which pass from production to consummation. There are no fixed systems of representation in the synthesis – only routes or paths of explanation. A reading (of a poem, picture, or building) assumes a permanent organisation – disorganisation – re-organisation – deconstruction. Any reading is, therefore, both possible and necessary.

If all cultural products are texts which intersect with each other, if those texts never finish by saying what they mean, if they don't mean what they say, then the facts of human life would be texts. Furthermore, each individual would be a text, a continuum of *différances* and signs, or a deconstructor that deconstructs itself.

Nevertheless, deconstruction does not provide us with analysis, techniques or methodology – instruments that one could apply in an authoritative manner, to be seen as valid objectives. The fact that they come from a preceding doctrinal body, outside of the work, or that they aim at universality, is not enough. Deconstruction estimates, according to Borges, that:

> The metaphysics of Tion? Do not seek the truth or verisimilitude, they aim to astonish. They consider that metaphysics is a branch of fictional literature. They realise that a system is nothing more than a subordination of every aspect of the universe into any one or other of them. Even the phrase 'all the aspects', can be rejected, as it supposes the impossible addition of present and past historic instances. The plural 'pasts' is justifiable, as it supposes once again surmounting the impossible . . . one of Tion's schools rejected time: reasoning that the present is undefined and that the future is not reality, but a present hope, that the past is only justified as a memory of the present (Tion, Ugbar, Orbivo, Tortivo, 1940).

Deconstruction developed a textual problem in ascertaining which element of truth limits fiction and which element of fiction limits truth. It tried to describe figurative, rhetorical articulations reversing established means of interpretation that made explicit what the author wanted to say, but did not say. The assumption is that they were subject to means of normalised intelligence and through this subjection to enforced models of universality. They disregarded observation of contradictions of language. Strictly speaking, it is man who is contradictory. It would be sensible to admit, paraphrasing Buffon, that language isn't a style, it is man himself.

Does a Deconstructionist architecture therefore exist? We can say that there are plans, as there are pictures and sculptures that are based on Deconstruction. Derrida himself sustained that Deconstructive architectural thought is impossible. Referring to Bernard Tschumi's designs for the Parc de la Villette in Paris (1985), Derrida departed from the bases of deconstruction by pointing out that, despite its appearance, Deconstruction is not an architectural metaphor, as it is not simply a question of dismantlement, but an affirmative, positive attitude. According to Derrida, the way in which architecture – places of habitat, the living space – is understood by philosophic and architectural thought, is evidence of logocentric thought. Yet, logocentrism, which can lead to Deconstruction through re-articula-tion of metaphysics, is centred on architecture, although transcending its marks.

Architectural thought, Derrida adds, 'can only be considered Deconstructive in the following sense: as an attempt at visualising that which establishes the authority linking architecture and philosophy'. Such an authority developed in the works of Aristotle, Descartes, Kant, Hegel, Heidegger *et al*, is the precise objective of Deconstruction.

For Derrida, architecture regulates everything that is called Western Culture, everything which of course transcends architectural practice. However if Deconstructionist architectural thought is possible, an affirmative, positive, metaphysical 'Transarchitecture' would also be possible. This global idea, evident in Derrida's assertions, can be seen in the *folies* that cover the Parc de la Villette.

Tschumi's primary interest will not now be to organise space as a function, in accordance with economic, aesthetic or techno-utilitarian ideals. These norms will be taken into consideration, but they would find themselves subordinated, rewritten in some part of a text or space, where in the final instance they would no longer govern. To take architecture to its limits, each *folie* would have a determined use, with cultural, scientific, philosophical and pedagogical purposes. (These buildings contain an art gallery, performance space, work shops etc.)

Tschumi, perhaps the architect most influenced by Derrida, believes that it is now necessary to abandon Post-Modern architectural notions in favour of a Post-humanist architectural idea, characterised by the dispersion of subject and decentralisation. He chose disjunction in the same sense, that must not, however, be considered as an architectural concept. It is a question of a systematic exploration of one of various themes, that of sequence and of superposition (Parc de la Villette). Such explorations are not carried out in the abstract, but in relation to the field of architecture, even through other cultural domains such as cinema and literature.

This disjunctive architecture has three common denominators, according to Tschumi:

1) Rejection of the notion of syntheses in favour of the notion of disassociation and disjunctive analysis.

2) Rejection of the traditional opposition between use and architectural form in favour of a superposition or juxtaposition of two terms that can be both independently and equally applied to the same methods of architectural analysis.

3) Emphasis on the methodological plan, on fragmentation, superposition and combination, which undoes a disassociating strength that extends itself to all architectural systems; and at the time of breaking free from its limits, it is given a new definition.

The idea of transferring or abolishing frontiers is repeated by Peter Eisenman, whose work Derrida has commented on, although this American architect is dubious when calling himself or being called Deconstructionist. For Eisenman, what propels this new method is an expansion further away from the limits of the classical model towards the realisation of architecture as an independent power, free from external duties, this is the intersection of what is significant, arbitrary, timeless and artificial. Philip Johnson, in 1988, presented the works and designs of Tschumi, Eisenman and five other architects, in the Museum of Modern Art in New York, under the title of 'Deconstructivist Architecture'. The title was dedicated to clearing up any misconceptions, to point out that the show did not indicate the presence of a new style, movement or creed, but that it was only presenting the existence of serious similarities in the seven architects' works.

In 1959, Johnson declared at The American Institute of Architects that Modern Architecture was dead and that its final product had been Mies van der Rohe's Seagram building in New York. Johnson saw the seven architects' works as a continuum of the Soviet Constructivist experiences of 1920-32. He contrasted the irregular images of Deconstructivist architecture with the regular images of International Style, a contrast of perfection and violent perfection.

The show's curator, Wigley, agreed with Johnson's thesis and developed and rounded it off by affirming that the seven architects had departed from the point arrived at by the Soviet Constructivists. The architects had transformed the Soviet Constructivists' initial ideas, had branched off from them; it is these transformations that the Deconstructivists are practising.

In short, everything indicates a Deconstructivist, or Deconstructionist, architecture. Not only does it come from a utopic Constructivist background (and as is known, a utopia is neither a chimera nor an illusion but a forward thinking plan, a hopeful anticipation). The Deconstructivist architect should stop being a decorator of life and become an organiser of life, creating a new concept of architectural space. Moreover, through Deconstruction, the architect has his programme, his tool, his means and a message.

Bernard Tschumi, Zentrum für Kunst und Medientechnologie, Karlsruhe

Bernard Tschumi, Parc de la Villette, Paris

THE ARCHITECTURE OF DECONSTRUCTION

Whatever else happened in 1988 it is remembered in architecture as the year Deconstruction was promoted. For example, Andreas Papadakis of Academy Editions in London held a Symposium at the Tate Gallery and published associated issues of the two magazines, *Architectural Design* and *Art and Design;* then there was an Exhibition at the Museum of Modern Art in New York on 'Deconstructivist Architecture' instigated by Philip Johnson and with a Catalogue by Mark Wigley. So what was it all about?

It was clear from pictures such as these that something strange was going on. What's more all those jagged shapes and fragmented forms suggested that 'Deconstruction' was quite a good name for it. But there seemed to be problems too. The word 'Deconstruction' was actually used in London whereas in New York Wigley wrote of 'Deconstructivism'. In London most of the speakers and writers assumed that the French philosopher Jacques Derrida was somehow involved; indeed, Academy showed a film of him being interviewed by Christopher Norris. Mark Wigley in New York, however, denied any connection with Derrida as did some of those he exhibited, such as Frank Gehry. Attempts to relate architecture, even this architecture, with esoteric philosophies seemed to them not only misleading but misguided.

This is an attempt, by an architect, to find out. There have been books before about 'Deconstruction' and architecture written largely by philosophers who assumed that, like other philosophers, their architect-readers would have enough background in philosophy to put the work of Derrida and his architect-associates into context. Most of us did not, which is why we found their writing not only difficult to read but obscure; much in fact like Derrida's own, which for reasons we shall be exploring, is notoriously 'difficult'.

Furthermore, it is clear that Derrida and his interpreters actually intend it to be difficult. It's meant to make us feel inadequate on the grounds that it will make them seem cleverer than we. It doesn't, of course. There's nothing easier for a specialist in any field than to blind those 'outside' with the complexities of his subject but, as we shall see, it's fundamental to Derrida's extraordinary view of the world that nothing has much meaning anyway. That's why he struggles so hard not to communicate with us.

But what are we talking about anyway? What, for heaven's sake, is this 'Deconstruction'? Insofar as anything *is* clear from Derrida's writings and what his interpreters write about him, he sees himself as a general scourge of that great tradition in philosophy known as 'Metaphysics' – to do with what it means to be, to exist – which started with the ancient Greeks and has continued, well into the 20th century, with the writings of Husserl and Heidegger; a tradition to which Derrida brings:

1) An attitude: an irreverent approach to the wisdom of the ages, the things which most people take for granted, and
2) Working methods: his clever use of language, puns, alliterations and so on which can at times be fun to read.

The crucial question, of course, is what relevance, if any, can this most complex – even wilfully obscure – of philosophies conceivably have for architects and architecture? How can this intense intellectualising have anything to offer the most practical, the most pragmatic art of all and its exponents: architects? What, really, is the point of struggling with all this if there's nothing much solid there to start with? Because in his desperately clumsy way Derrida has stumbled on a truth or two. Because these actually throw a little light on to problems which beset us all; because certain architects, especially Bernard Tschumi and Peter Eisenman, have drawn directly on Derrida for some of their more remarkable ideas, and because others, quite oblivious to Derrida, have had very similar thoughts and done very similar things without even knowing there was a Derrida connection. These all seem to me good reasons for pursuing what is, at times, difficult stuff. But the ultimate reason, I suppose, is George Mallory's for climbing Mount Everest: 'Because it is there'. Deconstructionist architecture is there; there's a lot of it about and there's more to come. Neither blind acceptance nor blind rejection seems to be a very healthy view. So the book is offered in the hope that it may aid the reader in making up his or her own mind.

Peter Eisenman, Bio-Centrum, Frankfurt

Deconstruction in Architecture

Whilst 1988 was the year in which Deconstruction was promoted, architects had been working towards it for some time. It was clear by the early 1980s that something new was happening. Very different architects, in very different places, seemed to be placing buildings and bits of buildings at odd angles so that they clashed and even penetrated each other. They made immensely complicated drawings and models, sometimes so packed with detail that you could hardly see the building for the drawing. It all seemed, to say the least, unsettled and unsettling – if not confused and confusing. There were rumours even then that this strange French philosopher Jacques Derrida was involved and if you started trying to read his books confusion got even more confounded!

But let's look first at the architecture that was beginning to emerge. The kind of work I have in mind includes Richard Meier's Museum fur Kunsthandwerk in Frankfurt (designed in 1979), his High Museum for Atlanta, Georgia (1980), Eisenman and Robertson's Housing Block 5, just outside Checkpoint Charlie in Berlin (1981), their Center for the Visual Arts at Ohio State University (1982), Zaha Hadid's scheme for the Peak in Hong Kong (1982-3) and Bernard Tschumi's Parc de la Villette in north east Paris (also 1982-3).

In each of these designs some kind of geometry had been set up and then at least one other superimposed to clash with it. In Frankfurt, for instance, Meier wrapped the three main pavilions of his new Museum around the existing Villa Metzler in an L-shape. But the Villa is not parallel to the road, so Meier set up a second geometry of corridors, ramps and courtyards square to the road but tilted at 10 degrees to the Villa and therefore to the rest of his own design. His Atlanta Museum has an atrium – a quarter Guggenheim – enclosed by an L-shape of galleries. This atrium radiates from the internal corner of the L and one ascends the five storeys by means of ramps. Externally also a (straight) ramp from the road crashes into the atrium at an angle of some 40 degrees to the galleries whilst within, balconies radiate from the central point at several different angles. The High Museum is notable too, in the light of future developments, for the clearly 'Constructivist' flavour of the external beams and columns of the central atrium, not to mention the forms of the railings, windows and other details.

Eisenman and Roberston had quite different motives for their first uses of equally disparate angles. Their Apartments for Check-

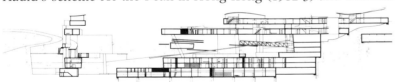

Zaha Hadid, The Peak, Hong Kong

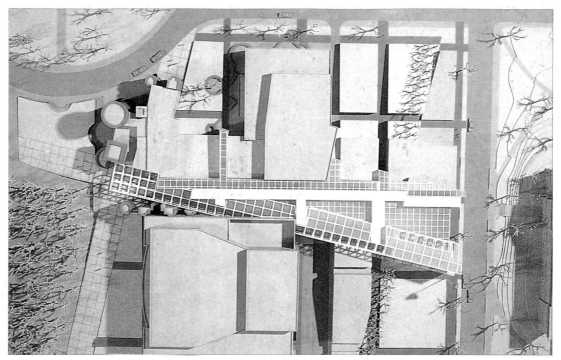

Peter Eisenman, Wexner Center for the Visual Arts, Columbus, Ohio

point Charlie lie immediately west of the Berlin Wall, the desperate implications of which at the time were by no means lost on them. So they planned not just the Apartments but an entire city block right up against the Wall, including existing buildings, around which they envisaged a highly symbolic park, dug deep into the ground – 'The City of Excavations'. They hoped to find real foundations there from Berlin's past but they also 'constructed' an imaginary history for the site which Eisenman describes (quoted Doubilet PA 4/1987):

> Working downward; the grid discovers . . . the trace of the absent wall of the eighteenth century. This invisible wall is plotted . . . as a shadow. Next (come) . . . foundation walls of nineteenth-century Berlin – not the actual, walls . . . but an artificial reconstruction, a hypothetical reconstruction of what . . . might have been. These walls derive . . . from the three existing buildings which, taken together, provide the fragments of a former grid.

Elsewhere Eisenman likens a site with various layers of this kind to a 'palimpsest' – a favourite conceit of Derrida's – which, according to the Oxford English Dictionary, is a parchment on which an earlier manuscript has been erased to make a 'clean' surface for a new one.

Thus, an ancient Greek text may be overlaid by a Christian one. Eisenman's 'former' grid conforms to the part of Berlin laid out for Frederick the Great in the 17th and 18th Centuries as the Friedrichstadt, with the Friedrichstrasse as its main central axis (see Leatherbarrow, 1983). Checkpoint Charlie, literally, cuts the Friedrichstrasse. So far only the Apartments have been built incorporating, at ground level, the Museum of the Berlin Wall. At first sight, Eisenman has simply enlarged the kind of complex, three-dimensional grid geometry which he had used so often in his early houses. His aim at that time had been an architecture of pure 'syntax' with no 'semantic' references of the kind which we call, loosely, 'meaning'. So Eisenman had used geometric rules derived from those which, according to Noam Chomsky (1956), we humans apply subconsciously whenever we formulate and speak or write a sentence (see Eisenman 1973, Gandelsonas and Morton 1972).

Chomsky had argued (1956) that these rules are of two kinds: generative – by which we formulate our basic sentences; and transformational – by which we convert them into active, passive, negative, questioning or other forms. Of course there is much more to it than that, but there are two crucial points here: one, that

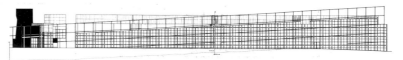

Peter Eisenman, Wexner Center for the Visual Arts, Columbus, Ohio

Zaha Hadid, The Peak, Hong Kong

Eisenman was trying to create an architecture of pure geometric syntax with no semantic 'meaning' at all; and two, that he drew on Chomsky to give his work a certain 'intellectual' stiffening (see Evans 1985). Clearly he did not feel it sufficient to stand alone *as architecture*.

So the Friedrichstrasse/Kochstrasse Apartments represent typical Eisenman three-dimensional grids writ large conforming, in plan, to the Friedrichstadt grid. Eisenman's eight-storey facade to the Kochstrasse is covered by a grid of small squares which determine not only the joints to the grey cladding tiles but also the pattern of the glazing bars. But at its Friedrichstrasse, Checkpoint Charlie, end this facade is broken into by a six-storey block *embedded* by about half a bay. And the 'embedded' block tilts outwards along the Kochstrasse to project by about half a bay at the far end.

It is clad with quite a different system of grids: large white squares, two storeys high and two bays wide interlocking, tartan-like, with dark grey squares and by a still larger grid of red lines – so large that the squares are never completed! Then one sees that on plan Eisenman has two square grids, red and white, covering both park and buildings; furthermore, these grids clash at 3.3 degrees. Eisenman explains this by suggesting that much of Berlin's tragic history was played out on the Friedrichstadt grid: the appalling horrors of the Nazi regime – Hitler's Bunker was just over the Wall to the east – and the rupture of East Berlin from West; both of which enormities he wished to challenge.

He felt that he could do so by imposing another grid on to that of Friedrichstadt choosing, for this purpose, the thoroughly humanist grid of Mercator's map projection 'upon which so much Enlightenment history has been acted out'. The Friedrichstadt grid departs from Mercator's 'neutral and artificial' one by 3.3 degrees. So Eisenman's Friedrichstadt Block encloses his Mercator Block and the two are distinguished from each other by differences of alignment, of facade treatment and so on. Thus Eisenman makes extraordinary use of pure, geometric syntaxes to give his Apartments 'semantic' meaning which you can't read directly from the forms – in fact you can only 'read' them after you have perused Eisenman's explanation!

There is an equally site-derived geometry in the now built Center for the Visual Arts at Ohio State University which Eisenman

Bernard Tschumi, Parc de la Villette, Paris

Zaha Hadid, The Peak, Hong Kong

and Robertson designed in 1982-3 (see Arnell and Bickford 1984). Like Berlin, the City of Columbus, Ohio, has a grid, but the University Campus has another, shifted from that of the city by some 12.5 degrees. So Eisenman and Robertson took an axis from the Columbus grid and projected it into and across the campus, marking the entrance to their Center with a 'frontispiece', the partial rebuilding, in concrete, of an old brick armoury which had stood on the site. So once again history is evoked – this time by direct, visual likeness – to give 'meaning' to the concept. A long, glazed 'spine' runs north from this 'armory', perpendicular to the new axis and between the existing Mershon Auditorium and Weigel Hall which of course conform to the University grid. This leaves a long, thin, triangular space west of the 'spine' towards Weigel Hall, on which the (tapering) galleries are built. Whilst the Frankfurt, Atlanta and Berlin schemes all have clashing angles in plan, there are clashing angles in section too at Columbus where, for instance, the roof of the spine, which slopes along its length, is penetrated by service 'bars' – all at the same level – under, across and over it according to where they occur on plan.

Such three-dimensional clashes were carried very much further by Zaha Hadid in her scheme for the Hong Kong Peak (1982). She planned to excavate and rebuild the landscape to form 'a man-made polished granite mountain' of vast, abstract, geometric forms. Then she thrust four enormous 'beams' horizontally into this man-made part of the mountain. The lowest, buried partly in the ground, contains two-storey, glass-fronted studio apartments, as does the second which rests partly on the first but skewed from it at an angle of some 30 degrees. Each 'beam' has traces in its internal planning of the angle of the other.

There is a void, some 13 metres high, over the second beam and under the third, which marks the transition from apartments to a club, the facilities of which include a long, narrow swimming pool skewed at 15 degrees from the second beam and spanning back into the mountain. At this level the man-made landscape contains squash courts, a health club and, above these, a cocktail bar. Other elements, such as entrance decks, circulation areas, a snack bar and a library, hover suspended in the void between the second and third 'beams'. Internally a ramp leads from the lobby to the club facilities within the mountain, whilst externally a long S-curved ramp, for cars and pedestrians, swings dramatically up from the road, across

Bernard Tschumi, Parc de la Villette, Paris

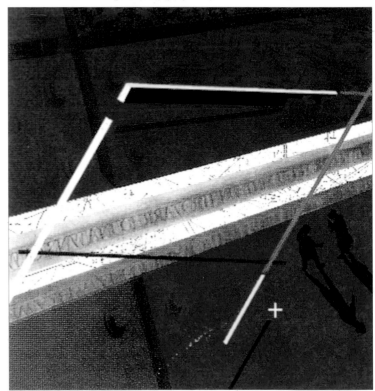

Daniel Libeskind, City Edge, Berlin

the main deck, round to the mountain where there is parking, and back to the road again.

The third beam, supported on columns over the void, has four penthouse apartments distributed along its length with roof terraces over which, after a 2.7 metre gap, there is the fourth 'beam' almost parallel to the third. It contains the owner's apartment with a lavish dining room, an even larger living room and a private swimming pool. In drawing after drawing, in the Hong Kong context, the Peak itself, the artificial mountain, the 'gathering together' of the 'beams', one sees apparently random forces at work, chance juxtapositions on to which Zaha Hadid somehow has imposed an exceedingly complex kind of order.

Chance, too, played its part in the way Bernard Tschumi designed his Parc de la Villette. Indeed he describes his chance procedures in some detail.

Before exploring what he did, however, we ought to note – and it is no coincidence – that Tschumi was teaching at the Architectural Association in London, from 1970 to 1979, where Hadid was a student from 1972 to 1977. Hadid's more sympathetic tutors included Leon Krier, Elias Zenghelis and Rem Koolhaas. What's more, Koolhaas went to Moscow to seek out the work of Leonidov, one of the great unbuilt Constructivists, an enthusiasm for whom he passed on to Hadid. As Alvin Boyarsky points out (1986), other influential figures also around at the time included: Peter Wilson, Dalibor Vasely, Cedric Price, Peter Cook and Nigel Coates.

Tschumi won the competition for La Villette in 1982. His site is bound to the north by Fainsilber's vast City of Science and Industry (1976) built into the steel frame of an aborted abattoir building. South of that there is Fainsilber's shining spherical Geode (a cinema); south and west of that again is Baltard's mid-19th century cast-iron-and-glass Cattle Market, converted by Fainsilber into a Grand Hall. Whilst Eisenman simply uses clashing grids, Tschumi uses clashing geometric systems. He laid a 120-metre grid across the site some eight squares from north to south and five from east to west. Tschumi saw this as a system of points and at every point of intersection, except where it would be inside one of the grander buildings, he places a 'folie' – a notional 10 metre cube. He has Eisenman-like rules, although more complex, for developing these 'folies' in various ways. Some of these ways, as we shall see, take their inspiration from Russian Constructivism; indeed Tschumi proposes to reconstruct, as one of them, a replica of the Pavilion which Melnikov – a Constructivist if ever there was one – built for the Paris Exposition of 1927.

Between and around his folies, Tschumi designed a multiplicity of paths to soar and swoop, some of them rigidly geometric and others taking very free forms. The paths, collectively, afford a *promenade cinématique* of a kind he had exhibited and described in his *Manhattan Transcripts* over and around 'thematic' gardens to be designed by Tschumi and others. He sees these walkways as presenting a system of 'lines'. Underneath all this, at ground level,

he laid a basic, geometric system: a square enclosing the City of Science, a circle south of this and, south again, a triangle which also lies east of the Great Hall. Tschumi sees these geometric forms as presenting a system of planes or 'surfaces'. Point, Line and Plane, of course, were basic Bauhaus exercises whilst the square, the circle and the triangle have ancient, mystic connotations going back to Classical Greece and even the foundations of Buddhism.

Tschumi's Parc is the superimposition of three quite different ordering systems: of points, of lines and of surfaces. Each is 'perfect' within itself but as they are overlaid, so they interact. Sometimes they clash and interfere with each other, the one is distorted against the other; sometimes they meet and match and thus the one is reinforced by the other and sometimes they merely co-exist, indifferent, as it were, to each other. Mark Wigley writes in his Catalogue (1988):

> The result is a series of ambiguous intersections between systems . . . in which the status of ideal forms and traditional composition is challenged. Ideas of purity, perfection, and order, become sources of impurity, imperfection, and disorder.

So Tschumi's 'layers' interact, as moiré patterns interact, when two or more systems of lines or grids are superimposed, or as in, the work of Bridget Riley or Victor Vasarely, the systems specifically interfere with one another. It's important for Wigley that Tschumi set up pure geometric systems and then force them to interfere with each other thus forming 'hybrid' distortions of some kind, since such distortions of once 'pure' forms is fundamental to Wigley's concept of 'Deconstructivism'.

So what is there in my descriptions so far, of work by Meier, Eisenman, Hadid and Tschumi to suggest that by 1988 a clear, coherent and consistent new form of architecture had emerged: 'Deconstruction', a new paradigm that marked as Bruno Zevi supposed (1988): 'the end of Post-Modernism, of Neo-Neo-Classical academy and of Eclectic escape'? Quite frankly, nothing very much!

The Meiers and the Eisenmans have clashing angles in common if only in plan. Eisenman and Hadid have clashing 'beams' in three-dimensions, whilst Tschumi has clashing geometric systems. Meier and Tschumi make Constructivist references, or even quotations, and that's about all in purely architectural terms.

All of which could have been described in Robert Venturi's memorable title, from 1966, as *Complexity and Contradiction*! Indeed, Venturi shows in his book clashes of very many kinds: historic and modern, clashes in plan, clashes in section or elevation and clashes in three dimensions. There are clashing angles, naturally, in many of the Baroque Plans he shows, for example, Bernini's for the Piazza to Saint Peter's in Rome, not to mention Michelangelo's Campidoglio. There are clashes between Vignola's Villa Lante and the town in which it stands, Bagnaia, as well as clashes within Viattone's S Chiari in Bari and so on. There are site-determined clashes within Soane's Bank of England, although a

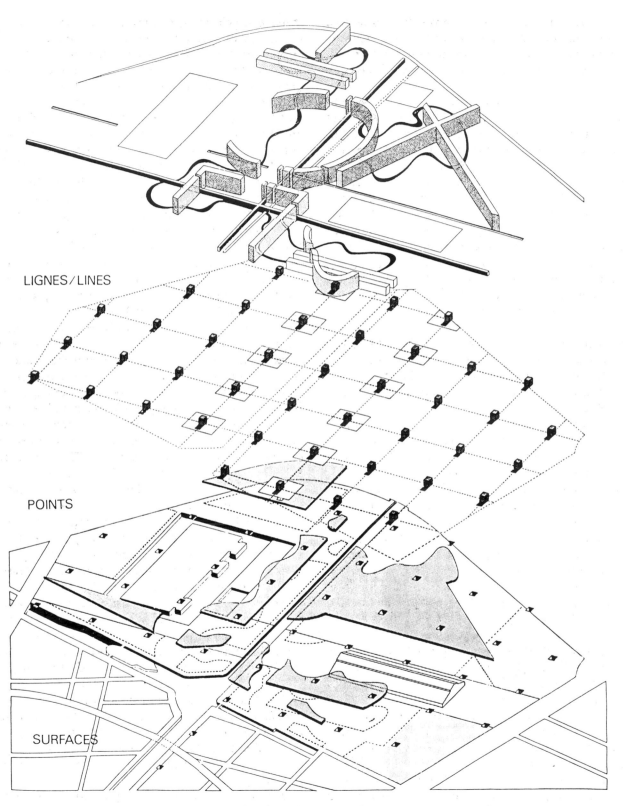

LIGNES / LINES

POINTS

SURFACES

Bernard Tschumi, Parc de la Villette, Paris

multiplicity of small and not-so-small rooms gives the whole plan an autonomous unity that others may have sought to achieve by symmetry, balance or some other conventional ordering device of the kind which Rob Krier describes so compulsively in his *Architectural Composition* (1988).

There are clashing angles, too, in the plans of many Alvar Aalto buildings: the Baker House Dormitories at MIT, the Apartment Building: in Bremen and so on. As for clashes in section, Venturi points out that you get them with Gothic flying and other buttresses. You get them, inevitably, every time you put a ramp within a rectangular frame – as Le Corbusier did in the Villa Savoye – which, with its U-shaped ground floor plan-within-a-square is a classic example, for Venturi, of *Complexity and Contradiction*. There are three-dimensional clashes in the Baroque and Rococo Churches which take up so much of Venturi's book and also in several of the Aalto buildings he shows: the Cultural Centre in Wolfsburg, the Church near Imatra and Aalto's own Studio at Munkkiniemi. He shows even more exaggerated clashes in Michelucci's Church on the Autrostrada near Florence and Scharoun's Philharmonie in Berlin.

So there wasn't much new about clashes and, indeed, by 1986 L M Farrelly had published in *The Architectural Review* a much more comprehensive, if thinner, catalogue of such things that Wigley was to do. She saw them as forming an emergent 'tendency' which she called: 'The New Spirit'.

Farrelly opens with an uncompromising statement: 'Post-Modernism is dead'. By this she means the 'small scale, the complex, the vernacular, the historical, the decorative, the popular' of Schumacher, Venturi and others. Their work had been 'ousted' and so had Post-Modern Classicism which she saw as the architecture of 'death merchants' who had contributed 'absolutely nothing' to the development of architecture. All of which seem in retrospect rather hasty judgements, for the spirit of Schumacher has grown with the Greens and apart from many journals in many parts of the world, Farrelly's 'death merchants' have published some 30 monographs on 'Post-Modern Classicists' of various persuasions and major books by Charles Jencks (1987) and Robert Stern (1988). Venturi, as we shall see, anticipates much that is in Derrida or his 'translators' into architecture.

But for Farrelly's 'New Spirit' to mean very much, such things had to have died. She saw her 'Spirit' as concerned with 'openness and honesty' with 'the thrusting, dynamic imagery of Constructivism and . . . Futurism's savage beauty'. Above all she saw it as a Dada 'state of mind' out of which 'Surrealism, arte povera, Pop Art, Action Painting, Conceptual Sculpture, Performance Art, 60s "Happenings", the Situationists and Punk, New Wave' were all generated. The architects of Farrelly's 'New Spirit' seem to have been essentially backward-looking, although she sees their 'state of mind' as 'a resurgent spirit of enquiry, a renewed interest in space and movement, in the use of real materials – steel, concrete, timber, stone, even plastic, appearing as itself – in a stripping-back towards the essentials of architecture and, most important, the dynamism of asymmetry, the very genesis of freedom'.

I say 'backward-looking' because this 'Spirit' had an extraordinary number of ancestors. Farrelly illustrates no less than 72, ranging from Leonardo da Vinci to Picasso, from James Watt, Brunel and Babbage – not to mention Buckminster Fuller – to Paul Klee and Kurt Schwitters. She shows the work of obvious architect-heroes, such as Le Corbusier, Oscar Niemeyer, Jean Prouvé and (no less than three times) Ray and Charles Eames. Also not-so-obvious heroes as Darbourn and Darke, Powell and Moya, Lucien Kroll and squatter house-builders from Chile and Finland. She shows 60s exponents of High-Tech, such as Archigram and Cedric Price, and more recent ones such as Piano and Rogers of the Centre Pompidou, Michael Hopkins and Richard Rogers of Lloyd's.

Farrelly's major 'shareholders', however, are the Russian Constructivists including El Lissitzky, Melnikov, Popova, Rodchenko and the Vesnin brothers. But if these are the precursors, who are the exponents of Farrelly's 'New Spirit'? Not only Moser and Goodwin, Honold and Pöschl, Neville Brody, Hacksaw, Zambia, Kevin Rowe Botham, Rambali, Leplastrier, Eduard Samso, Alfredo Vidal, but also Frank Gehry, Zaha Hadid, Daniel Libeskind and above all Coop Himmelblau. Insofar as, the works she shows have common elements, these tend to be linear: skeletons or cages of metal rods and strips crossing at clashing angles in plan, section and elevation, floors, partitions, ceilings or other space dividers consisting, as necessary, of thin plates in metal, timber or even concrete. These, too, meet or cross at clashing angles. The crucial point for her is a latter-day Dadaism: 'strange, wilful, even at times subversive' but also, so Farrelly says, 'unfailingly vigorous, exploratory . . . very much an architecture of now'.

Clearly Farrelly was on to something, but her 'New Spirit' hasn't stuck. It is interesting to conjecture why. In the late 1970s when her 'death merchants' were emerging, C Ray Smith called their work 'Supermannerism', Vincent Scully called it 'The Shingle Style Today' and Charles Jencks called it 'Post-Modern Architecture'. 'A strange name indeed, and at the very Academy Forum where Jencks' book was launched, Robert Stern and I found his title quite meaningless – 'Modern' is now and you can't get 'Post' that in any way. So we spoke instead of 'Post-Functionalism'. Yet 'Post-Modern' rang true and Jencks' title caught on; it even made Time magazine, because it captured the spirit of an age. We know from Jencks' explanation (1986) that he found it in literary criticism, in the writings of Leslie Fiedler and Ihab Hassan, critics of the 'Beat Generation', of student revolution and Buckminster Fuller's 'Hi-Tech'. Jencks' 'Post-Modern' had nothing to do with theirs, which his usage usurped, and now in any field, including literature, most critics use 'Post-Modern' in Jencks' sense.

Farrelly's 'New Spirit' never quite caught on but 'Deconstruction' did – pure or corrupted as 'Deconstructivism' – and it may be that in

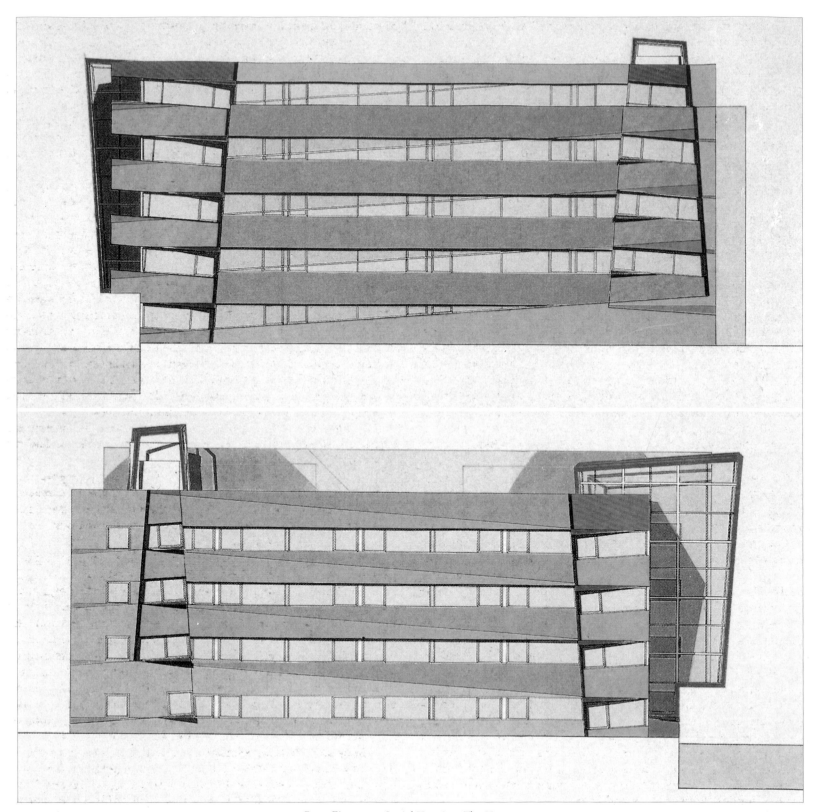

Peter Eisenman, Social Housing, The Hague

time architectural uses will usurp Derrida's to define 'Deconstruction' as a wider cultural enterprise!

But what was common to Farrelly's 'New Spirit', Academy's 'Deconstruction' and Wigley's 'Deconstructivism'? Meier was ignored by all three; perhaps he wanted to be, as did Gehry. Eisenman, Hadid and Tschumi all spoke at the Academy Forum. Work of theirs is shown in the relevant magazines: Tschumi's Parc, Hadid's Peak and her offices for Berlin, Eisenman's Center for the Visual Arts, his Bio-Centrum for Frankfurt and various other projects, including one with Jacques Derrida, Koolhaas/OMA Housing for Checkpoint Charlie, Frank Gehry's Winton Guest House, an Ambasz Conservatory in San Antonio, Texas and a project by Morphosis for Sixth Street, Los Angeles.

But having been displayed in London as exponents of 'Deconstruction', Eisenman, Hadid and Tschumi were also exhibited in New York, along with Coop Himmelblau, Frank Gehry, Rem Koolhaas and Daniel Libeskind as exponents of 'Deconstructivism'. One name only is common to all three 'definers' – Farrelly, Academy and Wigley: that is Zaha Hadid, but Farrelly and Wigley both included Coop Himmelblau, Gehry and Libeskind whilst Academy and Wigley both had Tschumi and Eisenman. There were some notable omissions. Given the nature of their work one would have expected that someone, somewhere, in those early days would have included James Wines and SITE with their many 'deconstructed' buildings not to mention Benisch and Partners, especially their Hysolar Institute in Stuttgart. But let's look at further projects represented in New York such as Eisenman's Bio-Centrum. Since it is a Bio-Centrum, Eisenman had looked for roots in the '20th century Biology' of Watson and Crick's 'double helix' (see Watson 1968, 1980). The 'double helix' spiral of DNA has four components: adenine, guanine, cytosine and thiamine which are represented by the letters: A, G, C and T. These, and the ways in which they interlock (A with T, G with C, T with A and C with G) can also be represented graphically, or even by models with bars. These 'bars' have concave or convex ends, curved or pointed like shallow Cs or shallow Vs. These forms can interlock like pieces of a jig-saw puzzle but concave or convex Cs won't interlock with Vs nor Vs with Cs.

Eisenman took such 'bars' as 'bases' for his Biocentrum; he has nine of them, interlocking as they would in a model of DNA. Having set up these basic forms, he cuts between and through them with an Ohio State-like glazed Mall. Furthermore, he complicates them with smaller versions of themselves. Wigley sees it as a 'world of unstable forms' which 'emerges from within the stable structure of Modernism'. As in Tschumi's Parc he sees forms meeting in three ways: 'sometimes there is no conflict, as one form passes over or under another; sometimes one form is simply embedded within another; sometimes both forms are disturbed and a new form is produced'. So the project becomes a complex inter-relationship between solidity, transparency and void.

Wigley sees Eisenman, too, as setting up (fairly) simple geomet-

ric forms and then distorting them by additions and subtractions. As indeed does Rem Koolhaas in his Apartment Building for Amsterdam, which is essentially a tall, thin slab with towers which project and penetrate. So one isn't quite sure whether to read it as a slab distorted by towers, or towers distorted by a slab. 'The struggle between towers and slab opens up gaps, either as a narrow slit, a huge hole in the volume, or a complete void'. Wherever there are gaps, whenever the volumes are punctured, floors, apparently floating, are exposed. Hence the ambiguity. Is the Apartment Block a row of towers, a slab, both or neither?

Then there was Daniel Libeskind's massive City Edge project for Berlin (1987): an 'architectural object' – a Hadid-like 'bar' – some 450 metres long, 10 metres wide, 20 metres high and cantilevered upwards along the Flottwellstrasse at an angle of six degrees and rising to a height of 56 metres. Libeskind's drawings show networks of fine lines clashing at disparate angles. Some of these represent delicate supports associated with staircases and elevators which are meant to come down to earth every 60 metres or so. There is also an external elevator at the lower end of the 'beam', mounted on a 20-metre disc, to rise and fall in a circular path. Internally, the structure is a jumble of folded concrete plates forming slabs and partitions to contain housing, offices, public administration, shops cinemas and so on. Since they span between the side walls, these *are* the structure. As Wigley says, 'The internal disorder produces the bar even while splitting it, even as gashes open up along its length'.

Libeskind is also fascinated by the space under and around his bar. For it rises from Karlsbad where Mies van der Rohe had his office. Libeskind's aim was to:

> . . . realign the sky against diagonal intersections; the ground-prop instead of a sky-hook. By opening up the space between the fulcrum and its virtual arc, the solid line grounds itself in the sky. Now the unsupportable supports the support . . . retrieving Utopia from the pit.

So the whole thing reminds Wigley of 'Walter Benjamin's unexpected encounter with the locomotive in the clouds'.

Frank Gehry's House is on a much smaller scale and Wigley sees it as a tilted cube which 'bursts through' the structure, peeling back the layers of the house. He sees the forms pushing out and thus lifting off the skin of the building. The structure is exposed and the gap between is a zone of conflict 'in which stable distinctions between inside and outside, original and addition, structure and facade, are questioned'. This is all a bit odd since, as Gehry points out, the small house which he – or rather his wife – originally had, remains almost intact. He added various elements to it but addition is by no means a 'deconstruction' of what is there already!

Wigley seems to have been anxious to add to the Deconstructionist devices we have seen already: 'beams', clashing angles and so on, a new dimension – a sense, so he says, of 'breaking out'. He finds this too in Coop Himmelblau's design for a lawyer's office, a Roof Space in Vienna which according to Wigley is a form which has been

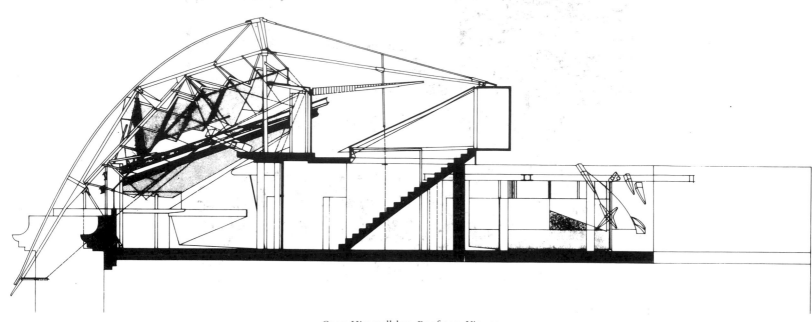

Coop Himmelblau, Roof-top, Vienna

distorted by some alien organism: 'a writhing, disruptive animal breaking through the corner.' Twisted forms 'infect' the rectangular box. The Roof Space is 'a skeletal monster' which breaks up the form as it struggles out. So, released as it is from the basic rectangular structure, 'the roof splits, shears and buckles'. This distortion is 'particularly disquieting' in that it 'seems to belong to the form, to be part of it'. Somehow it seems to have been 'latent' there until released by the architect. So 'the alien emerges out of the stairs, the walls, and the roof plane . . . an outgrowth of the very form it violates'. Others see it as an 'eagle' that has landed or even an 'insect' that has touched down and 'eaten' the building. Yet Wigley's description sounds remarkably like one by Derrida himself. Discussing death and mourning Derrida suggests that those who cannot mourn 'vomit' their bereavement and swallow it into some secret, internal chamber – a 'vault' or 'crypt'. There the forces of the trauma 'support the internal resistance of the vault like pillars, beams, studs, and retaining walls, leaning the powers of intolerable pain against an ineffable, forbidden pleasure'. The 'crypt' hides its dark secret and is hidden itself so it cannot take its place 'in the topography it preserves', but:

The demarcations between inside and outside, the closure established by the drawing of a line, the division of space by a wall, is disturbed by the internal fracturing of the walls in the crypt. The crypt organises the space in which it cannot simply be placed, and sustains the topography it fractures.

Which reads very much as if Derrida had written the actual brief for Coop Himmelblau! Except that Coop Himmelblau designed a light, airy, roof-top space whereas Derrida was describing a buried, claustrophobic crypt.

However, Coop Himmelblau has things in common with others in the Exhibition, such as Hadid and Libeskind. As Wigley points out, an Apartment Building in Vienna consists of four suspended bars, twisted in all dimensions. As with Hadid's, the internal formation of each bar is distorted by the conflicts with the others, and as the bars intersect between them they produce 'warped spaces'. As ever, Wigley looks for 'internal impurity': contorted interiors determined by lifts, stairways and a ramp ascending diagonally through the complex. And the building leans over precariously, held together only by vertical shafts and supported in place by angled struts. 'The skin of the bars is cut open and peeled

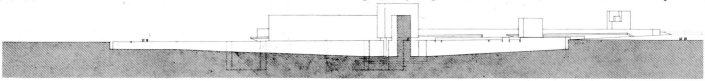

Peter Eisenman, Parc de la Villette, Paris

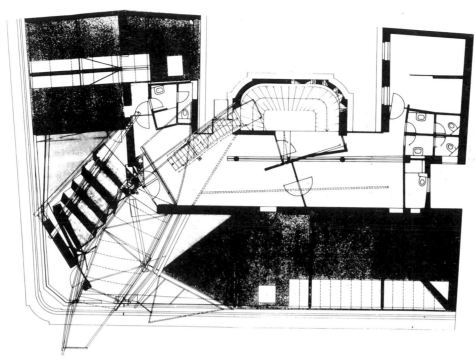

Coop Himmelblau, Roof-top, Vienna

back to expose this twisted structure.' – bars again, albeit on a smaller scale, each 'disturbing' the others as Hadid's did. The contortions of Coop Himmelblau's elevators, their stairways and ramp seem fairly 'normal' by comparison and so does the building's precarious 'lean'; it's nothing like as 'precarious' as Libeskind's! The 'skin . . . cut open and peeled back', of course, is the kind of thing that Wigley found in Gehry.

But why was all this called 'Deconstructivism' when the London – not to mention the Paris – title had been 'Deconstruction'? Wigley believed that, far from deriving from the writings of Jacques Derrida, such work was, in its way, an homage to Russian Constructivism; which of course is why Wigley wrote of 'Deconstructivism' to emphasise the Russian connection. At the same time he declared himself suspicious of an architecture designed by applying 'Deconstructivist' procedures from other disciplines – such as philosophy – which seem to Wigley no more than:

. . . provocative architectural design which appears to take structure apart – whether it be the simple breaking of an object or (its) complex dissimulation into a collage of traces.

These procedures may produce 'formidable projects' but for Wigley they are mere simulations of Deconstruction. However, only six months earlier (1987), Wigley had argued that models for such distortions were to be found in Derrida, who, he had said: 'deconstructs aesthetics by demonstrating that the constructional possibility of form is precisely its violation by a subversive alien, foreign body that already inhabits the interior and cannot be expelled without destroying its host'. Even in his exhibition, Wigley made much of such 'violation' from within, as we have seen from his descriptions of work by Coop Himmelblau, Gehry and others.

So what, in his view, do the 'Deconstructivists' take from the original Russian 'Constructivists' of the 1910s and 20s: Chernikhov, Ginzburg, Golosov, Krinskii, Leonidov, Melnikhov, Rodchenko, Tatlin, the Vesnin Brothers and so on? Wigley sees precedents, not so much in their many completed buildings in Moscow and elsewhere – housing slabs, offices and workers' clubs for instance – as in their sketches and drawings, often for competitions, such as Rodchenko's Experimental Design for a Newspaper Kiosk (1919) and a Radio Station (1920); Krinskii's Communal Housing (1920); the Vesnin Brothers' Palace of Labour (1922-3); and stage sets by Tatlin (1923 and 1935) not to mention his vast Monument to the

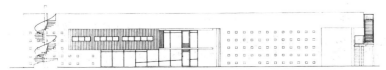

OMA, Checkpoint Charlie, Berlin, and Coop Himmelblau, Funder Factory 3, Carinthia

Third International (1919) in which pure, glass-faced geometric forms, a cube, a pyramid and a cylinder, containing, respectively, a Legislative Assembly, an International Executive and Information Services, were meant to rotate within his vast, skewed, spiral tower.

Such sketches, Wigley suggests 'posed a threat to tradition' by taking pure geometric forms and using them to produce 'impure', distorted, tortured and clashing compositions. Yet his 'Constructivist' examples also include some of Malevich's Suprematist compositions in which geometric forms are skewed at 'dynamic' angles. But whilst they confirm Wigley's point about clashing compositions, Malevich was no Constructivist – as Catherine Cooke points out (1988). He was, he insisted, *the* 'Suprematist' and his aims were quite different from those of the Constructivists, which renders him by no means irrelevant to the development of Deconstruction.

Take the case of Hadid, for instance. A scheme as complex as her Hong Kong Peak could not have emerged without precedent full-blown from the mind even of Zaha Hadid. As we have seen she knew of Leonidov but she seems to have derived more direct inspiration from Malevich. She even called a student design, for a club, hotel and other accommodation, 'Malevich's Tektonik'. In this she drew on two aspects of Malevich's work: his Suprematist Paintings and his model 'Tektoniks'. The paintings consisted largely of square and rectangular blocks, bars and lines of colour clashing at odd – and often very acute – angles. Malevich saw these as expressing the 'dynamism' of the 20th century and compared them to biplanes flying in formation! His 'Tektoniks' were somewhat different: plaster models of potential buildings each consisting of a large rectangular block, vertical or horizontal, with smaller, often long, flat and thin blocks attached to it stepping out, in the most complicated cases, to eight or ten layers as 'set backs', diminishing in size. Hadid's Malevich Club is just such a design but the Hotel is somewhat different: long and narrow on plan with, at water level and below, beginnings evident of the clashing angles which were to become such a feature of her work. Such things are much more marked in her Museum of the Nineteenth Century for London (1977-8) which is also notable for her first essay in clashing 'bars' with intersecting geometry. And one can trace increasing complexity in her entry, with OMA (including Koolhaas and Zenghelis) for the Parliament Extension in The Hague (1978-9); her Residence for the Prime Minister in Dublin (1979-80) in which great curving ramps make their appearance; various interiors for London and her Parc de la Villette scheme (1982-3). The Peak is simply the most confident expression in a 'language' which Hadid had been developing over six years or so.

So what is the real Constructivist connection?

Of course there are quotations from Constructivist forms, such as the Vesnin Brothers' Palace of Labour in Meier's High Museum for example, and their Pravda Building in some of the Folies at La Villette. But Wigley sees his Deconstructivism as no mere Constructivist Revival. The Constructivists, he felt, 'interrogated Modern Movement forms' and since his Deconstructivists follow similar procedures it is hardly surprising that they 'discover' forms much like those of the Constructivists. Or, as Wigley puts it: 'in dismantling the ongoing tradition . . . they find themselves inevitably rehearsing the strategies rehearsed by the (Russian) avant-garde. They 'irritate modernism from within, distorting it with its own genealogy'.

Indeed, he claims that the architect has always dreamt of pure form 'from which all instability and disorder have been excluded'. He sees buildings as constructed of pure geometric forms – 'cubes, cylinders, spheres, cones, pyramids, and so on' – combined into stable 'ensembles' by rules of composition 'which prevent any one form from conflicting with another'. This structure of pure forms 'becomes the physical structure of the building' and the architect develops his final design in ways which preserve his pure forms; any deviation would threaten, not just the formal purity but the very stability of his building. So, for Wigley: 'Architecture is a conservative discipline that produces pure form and protects it from contamination.'

Architects who have tried to do this include: Boullée, Ledoux, Schinkel, Mies, Kahn, Eisenman, Meier, Gwathmey, Grassi, early Rossi and Botta for example. But there is a snag to Wigley's thesis. As David Pye points out (1964) 'pure form' is an abstract ideal which in practice can never be achieved. However sophisticated his tools, the craftsman can never make a perfect cube, a perfect sphere and so on. His best efforts will always have blemishes, flaws, inaccuracies however minute. And even when Wigley's 'Purist' architects have come as close as practicalities allow to the achievement of pure form, wear, weathering, settlement and so on have taken over to streak, stain, pit, crack, twist and bend their buildings thus destroying whatever 'purity' they may have had in the first place. So nature literally achieves 'deconstructions' of the kind towards which Wigley says that his architects aspire! Except that, in comparison, they make exaggerated forms until, of course, Nature exercises her powers of gravity to make the building deconstruct itself by falling down.

What is more, for every architect who pursued 'pure' geometry

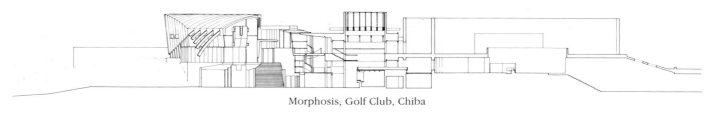

Morphosis, Golf Club, Chiba

one can think of many others who did not: Michelangelo, Vignola, Bernini, Borromini, Guarini, Fontana, Fischer von Ehrlach, Hawksmoor, Vanbrugh, Zimmerman, Soane, Pugin, Butterfield, Shaw, Webb, Richardson, Sullivan, Wright, Gaudí, Voysey, Lutyens, Le Corbusier, Aalto, Michelucci, Scharoun and all those others Venturi admired so much. Indeed *Complexity and Contradiction* was a full-frontal attack on just those qualities to which Wigley's purist architect apparently aspires.

So how do Wigley's Deconstructivists differ in motivation from them?

Wigley, as we have seen, distrusts the application of Derrida's form of 'Deconstruction' on to architecture. He feels that just as Derrida deconstructs language from within, so architecture, too, should be 'deconstructed' from within itself. Wigley's architect should locate dilemmas inherent in the nature of architecture by laying pure architectural forms 'on the couch' and then interrogating them by alternating gentle coaxing with violent torture, thus drawing their impurities to the surface. But that, surely, is what the Baroque and those many other architects did anyway, except that they 'interrogated' Classicism whereas Wigley's architects start with the 'pure' forms of the Modern Movement.

Wigley's distortions are produced within the forms themselves out of the very structures of which they are composed. They are simpler than merely 'fracturing, slicing, fragmentation or piercing'. The crucial point is that the forms 'are disturbed from within, the disturbances incorporated into the internal structure, the actual construction'. 'It is,' says Wigley 'as if some kind of parasite has infected the form and distorted it from the inside!' Which of course is rather different from drawing out 'impurities' inherent in the forms themselves – savouring rather the infection of congenital disease!

So Wigley seeks a form of 'Deconstructivism' in which architecture will be free from the influence of any language or philosophy. But his 'Deconstructivism' opens the flood gates, for if 'Constructivism' was an influence – as clearly it was, if only in the works of Meier and Tschumi – then many other Modern '-ists' and '-isms' can be seen as equally legitimate sources.

One is amazed to find, for instance, that neither Farrelly nor Wigley so much as mention Expressionism, that anguished attitude which permeated (largely German) painting, sculpture, architecture, literature, drama, cinema and music from the 1910s to the 1930s. The hard core of painters included Feininger, Kandinsky, Kirchner, Klee, Kokoschka, Mack and Marc, Meller, Nolde, Schiele and Schmidt-Rottluff. Most of their subjects were anguished human beings but Kandinsky's also experimented with clashing geometries from Malevich and the Constructivists (c1915) and practised them from 1922, most particularly, in that most conducive of environments: Gropius' Bauhaus. Indeed the prototype for all Deconstructionist architecture may well be Lionel Feininger's cover design for the Bauhaus Manifesto (1919).

Yet as early as 1904 Paul Scheerbart was producing vignettes, such as his 'Bibliothèque théâtrale révolutionnaire' which, whilst by no means architectural drawings, anticipate some of Coop Himmelblau's forms, as do his writings from 1898 onwards, culminating in his book on *Glass Architecture* of 1914:

> We live for the most part in enclosed spaces. These form the environment in which our culture grows . . . If we wish to raise our culture to a higher level, we are forced . . . to transform our architecture. And this will be possible only if we remove the enclosed quality from the spaces within which we live. This can only be done by the introduction of glass architecture that lets in the sunlight and the light of the moon and the stars . . . through the greatest number of walls that are made entirely of glass . . .

Given such constructions, according to Scheerbart: 'we should have paradise on earth and would no longer need to gaze at the paradise in the sky'. What's more, with iron supports, walls need no longer be vertical; 'dome effects up above' could be displaced to the sides, including the lower parts of the walls; smaller rooms would be freed entirely from the need for vertical walls.

Surely a better description altogether than Wigley's of Coop Himmelblau's Roof Space?

Scheerbart's thinking was applied fairly quickly by Bruno Taut in his Pavilion for the Glass Industry at the Cologne Exhibition of 1914, which surprisingly, like most other Expressionist buildings that were actually realised, turned out to lack those features which seem indispensable to Deconstruction: fragmentation and asymmetry.

In 1919, Taut published his *Alpine Architecture* in which the mountains and valleys of the Alps were transformed, by facetted glass and concrete vaults and other structures, into vast cities. A year earlier Taut and other revolutionaries such as Gropius had set up the Arbeitsrat fur Kunst – a 'Working Council for Art' and amongst the works they exhibited were clearly Deconstructionist drawings such as Golyscheff's of 1919 and Krayl's of 1920. But some of them wished to go further in their experimental work and in November 1919 Taut initiated the *Glass Chain* to which he and

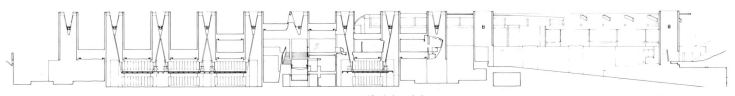

Morphosis, Golf Club, Chiba

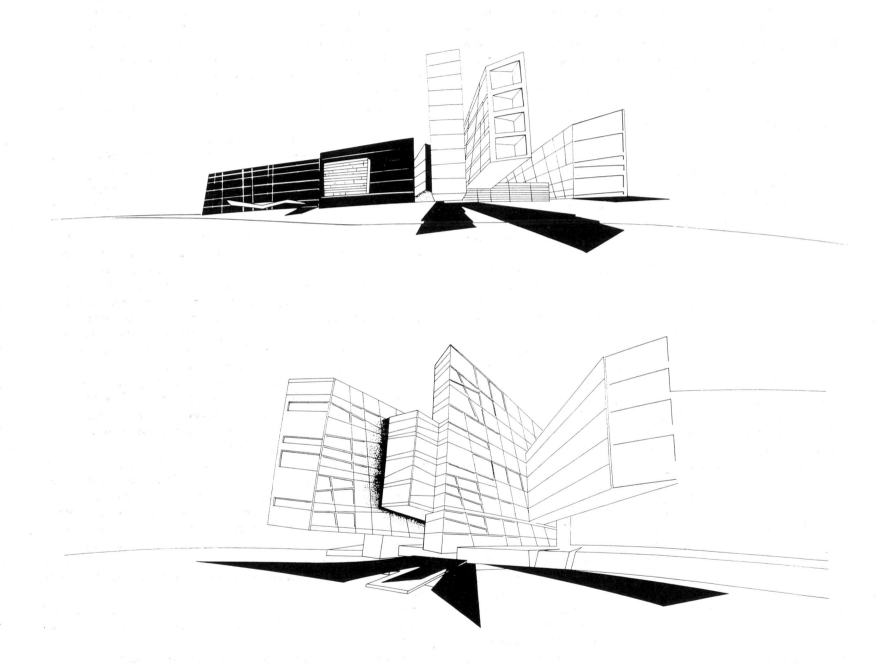

Zaha Hadid, Zollhof 3, Düsseldorf

others such as Gropius, Scharoun, Finsterlin and the Luckhardts contributed anonymously, and some of the more extreme of their fantastic projects certainly were pioneering exercises in Deconstruction.

So it was in the context of of the *Arbeitsrat*, or the more private *Glass Chain* that Karl Krayl published his Cathedral of Christian Science, the Luckhardts their Form Fantasy of 1919, Finsterlin his many studies for (very plastic) houses and other building types, Scharoun his Skyscraper Project for the Friedrichstrasse and Mies van der Rohe his Glass Tower also for the Friedrichstrasse (1919).

A few such structures were actually built, such as Max Taut's Wissinger Tomb of 1920, Gropius' jagged Memorial to the March Victims in Weimar (1920-21) and, as practical buildings on a larger scale: Mendellsohn's Einstein Tower (1920-1921), his Luckenwalde Hat Factory (1921-3) and Hugo Häring's Farm at Gut Garkau near Lubeck (1923-4).

Häring's Farm indeed demonstrates a crucial point: that whereas for Giedion, Pevsner and other advocates of the International style the simple rectilinearity of, say, Gropius' Fagus Factory office symbolised 'Functionalism', the sloping staircase roofs and other 'eccentric' forms of the Farm actually followed, and therefore were direct expressions of function.

Nor did Expressionism die; Scharoun continued in this vein for the rest of his life up to and including the Chamber Music Hall for the Philharmonie in Berlin (1978) and Gottfried Bohm picked up the tradition with his Bensberg Town Hall (1962) and, especially, the Pilgrimage Church at Neviges (1972).

In painting, too, the clashes of the Expressionists were continued in the 'Abstract Expressionism' of, for example, Jackson Pollock (1949 to 1951) and, more rigidly geometric, in Sol Lewitt's *Ten Thousand Lines* of (1971), *Lines through, towards and to Points* (1973), his *Lines from Two Points* (1975). Pollock and Lewitt share that 'all-of-a-piece' quality that unity-of-complexity that we saw in, say, Soane's Bank of England plan. One finds it too in Daniel Libeskind's *Arktische Blumen* (Arctic Flowers) of 1979, composed, in Libeskind's case, of exquisitely drawn architectural detail.

Such things clearly encouraged a mood – a flavour – but there are other more specific sources. Gehry, for instance, is quite clear about his. Indeed Gehry's own account of his House (1987) suggests something rather different from Wigley's 'bursting out'. It was, rather, a matter of 'containing', for as Gehry says: 'My wife . . . found this beautiful . . . anonymous little house, and I decided to remodel it, and . . . since it was my own building . . . explore ideas I'd had about the materials I used here: corrugated metal, and plywood, chain link . . .' The point was to make the little old house: 'appear intact inside the new house, so that, from the outside, you would be aware always that the old house was still there . . . some guy just wrapped it in new materials . . .' Clearly if you leave something intact you cannot be 'deconstructing'. Gehry's process was other than Wigley describes. Gehry's 'wrappings' consist at ground level of corrugated metal extensions to the north and west of his

little house: kitchen, dining room, entrance and back yards. Over these there are decks 'contained' by chain-link screens and their slender framing but the crucial clues to his sources are given in Gehry's decriptions of his windows. He says:

> I started a dialogue with (the) new kitchen window and the existing bay window . . . I became interested in opposing the bay window with a different kind of geometric activity, something that was more active. I fantasised that when I closed the box (the old house) there were ghosts . . . that would try to creep out, and this window was a cubist ghost. I became fascinated by that and started making models of windows that looked like the ghost of Cubism was trying to crawl out.

Cubism was clearly a source and not just for Gehry but also for other 'Deconstructivists'. Hadid's 'artificial landscape' for Hong Kong looks like nothing so much as one of the facetted paintings – the colours, even, are similar – which Picasso and Braque produced in the first, Analytical, phase of Cubism. Then Gehry describes the corner window of his dining room:

> I was interested in the corner window. How you turn the corner. I thought of Duchamp's nude going down the staircase, and tried to figure out how I could rotate the corner so as you walked around it, it would rotate . . . that piece of glass slides beyond the corner. It works from the inside and outside to rotate the cube. Another source, obviously, for others as well, especially when one remembers that at the time of its first showing in New York, at the Armory Show of 1913, Duchamp's 'Nude' was called by very many names: from 'Sunrise is a Lumber Yard' and 'Pack of Brown Cards in a Nightmare' to 'An Explosion in a Shingle Factory' (see Dunlop 1972). Although there is no direct Duchamp derivation, some of Hadid's perspectives of Hong Kong are bigger and better packs of cards, sunrises or even explosions!

Duchamp himself, of course, was the founding-father of chance as a generator of form in modern art. In 1915 for instance, when he was working on the 'Large Glass', Duchamp used chance events of various kinds: photographing a piece of white cloth as it flapped in the breeze to get three irregular squares, firing a match stick dipped in paint from a toy gun to get random points for holes in his glass; dropping a one-metre thread from a height of one metre and fixing the curve it took on the floor to provide 'a new image of the unit of length'.

A year later the Zurich Dadaist Hans Arp was making collages by chance, such as Selon *les lois du hasard*. Hans Richter describes Arp's process:

> Dissatisfied with a drawing he had been working on . . . Arp finally tore it up, and let the pieces flutter to the floor . . . Some time later he happened to notice these . . . scraps . . . as they lay on the floor, and was struck by the pattern they formed. It had all the expressive power that he had tried in vain to achieve.

How meaningful! How telling!

Tristan Tzara, too, offered equivalent methods, sometime between 1916 and 1920, for making poetry by chance in which he took a newspaper, chose an article as long as he wanted his poem to be, cut it out and cut it up, put the words into a bag, drew them out at random and wrote them down.

Dada itself was a pre-echo of much that 'Deconstruction' was to say. Its fundamental tenets were described in many manifestos of which the most significant, from our point of view, was Tristan Tzara's of 1918. Tzara says:

> Does anyone think he has found a psychic base common to all mankind? . . . How can one expect to put order into the chaos that constitutes that infinite and shapeless variation: man?
>
> . . . Dada was born of a need for independence, of a distrust towards unity. Those who are with us preserve their freedom. We recognise no theory . . .
>
> Some people think they can explain rationally, by thought, what they think. But that is extremely relative . . . There is no ultimate Truth. The dialectic is an amusing mechanism which guides us, in a banal kind of way, to opinions we had in the first place. Does anyone think that, by a minute refinement of logic, he has demonstrated the truth and established the correctness of these opinions?
>
> . . . Logic is a complication. Logic is always wrong. It draws the threads of notions, words, in their formal exterior, towards illusory ends and centres. Its chains kill; it is an enormous centipede stifling independence.
>
> Let each man proclaim: there is a great negative work of destruction to be accomplished. We must sweep clean . . . Without aim or design, without organisation: indomitable madness, decomposition.

Another branch of Dada, Schwitters' in Hanover, gives us certain other clues to 'Deconstructivism'. Wigley, as we have seen, made much of 'alien organisms' somehow subverting forms from within.

That may not have been true of Gehry's House or Coop Himmelblau's Roof Space but both of them rejected also any connection with Derrida. Indeed as Cohen says of Gehry (*Architecture d'Aujourd'hui*): 'An exhibition and a recent debate have tried, timidly, to associate him with some kind of Deconstructivism: lost cause. His presence at MoMA with the old project of his house is incongruous, and his name remains absent from the debate'.

Frank Werner wrote on behalf of Coop Himmelblau (1989): Everywhere one . . . reads that the literary critic and American by choice Paul de Man discovered 'Deconstruction', and that the French philosopher Jacques Derrida has made it instrumental by rendering essentially doubtful the authenticity of visual forms and their historically derived meanings. But haven't older architects like Peter Eisenman and Frank O Gehry, as well as younger architects like Bernard Tschumi, Daniel Libeskind, Zaha Hadid, Rem Koolhaas or Coop Himmelblau been working out the same ideas in practice, producing buildings without any of this philosophical help and support?

And certainly Schwitters, with his Merzbau (*c*1925-8), seems to have presented the very prototype of forms 'bursting through'. 'Merz' was for Schwitters an ironic reference to 'Kommerz' and of course it is no coincidence that one of Coop Himmelblau's earlier projects (1981) – a series of prefabricated rooms for pupils arranged in 'whale' – like 'bars', supported over an atrium by a by a complex of columns and struts – is actually called the 'Merz School'!

The original Merzbau was the 'Column' with which Schwitters had 'invaded' his house in the later 1920s. As Richter says (1965):

> When I first saw it, about 1925, it filled about half the room and reached almost to the ceiling. It resembled, if anything . . . earlier (De Stijl) sculpture by Domela or Vantongerloo (he might also have mentioned Malevich). But this was more than sculpture; it was a living, daily changing document of Schwitters and his friends . . . the whole thing was an aggregate of hollow space, a structure of concave and convex forms which hollowed and inflated the whole scuplture.
>
> Each of these forms had a 'meaning'. There was a Mondrian hole, and there were Arp, Gabo, Doesburg, Lissitzky, Malevich, Mies van der Rohe and Richter holes . . . Each hole contained highly personal details from the life . . . He cut off a lock of my hair and put it in my hole. A thick pencil, filched from Mies . . . lay in his cavity. In others there were pieces if shoelace, a half-smoked cigarette, a nail paring, a piece of tie (Doesburg), a broken pen . . . a dental bridge with several teeth in it . . . a little bottle of urine . . . Schwitters gave us several holes each . . . and the column grew.

Indeed, Richter describes how it had grown three years later:

> . . . the pillar was totally different. All the little holes . . . were no longer to be seen. 'They are all deep down inside,' Schwitters explained. They were concealed by the monstrous growth of the column, covered by other sculptural excrescences, new people, new shapes, colours and details. A proliferation that never ceased. The pillar that had . . . looked . . . Constructivist . . . now was more curvilinear.

And crucial for its status as proto-Deconstructivism:

> . . . the column, in its overwhelming and still continuing growth, had, as it were, burst the room apart at the seams. Schwitters could add no more breadth, if he still wanted to get round the column; so he had to expand upwards. As landlord of the house . . . he got rid of the tenants . . . above . . . made a hole in the ceiling and continued the column on the upper floor.

So there's an 'alien growth' if ever there was one. Just to cement the Dada connection let's remember the word-games which Duchamp used to play long after the heroic days: Take these from L' Usa*ge de la Parole* No 1, Paris, December 1939:

SURcenSURE
[RErePROACH]

On which, clearly, I drew for my title; not directly after Duchamp but after Derrida and Eisenman! Or even more Derrida-like, this *Homage to Man Ray* of 1963:

La Vie on Ose
on suppose
on oppose
on impose
on appose   Man Ray
on dépose
on repose
on indispose

Not that Duchamp invented such typographical games. The Romans had played them and even in recent French poetry there had been *Un Coup de Dés* (A throw of the Dice) by Stéphane Mallarmé (1866) and the *Calligrammes* of Guillaume Apollinaire (1900-1910).

Derrida has much to say about Mallarmé in *Dissémination* (1972) but surprisingly little about Dada or the Surrealism which emerged out of it, except for an oblique reference to that concept of Lautréamont's which the Surrealists found so significant: 'Beautiful as the chance encounter of an umbrella and a sewing machine on a dissecting table'. Derrida's version is in *Spurs* (1978); it's Nietzsche's umbrella and he says: 'One doesn't just happen on to an unwanted object of this sort in a sewing machine on a castration table.'

That is typical Derrida, but, if nothing else, he shows that the spirit of Dada/Surrealism, is by no means dead!

Its life was never threatened much anyway. Dada/Surrealism transmogrified into things like COBRA, Lettrisme, the Internationale Situationiste and so on. Indeed the latter can be seen in many ways as a very close precursor to Deconstruction; not just in the thinking behind it but in the urban and building forms it produced; including clashing 'beams' much like those of Eisenman, Hadid and Libeskind.

Guy Debord and the 'Internationale Situationniste' declared their stance in the first issue of the Journal to which they gave their name, published in 1958.

Their Manifesto makes interesting reading these days, in the light of 'Deconstruction'. Some of their tenets are deeply political – Marxist, of course – whilst others, such as *dérive* are concerned with the sensory experience of being in and moving around the city.

Other terms had distinctly 'Deconstructivist' flavours such as: '. . . *détournement*: the re-use and even misappropriation of . . . existing aesthetic elements, by, say, buying a painting and painting over it, building into and around an existing building, and so on'.

The Situationists intended by such things to integrate artistic products, present or past 'into the construction of a superior environment'. In this sense, they said 'it is not possible to have situationist painting or music, but only a situationist use of these media'. The point was to make propaganda 'within the old cultural spheres' which demonstrated that they were worn out and had lost their former consequence.

By unitary urbanism they sought to bring art and technology together 'for the integrated construction of an environment in a dynamic liaison with experiments in behaviour' whilst by 'psychogeography' they meant a study of the precise effects which geographic environments, consciously organised or not, had on the emotional behaviour of individuals.

But their key term was: '. . . decomposition: a process by which, as superior forms appear for the domination of nature, the traditional cultural forms destroyed themselves, thus permitting and demanding superior cultural constructions'.

The Situationists distinguished between an active phase of 'decomposition', the effective demolition of antiquated superstructures – which they saw as having stopped around 1930 – and a phase of repetition which had held sway since then. Naturally they felt that 'the delay in the transition from decomposition to new construction is linked to the delay in the revolutionary liquidation of capitalism'.

So what kinds of forms emerged from such concepts? The most pertinent are to be found in the work of Nieuwenhuis Constant, Dutch painter and architect who exhibited his *ilôts-maquettes* (model precincts) at the Stedelijk Museum, Amsterdam in 1959.

They included such projects as 'Neue Babylon' a city to be formed from a vast chain of mega-structures, each of which could be reorganised at will, much in the manner of the (later) Archigram.

Some of Constant's drawings look remarkably like pioneering works of 'Deconstruction'. His 'Neue Babylon Nord', for instance, is a city plan with white, bar-like buildings – rather like the medium-rise flats of Le Corbusier's 'Cellular System' suburbs – but clashing at Hadid-like angles, with red and black 'incidents' along the bars and black lines crossing and curving over them. The 'Groep Sectaire' of 1959 is another city plan; a collage of bar-like buildings – made from one millimetre graph-paper – which also clash like those of 'Babylon Nord', with thin red 'railway lines' curving and crossing over them.

Constant's models of individual buildings seem even more 'Deconstructionist'. The 'Bode Sector' of 1958 has plexiglass decks with metal partitions between them clashing at odd angles; whilst the 'Kleine-labyrinth' (also 1958) has a black metal frame of irregularly-spaced columns and beams containing clashing panels, tubes, ramps and metal discs.

So the Situationists as a whole and Constant in particular, could have provided the Deconstructionists with all source material they needed to develop their clashing forms from 1967 onwards. Constant's influence certainly is acknowledged by Gruppo Strum, Nigel Coates and his NATO Group – Narrative Architecture Today. Coates, of course, was at the AA with Hadid and Tschumi.

The crucial point of course is that the Situationnistes declared themselves, and Constant exhibited his projects, long before 1967 when Jacques Derrida published the three major works on which

'Deconstruction', literally, was founded. This raises the fundamental question: who needs Derrida anyway?

Well two of the architects at least, Tschumi and Eisenman, do. They draw on Derrida in their work. Clearly they see his writing as endowing their work with a certain intellectual authority: Eisenman has found another guru. But there is more to it than that. Derrida himself acknowledges the connection and has commented on their work at some length; indeed, on Tschumi's Parc de la Villette in 'Point de Folie – Maintenant Architecture' (1985). He has analysed Eisenman, too, as Architect/Writer in 'Pourquoi Peter Eisenman écrit de si bonnes livres?' (1987) – a title, be it noted, derived from Nietzsche.

Tschumi, certainly, spoke of Derrida – but also of Barthes and Foucault – when he was teaching at my own School of Architecture (Portsmouth) in 1969-75.

Yet as late as 1985, Eisenman was writing of 'decomposition' in his work and indeed it was Tschumi who suggested that he collaborate with Derrida on a 'thematic garden' for La Villette; the stone, steel, glass and water Choral Work (see Derrida, 1987 and Eisenman 1988.

And whilst they seem few, two architects are enough to form a movement. 'Purism' had only one, albeit Le Corbusier. The only other 'Purist' was his sometime collaborator and friend Amedée Ozenfant, a painter. Yet one can hardly call them an insignificant group in the history of 20th century art and design!

And there may be more to 'Deconstruction' than a movement of only two fully-paid-up architect members. It may be that Derrida has struck some kind of chord, set in motion resonances which, even if they do not know it, permeate the work of other architects. Perhaps he even expresses some kind of 'Spirit of the Age'.

All this suggests that we might do well to look a little closer at Derrida, examine what he wrote and try to find if, conceivably, there is anything in Deconstruction for other architects and for the art and science of architecture.

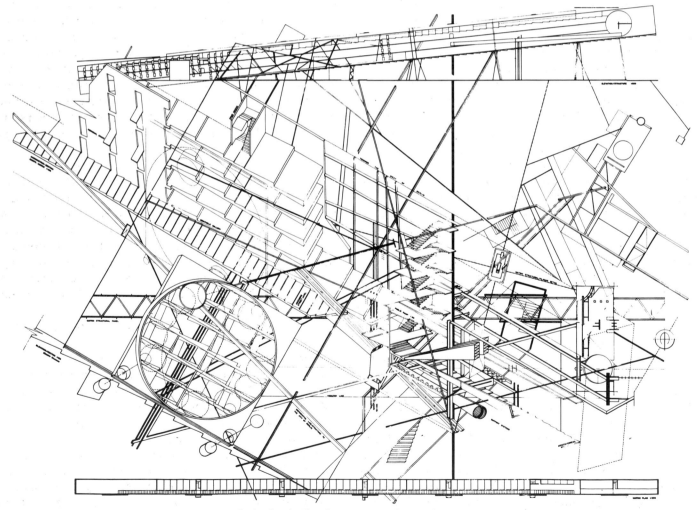

Daniel Libeskind, 'Cloud Prop', City Edge, Berlin

THE PHILOSOPHY OF DECONSTRUCTION

The founding-father of Deconstruction, Jacques Derrida, was born in Algiers in 1930. He teaches philosophy at the École Normale Supérieure in Paris and at various American universities, such as the University of California at Irvine, Johns Hopkins and Yale. Derrida first sprang to national attention in France with the publication, in 1967, of three major books: *La Voix et le Phénomène; L'écriture et la Différence* and *De la Grammatologie* which were translated into English, over the years, as *Speech and Phenomenon* (1973), *Writing and Difference* (1978), *Of Grammatology* (1974). He followed these with three more in 1972: *Positions; La Dissémination* and *Marges: de la Philosophie*. These too were translated as *Positions* (1981), *Dissemination* (1981) and *Margins of Philosophy* (1982). And of course there are many published lectures, papers, interviews and so on.

Like Karl Marx before him Derrida tends to work not so much by initiating ideas as by reacting, forcibly, to what others have written already. His targets have included not only philosophers such as Plato, Aristotle, Descartes, Leibnitz, Rousseau, Kant, Hegel, Nietzsche, Husserl, Heidegger, Freud, Saussure, Levinas, Merleau-Ponty and Bataille, but linguists such as Saussure and Hjelmslev, structuralists such as Lévi-Strauss, historians such as Foucault and, perhaps even more to the point, psychiatrists such as Freud and Lacan. But there is curiously little on such evident fellow-spirits as Sartre and Barthes. In each case Derrida aims to refute the author with arguments derived from the latter's own writings, to demonstrate – successfully in many cases – that the very premises on which the author bases his case will, if pursued to their logical conclusions, defeat the original arguments. Such writing contains within itself the seeds of its own destruction and Derrida sees his task, as a Deconstructionist, to find those seeds and nourish them!

As Norris points out (1987) Derrida began to formulate his ideas during a long series of encounters with the writings of Edmund Husserl, the founder of 'Phenomenology', his search for the 'ultimate truths' of human existence by contemplating, in a state of total introspection, his own consciousness and nothing but his consciousness! Derrida saw this as a much-needed antidote to the then-rampant intellectual fashion of 'Structuralism' – the study of relationships between, say words in language, people in anthropological groups, incidents in myths and so on. Derrida saw such studies as essentially sterile; for the study of relationships between elements drained the elements themselves of any meaning, left them lifeless and desiccated. He rejected any kind of science – or as he put it 'scientificity' – on the grounds that it could not explain anything of interest about the human condition, or indeed about the world as a whole. For science rejects whatever we cannot experience directly with our senses, tests by scientific experiments and indeed regards such things as beyond our understanding and quite 'unknowable'.

Yet these are the things that matter most to Derrida. He had intended to explore them further in his PhD Thesis (planned in 1957) but as Norris suggests (1987) he had a growing sense that philosophy itself was in a state of crisis. Philosophy consists of written texts yet philosophers seem to ignore the problem of writing itself, which, for Derrida, proved to be of crucial importance. So he started to write on such things for the literary journal *Tel Quel* whose other (largely Marxist) contributors drew on Psychoanalysis, Semiology (Saussure's theory of signs) and 'Structuralism', initiated by Lévi-Strauss, which grew out of it.

So what is this 'Structuralism' which Derrida dislikes so much?

Structuralism

'Structuralism' started in the studies of language which Ferdinand de Saussure initiated in lectures at the University of Geneva from 1906 to 1911. Saussure never wrote the book of his lectures; it was compiled, after his death, by students who published it in 1915, as the *Cours en Linguistique Générale*.

Saussure had wanted to develop out of language a 'General Theory of Signs' which he calls 'Semiology'. He sees it as a branch of social psychology 'that studies the life of signs in society'. Saussure based his studies in language on the grounds that we all use language, constantly, for conveying ideas to other people, so:

'language, better than anything else, offers a basis for understanding the semiological problem'. Saussure aims to extract from language general laws of meaning and communication which others can then apply to other fields of culture. This means that language studies form only a part of his 'General Science of Signs', in which he applies the word 'Sign' to anything which conveys ideas from one brain to others. A traffic 'sign' obviously does this, so does a shop sign. So do words, strings of equations, diagrams, pictures, music and buildings.

Let's explore Saussure's 'Semiology' a little further. Saussure was worried (p 23) that most language studies up to his time had been based on analyses of written text. The words are there, unchanging, on the page and it's much easier to compare, contrast, or whatever else one wants to do with them than it is – or was – to analyse the transient sounds of speech. These days, of course, we have tape recorders so speech can be made as permanent as writing. But that was hardly true in Saussure's day. What's more, he says (p 25) '. . . literary language adds to the undeserved importance of writing. It has dictionaries and grammars; . . . children are taught from and by means of books; language is apparently governed by a code . . . a written set of strict rules of usage . . . that is why writing acquires primary importance'.

What's more, language studies are conducted by people who actually write themselves. They come from cultures that see writing as the normal, natural, indeed inevitable means of communication and yet there have been, and still are, many cultures in which writing is or was quite unknown. But of course those cultures that are based on writing see themselves as far superior. Webster's Dictionary has a name for such an approach: ethnocentrism, which is defined as 'a habitual disposition to judge foreign peoples or groups by the standards and practices of one's own culture or ethnic group . . .'

Saussure deplored that and believed we could dig much deeper into the roots of language, at all times and in all places, by studying speech as well as an antidote to purely writing-based studies. So he saw 'language' as his primary study, divided into two different modes of expression: 'writing' and 'speech', one formed of words on paper – that is 'graphic' – and the other formed of the sounds we make as we speak – in other words 'sonic'.

So like many others before him Saussure tended to think in pairs, or 'binary oppositions', in which, as Derrida points out many times, he was part of a great tradition which reaches back to the ancient Greek founding-fathers of Western Philosophy: Pythagoras, Socrates, Plato and Aristotle.

'Language' for Saussure is as 'a collection of necessary conventions that have been adopted by a social body' as their means of communication. He stresses, absolutely, its *social* function. English, as a 'Language', comprises a set of words, and a set of rules – a syntax – for using them, from which each of us gets to use a personal vocabulary and develops ways of applying the rules: the two together then form our individual 'Speech'.

Saussure has other 'binary oppositions' and 'Structuralism' was based on two of them in particular: his division of Linguistics into Diachronic/Synchronic and his idea that words have two ways of relating which he describes as Syntagmatic/Associative.

Saussure's Diachronic Linguistics, his study of changes in language over time, takes 49 pages of the *Cours* whereas his Synchronic Linguistics takes only 36. The latter is a study of things which are static in language, 'synchronised', as it were, at a moment in time, which in language, or so Saussure suggests, are relationships between words of which he identifies two kinds: Syntagmatic and Associative. The first stem from the roles which different words play in the structure of a sentence, its syntax. That is why Saussure coins the adjective 'Syntagmatic' to describe them.

His second set of relations is those with words 'outside' the sentence which we associate with those within it. If I use the word 'architect' then you might well associate this – in your mind – with 'architecture', 'design', 'construction' and so on. So, not surprisingly, Saussure calls these 'Associative Relations'.

Let's see such relations at work in a simple sentence:

						A
						S
						S
	kitten	lay			floor	O
					rug	C
SYNTAGMATIC The	cat	sat	on	the	mat	I
					carpet	A
	dog	stood			tiles	T
						I
						V
						E

Saussure's successors, such as Claude Lévi-Strauss and Roland Barthes, muddied the waters by giving his relations different names but the relationships themselves, 'Syntagmatic' and 'Associative', became the basis of the 'Structuralism' which Lévi-Strauss and others were to apply to many kinds of relations in anthropology: between kith and kin, between incidents in myths, and so on. Lévi-Strauss announced that he would apply them to such things in his Inaugural Lecture (1958) as Professor of Social Anthropology at the Collège de France. He displayed the results in his voluminous writings, such as his *Structural Anthropology* (two volumes, 1958 and 1973); *Totemism* and *The Savage Mind* (both 1961); *The Raw and the Cooked* (1964).

These studies are of the kind which Derrida found 'lifeless and desiccated'. He drew in his own work rather more directly on another of Saussure's 'binary oppositions': his 'Signifier/Signified'. We have within our brains ideas, concepts of some kind which we try to convey to other people. Being within our brains those concepts, says Saussure, are by their nature abstract, indeed 'immaterial'. They may be about concrete things and exist physically in the brain as patterns of chemical and electrical activity. But still they are *ideas*, not concrete things in themselves. We pass ideas from our own brains to other people's by putting them into physical – Saussure says 'material' – form. As I speak I 'encode' my 'concepts' into 'sound-images' which pass to your ears: your 'sensory' organs for hearing. Which is why Saussure says they have taken 'sensory' form. Your ears pass those 'sound images' towards your brain where they are 'decoded' back into 'immaterial' concepts. Those two very different elements, the 'sound image' and the immaterial 'concept' are joined, says Saussure, to form the 'sign' and he names them, with admirable clarity, the 'Signifier' and the 'Signified'.

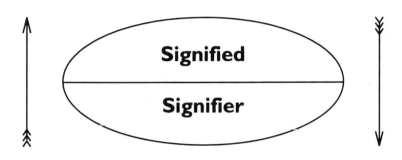

Whilst Saussure's 'Signifieds' exist *only* in the brain, their physical manifestations – their 'Signifiers' – may exist in many forms: as words written or printed on paper, as diagrams, drawings, paintings, sounds of music, or forms of architecture. Saussure himself says (p103) his two sided 'linguistic unit' has been compared, often, to a human being 'made up of body and soul'. But he doesn't think much of this comparison. 'A better choice' he says, 'would be a chemical compound, a combination of hydrogen and oxygen'. The crucial point being that, taken separately, 'neither element has any of the properties of water'. So the two parts of his sign are unified within quite a different thing: the 'sign-as-a-whole'. Crucial for Saussure is the inextricable linking of 'Signifier' and 'Signified'. Most of us think of a 'sign' only as the physical part, a 'Signifier' such as a shop sign, a traffic sign and so on. But that for Saussure is only half the story. His 'sign' is complete only with the linking of 'Signifier' and 'Signified' inextricably together.

They have to be because were they not, we could not communicate. Especially since their linking in the first place was quite arbitrary. It's an accident of history that the speech-sounds 'ox' got attached to a certain kind of large quadruped – or at least to a concept of that animal; it is so attached for English-speakers, but the French use 'boeuf', the Germans 'ochs' and so on. So the animal is lumbered with quite different 'Signifiers' in the different languages! Some words have firmer connections. They sound like the concepts they signify: 'hiss', 'gurgle', 'tick-tock' and so on. But such onomato-

poeiae are too rare to have much effect upon Saussure's general point.

But once 'Signifier' and 'Signified' have been linked, no one, unilaterally, can break them apart if he intends to communicate. Saussure says:

The Signifier, though to all appearances freely chosen with respect to the idea that it represents, is fixed, not free with respect to the linguistic community that uses it . . . the Signifier chosen by language could be replaced by no other . . . No individual, even if he willed it, could modify in any way . . . the choice that has been made; and what is more, the community itself cannot control so much as a single word; it is bound to the existing language.

There are several reasons for this: we inherit language from previous generations, the ways in which words are used, their dictionary definitions and so on. We have to respect all this if communication is to occur. But there's more to it than that. The speech-sound component of the sign – the 'signifier' – got attached to its 'signified' quite arbitrarily. The 'ox' might just as well have been called a 'cat'. But for Saussure the 'signifieds' – the concepts – are just as arbitrary; they stem from the way that the world around us has been 'carved up' by a particular language. Saussure gives examples of different 'values' (p111). There is, for instance, a certain kind of meat which the French call 'mouton'; from which the English derived their 'mutton'. But when the animal was alive, and frisking around, the French still called it 'mouton'; the English called it 'sheep'. Different things are differentiated in quite different ways in different languages; so any particular concept only 'achieves' its meaning within a whole cluster of other concepts. We have to have the others to know where it lies in relation to them, how it is different from each of them.

Having clarified this, Saussure is at pains to point out that changes do occur in meanings over time for 'language is always the product of historical forces'. And it is these which preclude 'any sudden widespread change'. Above all, language is a social institution. I am perfectly free, if I wish, to call our four-legged animal a 'cat'. But no one would understand me if I did. I would have broken the 'social contract' by which English-speaking people call it an 'ox'. This social basis of language, as we shall see, Derrida does his damnedest to destroy!

But language offers more than communication with others. Saussure suggests that if we had no language our thoughts could only be 'a shapeless and indistinct mass'. If we had no signs to use in our thinking we would have no way of making any 'clear-cut, consistent distinction' between ideas. 'Without language, thought is a vague, uncharted nebula.' Language, therefore, gives us the structures by which we think.

So what kind of structures are they?

Two kinds, of course, for Saussure: 'Relations' and 'Differences'. We have looked at his 'Relations' already: 'Syntagmatic' and 'Associative'. As for his 'Differences' these of course occur between our words in the sounds we make as we speak them, such as those which allow us to distinguish **c**at from **m**at, **m**at from **s**at and so on. Of course the sounds themselves are arbitrary. The '**m**at' could have '**c**at' on the '**s**at', if other equally arbitrary connections had been made! What matters are the differences between them and from other words, too, which 'surround' them such as **b**at, **f**at, **h**at and **p**at. Saussure says that the 'phonic substance' contained in a sign is less important than its difference from the other signs which surround it. Of course different speech-sounds give us different 'Signifiers'. And since these are linked inextricably to 'Signifieds', our 'Signifieds' also will be structured by 'Relations' and 'Differences'. It is, says Saussure, these which enable us to think:

> The conceptual side . . . is made up solely of relations and differences with respect to the other terms of language, and the same can be said of its material side . . . Everything that has been said up to this point boils down to this: in language there are only differences.

Spelt with an 'e'. But these are 'Differences' of rather a special kind: a difference usually means that we have set something up and then set up something else in opposition. Black seems even more black when we oppose it with white! The fact that one opposes the other means, in a curious way, that each gives a reason for the other to exist. As Saussure puts it:

> . . . a difference generally implies positive terms between which the difference is set up: but in language there are only differences without positive terms. Whether we take the Signified or the Signifier, language has neither ideas nor sounds that existed before the linguistic system.

Of course there is much more to Saussure than simply this but the concepts we have explored, especially his Language/Speech, Signifier/Signified and Relations/Differences at least give us a basis from which to tangle with Derrida.

Saussure

DIACHRONIC LINGUISTICS: Studies of changes in language over time.

SYNCHRONIC LINGUISTICS: Studies of the structure of a language at a particular moment in time, hence STRUCTURALISM.

SYNTAGMATIC RELATIONS: Relationships between words within the structure, the SYNTAX of a sentence.

ASSOCIATIVE RELATIONS: Relationships with words 'outside' the sentence called up by their ASSOCIATIONS with words 'within' the sentence.

LANGUAGE: A system of words and the rules for using them, such as Greek, Latin, English, etc which gives structure to our thoughts and by which the members of a culture communicate with each other.

SPEECH (1): The personal selection of words etc out of *language* by which a particular individual communicates with others.

SPEECH (2): Face-to-face communication by use of the spoken word.

WRITING: Communication by words written on paper as a permanent record of one's thoughts.

SIGN: Anything which conveys ideas from one person's brain to others consisting of two parts, inextricably linked, a SIGNIFIER and a SIGNIFIED.

SIGNIFIER: The 'physical' aspect of a SIGN consisting of the sounds which form a word in speech, the marks on paper which form a word in writing, a drawing, a diagram, a painting, a piece of music, a building; anything intended by the author to convey a certain 'meaning' to others.

SIGNIFIED: The concept, thought or idea part of the 'sign' which is brought to mind by the SIGNIFIER as perceived by one of the senses.

DIFFERENCE: Such difference in sounds or marks on paper as those which enable us to distinguish, say, between cat and mat, mat and sat etc. The DIFFERENCES between our thoughts, our SIGNIFIEDS, which these conjure up in our minds.

Saussure's ideas had very little impact until 1958 when Claude Lévi-Strauss took them up. And then the flood gates were opened. 'Structures' of Saussure's kind were identified in virtually every branch of culture from History to Mathematics to Politics (see Lane 1970). Roland Barthes (1957) found them in such disparate *Mythologies* as Blue Guides, Detergent Packets, Striptease, Toys, Wine and Wrestling. Thus 'Structuralism' became a rampant intellectual fashion. Barthes sees a 'sign' as a three-part thing: a 'Signifier', a 'Signified' and 'Sign' as a whole, greater than the sum of its two parts. He has roses, he says, which signify his passion and these amount to more than roses (Signifier) and passion (Signified). They are, he says, 'passionified roses' and it is these which constitute the 'Sign-as-a-whole'. Barthes finds equivalent 'tri-dimensional' structures in Freud's psychoanalysis, Sartre's literary criticism and so on. A dream, for instance, is a 'Sign' which unites certain manifest events: the 'content' one remembers of the dream (Signifier) with the 'latent or real' meaning (Signified) in one's subconscious.

Barthes' *Mythologies* were part of his rather obsessive rooting out of the bourgeois ideology which in his view permeated Western Culture. Thus every kind of 'Sign' within that culture was a 'signifier' of that 'essential enemy (the bourgeois norm)', signifying that vast 'collective representation' within a 'second-order semiological system'. So each of his 'signs-as-a-whole' becomes the 'signifier' of another 'sign' and so on in an infinite process of regression:

1) Signifier	2) Signified	
3) Sign		
	I SIGNIFIER	II SIGNIFIER
	III SIGN	

This suggests an infinite 'nesting' of significations which Derrida was to take a good deal further, as we shall see.

The trouble is that 'Structuralism' never really worked, largely because it was based on such a tiny fragment of Saussure and on Saussure's two-value logic at that! This, as we shall see, presented problems of a kind which for Derrida are fundamental to the whole tradition of Western Philosophy.

Post-Structuralism

Derrida was by no means the only Parisian to react strongly against Structuralism; so did Roland Barthes himself who presented the 'rationale' – if such it can be called, for the dense, impenetrable, ambiguous and incoherent style of writing which seems to be the 'essence' of French 'Post Structuralism'. He launched his attack on 'clarity' in French, writing in his *Writing Degree Zero* of 1953. 'Clarity', he says 'is a purely rhetorical attribute, not a quality of language in general . . . the ideal appendage to a certain type of discourse, that which is given over to (an) intention to persuade'. For writing is 'in no way an instrument of communication'! It is, rather, a device by which his bourgeois 'enemy' imposes his own 'social, economic, and political conditions' upon other people. Barthes deplores the way in which language, and particularly the French language, has been used as a vehicle – the vehicle – for disseminating bourgeois values, forcing them on to others and making them seem 'normal', even to those who were disadvantaged by them. Barthes saw such writing as aimed at a passive 'consumer' of the text; he called it 'readerly' writing. So according to Barthes, if I try to write simply, directly, clearly and unambiguously, this stems from my bourgeois intention; my evident desire is to insinuate my thoughts into your brain, to 'colonise' your mind! Barthes warms to this theme in *S/Z* (1970) where he distinguishes between his 'readerly' writing and what he calls 'writerly', which is deliberately unclear, diffuse, incoherent and ambiguous. It will get you so angry that, in your struggle to understand, you will be forced into having your own creative thoughts! Like Barthes – and Derrida – Foucault, too, despises 'clarity'. As White says (1979):

> . . . the thorniness of Foucault's style is . . . ideologically motivated. His interminable sentences, parentheses, repetitions, neologisms, paradoxes, oxymorons, alternations of analytical with lyrical passages, his combinations of scientistic with mythic terminology – all this appears to be consciously designed to render his discourse impenetrable . . .

Foucault writes 'discourse', based largely on 'catachresis' – the slight misuse of words, such as 'anachronism' for 'anomoly' or 'chronic' for 'severe'. But for White it is precisely this style that gives authority to what Foucault has to say!

So Barthes, Foucault, Derrida and other French 'Post-Structuralists' actually aim to make their writing dense and impenetrable. I for one shall try to engage your mind by putting my thoughts – and even theirs – as clearly and directly as I can. On the grounds that if you understand me then you can disagree, tell me, in whatever terms you choose, precisely where you think I have gone wrong. If you try to remonstrate with the Post-Structuralist, of course, he can always claim that you are wrong; that your interpretation of his impenetrable prose is a naive misunderstanding of what he had in mind. It's like trying to put your finger on a blob of mercury. Once you touch it, it isn't there any more!

Deconstruction

So having set the scene, let us now look at what Derrida seems to be trying so very hard (not) to say. Just what is his 'Deconstruction'? That is notoriously difficult to say. Ellis (1989) goes in some detail into the fog of obscurity which surrounds it. As he points out (p ix), it is a favourite Deconstructionist device to attack the credentials of its opponents. For crucial to Deconstructionist technique is the 'dramatic denunciation of the person of common sense and received opinion', an attack of course, which is greatly facilitated by the obscurity of many deconstructive writings. So few 'outsiders' are bold enough to claim any confidence in their interpretations. Ellis sees his role as not so much contributing to an on-going debate as helping to create the conditions under which such a debate will be possible!

For as Ellis says (p3) all attempts to explain or to analyse 'Deconstruction' and certainly attempts to criticise it have been rebutted, superciliously, violently, even on the grounds that such approaches violate the very nature of 'Deconstruction'. Its proponents insist that 'it cannot be described and stated as other positions can' because it is a new form of logic. Such things as description, analysis and so on are, by their very nature, couched in the old, outmoded, traditional logic which 'Deconstruction' has superseded.

The first reasoned criticism, probably, was Graff's in his paper (1980) on 'Nothing Fails Like Success' and his later reviews of 'Deconstruction'. (1981, 1983 etc). And Graff was subject to counter-attack by Riddell in his 1980 paper: 'What is Deconstruction and Why Are They Writing All Those Graff-ic Things About It?'·

Enthusiasts, even, have been under fire for trying to explain 'Deconstruction' to make it intelligible to ordinary mortals. Jonathan Culler tried this in 1981 and 1982. He too was subject to scathing attack by Lentricchia (1980), Zavarzadeh (1981), Rendall (1984) and others. Zavarzadeh accuses him of the ultimate heresy: of trying to tame 'radical new ideas' whilst his *unproblematic* prose and the *clarity* of his presentation (my italics) . . . are the conceptual tools of conservatism'. Clearly it threatens the 'Deconstructionists' when anyone tries to open up their esoteric cult!

So I am by no means the first to pit myself, David-like, against the Goliath of 'Deconstruction'. Indeed the most thorough demystification is to be found in John M Ellis' *Against Deconstruction* published in 1989. Would that it had been published a year earlier! For that would have saved me months of puzzling through volumes of obscure, impenetrable prose; wilfully obscure as we have seen. On the other hand I found things he did not, so the following account is largely as I wrote it but reinforced where I need him – and with due acknowledgement – by Ellis.

But let us look at what the man himself, Jacques Derrida, says about 'Deconstruction'. In one version (1986) he says:

> Something has been constructed, a philosophical system, a tradition, a culture, and along comes a de-constructor (who) destroys it stone by stone, analyses the structure and dissolves it . . . One looks at a system . . . and examines how it was built, which keystone, which angle . . . supports the building; one shifts them and thereby frees oneself from the authority of the system.

But there is more to Deconstruction than that. It is by no means a 'technique of reversed construction'. It is, rather, 'a probing which touches (the very) technique itself', the technique which is being deconstructed!

Derrida's Programme

So what does he 'Deconstruct'? And how does he set about it? Derrida lays out a programme in the so-called 'Exergue' to *Of Grammatology* which raises the obvious question: what on earth is an 'Exergue'? According to the *Oxford Dictionary,* it's that small space on the back of a coin, below the 'principal device' containing, for instance, the year of minting. Or it may be the date itself. So Derrida, as so often, hijacks a word from quite another context and distorts its meaning for his own peculiar ends! I shall try to clarify this 'inscription' of Derrida's in a way that neither he nor his interpreters would approve – since the last thing they want is 'clarity'. He seems to be announcing his attack on the following:

ETHNOCENTRISM: the belief that one's own culture or ethnic group somehow is superior to others and therefore standards by which the others can and should be judged.

LOGOCENTRISM: a belief that at the roots of all existence there are abstract 'truths' organised in absolute and inevitable 'categories'. These exist only in the Mind and Word of God but all 'real' things are formed from them. We can penetrate to them only by the use of language.

PHONOCENTRISM: the idea that speaking is better than writing since it came first and gives us direct access to the speaker's thoughts; speech is 'transparent' in a way that writing can never be.

And more generalised attacks on:

METAPHYSICS: the age-old search by philosophers for 'truth', divided by Aristotle's editors into three main studies:

Ontology: the nature of 'Being' and what it is, actually, to exist.

Cosmology: the nature of the Universe itself. Sun, Moon, the planets and the stars to rotate in Celestial Spheres around the Earth.

Theology: the nature of the 'Prime Mover' who causes such movement.

ONTOTHEOLOGY: Martin Heidegger's personal blending of Ontology and Theology.

THE CONCEPT OF SCIENCE: the idea that Empirical Science can tell us anything of interest about the nature of the Universe, the nature of human thinking, meaning etc. Derrida sees 'Science' as entirely a matter of rational thought; he has no concept of observation and experiment.

Derrida's work indeed turns out to be a sustained, repetitive, and inconsistent attack on all of these but with considerable emphasis on his 'Logo-centrism', 'Phono-centrism' and 'Onto-Theology'.

One has to query for these in his voluminous writings. He is, after all a post-Structuralist, even an anti-Structuralist, so it's hardly surprising that his books have little sense of order, little sense of structure of any kind. He is anxious that one should plough through, and savour, his every word, so there are no indices. For most of us life is not long enough. There are far more interesting things to do, such as architecture. Nor can we expect, even if we do the 'ploughing' – given Derrida's view that there are no 'roots', to his own, or anyone else's thinking – to 'get to the bottom' of what he has in mind. So my attempt to extract anything coherent from his writing is totally alien to his way of working. And his thinking! So since he refuses to define his basic concepts, as do most of his interpreters, I can but try!

Metaphysics

Derrida chooses some ludicrously easy targets for his attacks from the long and continuing tradition of 'Metaphysics' started by the Greeks, especially Pythagoras, Parmenides, Socrates, Plato and Aristotle. Whilst one reads these early writers with pleasure, if not entire agreement, that cannot be said of their 20th-century successors. Indeed with some of the latter one has to struggle mightily to extract any semblance of meaning.

The central theme of 'Metaphysics' is being: what it is, actually, to be in the world; the different ways of being that there are; the different kinds of beings there may be, whether finite or infinite; their particular features and relationships. The Greeks, too, dealt with the nature of the universe as a whole – its origins and structure, with the nature of whatever 'Prime Mover' may have created it, keeps it in motion, and so on. The Metaphysician tries to penetrate such things by pure thought – by the strict application of reason. He believes he can do this because neither we nor the things around us need exist; need be 'there' in any way we understand as 'real'. They might exist only in a 'mind' of some kind.

As Anaxagoras wrote in the 5th century BC: 'the mind . . . arranges and causes all things', which pleased his great successor, Socrates (469-369 BC) who thought it 'somehow right' that this be so. For if 'the mind' causes everything, then of course it 'establishes each . . . as . . . is best for it to be'. But Socrates refused to write his thoughts down. He left that to his pupils, especially Plato and Xenophon who recorded various dialogues between Socrates and other people. Typically, Socrates asks his 'stooge' for views on something, questions those views and exposes their inconsistencies to establish 'the truth'.

Plato (c 427-348 BC)

It was in such a dialogue, *The Republic,* that Plato set out the 'ground rules' for Metaphysics. There Socrates sees 'Goodness' as the highest object of Knowledge (Book XXIII), the ultimate truth. His colleagues, naturally, want to know what 'Goodness' is but when it comes to the crunch, Socrates opts out! Asked to describe the ultimate Good, he answers: 'I am afraid it is beyond my power; with the best will in the world I should only disgrace myself and be laughed at . . . it would call for an effort too ambitious for an enquiry like ours.' So he offers the next best thing: 'the offspring of the Good . . . most nearly resembling it', which, he says, is the Sun! Later, in Book XXXVI, Socrates explains the nature of illusions:

An object seen at a distance does not . . . look the same size as when it is close at hand; a straight stick looks bent when part of it is under water; . . . the same thing appears concave or convex . . . to an eye misled by colour. Every sort of confusion . . . is to be found in our minds; and . . . this weakness . . . is exploited, with . . . quite magical effect, by many tricks of illusion, like scene painting and conjuring . . . .

Such illusions confuse our senses of seeing, hearing and so on, but means have been found for dispelling them, by measuring, counting and weighing. So we need be at their mercy no longer. That part of the 'soul' which does the counting, the measuring or the weighing, can take control. And since no part of the soul can hold to conflicting beliefs, this 'calculating or reasoning' part must be different in kind from, better, and indeed 'higher' than the mere 'sensing' part. But measuring still involves sensing things with our eyes and we shall get closer still to the 'truth' if we ignore our senses and conceive things directly in our minds. Abstract numbers will bring us to 'pure truth'; so will the geometry of two-dimensional shapes and three-dimensional forms. We can use pure 'reason' too to think out the motions of the heavenly bodies, the harmonies of music, and so on. So:

. . . the summit of the intelligible world is reached . . . by one who aspires, through the discourse of reason, unaided by . . . the senses, to make his way . . . to the essential reality and perseveres until he has grasped, by pure intelligence, the very nature of Goodness itself.

Many of Plato's successors accept his two 'worlds': the world as perceived by the senses, the 'sensible' world; and the world built entirely by the intellect, his 'intelligible' world. They ignore the 'world' between the two which Plato described; that which could be measured and worked on by arithmetic and geometry which Plato himself dismissed. For Plutarch records, in his *Life of Marcellus,* that since certain geometric problems cannot be solved by the intellect alone, even using 'words and diagrams', Eudoxus and Archytas had 'embellished' geometry by solving them with physical models. They used 'mechanical illustrations . . . patent to the senses', which infuriated Plato who:

. . . inveighed against them with great indignation as corrupt-

ing and destroying the pure excellence of geometry which thus turned her back upon the incorporeal things of intelligible thought and descended to things of the senses, using, moreover, objects which required much vulgar handicraft in their making.

So at Plato's insistence such pragmatic devices were expunged from geometry. Philosophers despised mechanical aids for many centuries thus limiting what they could think. But, sometime around 1600, Galileo, seeking to correct what seemed to be errors in Aristotle's physics and metaphysics, pointed his telescope at the Moon and the planets, measured the speeds of balls rolling down inclined planes and thus – by sensory observation and 'vulgar handicraft' – launched modern science on its triumphant course!

Nor does Plato's 'intelligible' world exhaust even the worlds we can construct entirely in our minds. Poets, painters, scientists and other creative people literally 'dream up' new, strange and wonderful ideas. Theirs is the 'world' of the 'imagination' but there was no place for them in Plato's *Republic;* they threatened his claim that 'intelligible' philosophy gives us the only access we need to the 'truth'. And Plato himself believed, as we have seen, in a 'Good' he could not explain. We cannot see his 'Good', his God, who is by no means accessible to our senses nor can we 'get to' him by the application of sheer intellect. But there is a world clearly, where people – such as Plato – 'feel' the presence of their God. We shall call theirs the world of 'Divine Revelation'.

Therefore we have five 'worlds'; but ever since Plato's time his exclusive concentration on his 'intelligible' world has permeated Metaphysics and indeed much other philosophy. This crippled human development for almost 2000 years; for limiting one's thinking to the intellect alone is tantamount to wrestling with a single limb. An important limb no doubt: one of the very 'legs' on which all our thinking stands; the other being our 'sensory' thinking. But how absurd to forgo the riches which other kinds of thinking can afford us!

Plato: Modes Of Thinking

THE INTELLIGIBLE WORLD: A world such as that of geometry which can be understood by the sheer application of intellect. Plato saw this as vastly superior to:

THE SENSIBLE WORLD: The world as we perceive it with our senses.

He possessed, but could not explain:

DIVINE REVELATION: But dismissed as perverting 'all that is good in geometry'.

PRAGMATICS: The use of mechanical models for solving geometric problems.

And he excluded from his 'Republic':

CREATIVE IMAGINATION: The work of artists and poets which might challenge the conventions of his 'Intelligible World'.

Derrida on Plato

Derrida himself sees Plato's two-world division as 'the founding-principle of Western Philosophy' and one which he believes has had profoundly detrimental effects. So it has, but this does not stop Derrida himself from choosing to work entirely in the 'intelligible', intellectual world! He professes to dislike intensely any kind of two-value logic; of thinking by 'binary oppositions' and finds many examples in Plato, listing, for instance: in *Dissemination* (1972) (p 85): 'speech/writing, life/death, father/son' and so on. These oppositions are elements of myths but later he finds others also in Plato (p 103) such as: 'good/evil, true/false, essence/appearance, inside/outside' and so on. These seem pernicious to Derrida especially when, as in the case of 'male/female' one of the pair is seen as having some kind of precedence over the other. He calls these 'substitutes for thinking', especially since in each case Plato clearly prefers the first term over the second. We shall see many more examples.

Aristotle

Plato's pupil Aristotle (384-322 BC) was less than satisfied with the universal science of Plato's *Republic*. He presented his own much more ambitious version in a daunting series of works. Yet he built on his Master's division into 'sensible' and 'intelligible' worlds; indeed in the *Prior Analytics* he laid down rules for thinking based on self-evident 'premises' such as:

All men are mortal	(Major premise)
Socrates is a man	(Minor premise)
Therefore Socrates is mortal	(Conclusion)

Yet despite Plato's strictures, Aristotle thought we should study things in the world around us by means of our senses and this 'natural science' would be his 'First Science' or Physics, crucial to which are his ideas on the causes of things which he describes in considerable detail. Aristotle believed that earthly matter in motion seeks to find its natural home, at the centre of the earth. Hence what we call 'gravitational attraction'. So the heavier an object the faster it will fall, as anyone could see by dropping a rock and a feather. But of course as a follower of Plato he could not permit himself the 'vulgar handicraft' of, say, dropping rocks of two different sizes and measuring the speeds at which they fell.

But there are limits to what Physics can explain. All 'substances' (material things) move and change and something must cause them to do so. So Aristotle seeks to find the 'immovable (immaterial) substance' which causes this: 'the science (of which) must be prior (to physics) . . .' He calls this 'First Philosophy', 'Wisdom' or 'Theology' and later his editors called it *Metaphysics*. Aristotle opens his *Metaphysics* with a Derrida-like 'deconstruction' of his predecessors such as Socrates, Plato, Heraclitus, Anaxagoras, Empedocles, Parmenides and the Pythagoreans finding them deficient because they did not understand 'Causes' in the way he did. He notes that some of them think in unities, some in pluralities and that the Pythagoreans, not to mention Plato, think in 'corresponding pairs'.

And in Book IV of the *Metaphysics* he declares its central study to be the nature of being as such: 'Being *qua* Being'. He describes various ways of 'being': as 'Substance', such as a man; as a 'Quality', such as white; as a 'Quantity', such as ten feet; as a 'Relation', such as a double, and so on. He has ten such ways of 'being' altogether. But what then is *being* as a 'Substance'? Aristotle's detailed explanations vary from time to time but in principle each 'Substance' starts as 'Matter' and is subject to his 'Causes' which bring it to its final 'Form'. Thus a statue may have bronze for its 'Matter', which is caused by a sculptor to take on a human 'Form'. The soul provides the Form of a living body, animal or vegetable. Plants possess such functions as growth, nutrition and reproduction; animals possess these and also locomotion, sensations and desires. Humans possess all these together with the faculty of reason by which they perform the highest activity of all: the pursuit of knowledge. Man's 'rational soul' is neither 'sensible nor perishable' in which respect it must resemble God.

Having described the nature of 'things', Aristotle considers the universe as a whole (Book XII), assuming that the Earth is at the centre, with the Sun, Moon, planets and stars moving round it in 'Celestial Spheres'. He even worked out how many spheres there might be: 47 or 55 according to how many were needed to explain the movements of the Sun and the Moon! The spheres are in constant motion, and 'that which is moved must be moved by a something'. But to move other things, that 'something' must be fixed: 'immovable, and external'. So Aristotle's universe needs a 'Prime Mover' of some non-material pure form; nothing more nor less than 'Mind' or 'God'.

So Aristotle laid the foundations of both Physics and Metaphysics. The crucial elements of the latter seem to be: the nature of 'Being *qua* Being', later known as 'Ontology'; the structure of the Universe, later known as 'Cosmology'; and the nature and existence of God, for which Aristotle's term 'Theology' was adopted.

This is not the place to trace the after-life of Metaphysics but since Derrida's major motivation seems to have been its demolition, we will put his thinking into context by seeing what happened to its basic concepts. Like Derrida himself, I find Metaphysics quite impotent to explain the world as I know it. But my objections are vastly different from his. For whilst some of his apologists think it a virtue that Derrida sticks to 'intelligible' methods in trying to destroy such methods, that seems to me perverse. It means that by their very nature Derrida's objections to Metaphysics are no more susceptible to proof – or refutation – than the very tenets he attacks since they, too, are only 'in the mind'.

I prefer to attack Metaphysics – and Derrida – by using all our ways of thinking: 'sensible', 'pragmatic', 'creative' and so on. Of course I have a complex argument – if by no means as convoluted as Derrida's own – and since my writing is on Architecture, this is not the place to expand upon it too far. So I have prepared a series of charts to outline the contributions which various thinkers have made to the philosophical traditions which Derrida has tackled or, in my view, ought to have tackled!

There are some obvious gaps: Marxism, which he brushes aside in *Positions;* the philosophy, as distinct from the history of science, which he brushes aside in *Of Grammatology,* and so on. These certainly would be included in any comprehensive record of Western thought but the picture is complicated enough without engaging issues which are quite outside the Derrida canon!

Taking the three major divisions of Metaphysics: Aristotle's Ontology, the study of 'being' and his Theology, his study of the 'Prime Mover' were taken over by Christians such as St Augustine, Thomas Aquinas, Duns Scotus and William of Ockham. Thomas developed Aristotle's 'proofs' for the Prime Mover as 'proofs' for the existence of his Christian God. For Duns Scotus, such things cannot be proved by any kind of logical argument; God's existence is a matter of Faith – Duns Scotus clearly occupies my 'world' of Divine Revelation. Whereas William occupies the world of the senses, we experience reality and develop by analogy our understanding of things beyond our sensory experience. The third aspect of Metaphysics, however – Aristotle's Cosmology – was utterly demolished by the rise of modern Science. For which Galileo and others used various combinations of 'sensible' observation, 'pragmatic' experiment and 'intelligible' thinking.

Despite Derrida's reservation such science has increased our understanding of the world, the universe, even ourselves, immeasurably. We do comprehend, say, the structure and working of the solar system. Copernicus, Galileo, Kepler, Newton, Einstein and others have given us such understanding that thanks to the first four we can calculate where each planet is going to be at any time we care to state in the future. And do it with such precision that we could launch a Voyager space craft in September 1977 – at an 'escape velocity' calculated by Einstein – in such a trajectory that the gravitational fields of various planets would enable it to swing by, not just the planets themselves but, at carefully selected distances, individual moons such as those which Galileo observed around Jupiter, especially Io; those around Saturn, such as Titan; those around Uranus, such as Oberon and Titania; those around Neptune, such as Triton and Canopus; and on certain stated days, at certain stated times, two, four, nine and even twelve years into the future.

Spacecraft, of course require fantastic amounts of 'vulgar handicraft'. Their cameras, transmitters and so on make 'facts' of the universe accessible to our senses. But most people these days see such triumphs of pragmatic and sensory revelation as infinitely more interesting, more exciting, more rewarding, than the speculative fictions of Aristotle's Cosmology.

500 years of science have 'killed' these stone dead. Indeed they were looking very sick when in 1692 Jean le Clerc coined the word 'Ontologia' to salvage what was left to Metaphysics the study of 'Being *qua* Being'. This suggests three provisional conclusions:

1 That in rejecting the 'sensible', not to mention the 'mechanical' world, Plato delayed our understanding by some 2000 years – until the time of Copernicus.

2 That Aristotle's descriptions of the universe were mere unsubstantiated speculations.

3 That in dismissing 'Empirical Science' with its 'sensible' observations and 'pragmatic' experiments Derrida too is turning back the clock, resorting, like Aristotle, to mere speculative fictions. But given the impact of science, how can speculations of these kinds command a hearing of any kind?

Aristotle (384-22 BC)

ORGANON: Aristotle's six books on logic including discussions (In *Categories*) of 'form' and 'substance' (noesia). Introduces *(Prior Analytics)* Aristotle's method of syllogisms, based on self-evident 'truths'.

PHYSICS: Aristotle's 'First Science' – a sense-based analysis of physical objects, their 'matter' and 'form', the causes of such things, space, position, time and movement. Supplemented by treatises O*n the Heavens, Meteorology, Animals* etc.

METAPHYSICS: A later title for Aristotle's 'First Philosophy', his 'intellectual' study of 'reality' and universal principles including his own four 'causes' and aporiai – the basic problems of *Metaphysics*. Its basic divisions – much developed by later writers and with later names – are:

ONTOLOGY: studies of 'being' as such: 'being *qua* being'.

COSMOLOGY: studies of the structure of the universe.

THEOLOGY: studies of whatever form the 'Prime Mover', 'ultimate cause' or, with later scholars, 'creator' of the universe may take.

ETHICS, POLITICS, POETICS

Essential works of Aristotle of less direct bearing on 'Deconstruction'.

Onto-Theology

But still the Ontologists persist. The first great Onto-Theologist was the founder of French Rationalism, René Descartes (1591-1650). Despite Galileo's demonstration that 'intellectual, sensory' and 'pragmatic' thinking together could achieve far more than any of these on its own, Descartes would have none of this. He had no time for 'vulgar handicraft'; his *Method* of 'Logical Doubt' (1641) rather was to 'think through' something like the nature of light and it is hardly surprising that Newton, with a prism, proved him unequivocally wrong.

Like Plato, Descartes simply does not trust his senses. Of course they can be tricked and Descartes tries to transcend them. He really cannot know if, at the moment, he is sitting in his chair, reading, or lying in his bed dreaming about it. Indeed Descartes tries to imagine a world in which everything is mere illusion. He cannot do it so he tries to go further, to imagine a state in which he, Descartes, no longer exists. He cannot do either: 'in the very act of . . . thinking anything at all', he, Descartes, indubitably exists. 'Whence, after due thought and scrupulous reflection, I have to conclude that . . . I think, therefore I am is . . . true every time I state it or conceive it.'

Having 'proved' his very own existence, Descartes then meditates on God's. His idea of God is 'particularly clear and distinct' so it must contain within itself 'more objective reality than any other', which argument he backs up with reference to knowledge. His own knowledge seems to grow all the time; there must be more to which he has not yet had access; indeed infinite knowledge has to exist somewhere, so there must be some Being with a Mind to possess it. This Being can only be his God!

Since his God is a triumph of 'intelligible' over 'sensible' thinking, Descartes feels constrained to back up his claim! As a living being he, Descartes, possesses physical substance. But in Metaphysics of course everything has to be part of a 'binary opposition'. So if there is a finite substance, such as himself, there must be an infinite substance, such as his God: the ultimate triumph, surely, of non-thinking by 'binary oppositions'!

Derrida on Descartes

Naturally Derrida is suspicious of Descartes. He outlines his reasons in *Writing and Difference,* quoting Michael Foucault of *Madness and Civilisation* to the effect that Descartes dismisses from his pure *cogito* anything to do with 'madness, folly, dementia, insanity' – hardly surprising since Descartes was aiming for total Rationalism! It seems to worry Derrida that such things are 'dismissed, excluded, and ostracised from the circle of philosophical dignity'. So like Foucault, Derrida advocates madness! Why would he want to do that? One can think of a compelling explanation!

Descartes of course had many successors, such as Leibnitz and Spinoza, who reasserted the precedence of the senses, whilst the views were opposed absolutely by the British Empiricists (see chart). The two positions: Rationalism and Empiricism, were reconciled with exemplary skill by Immanuel Kant (1724-1804) who argued that whilst our knowledge is based on experience, experience itself will be disordered unless we 'project' onto it our innate understanding of space and time.

Again one could write of many successors, such as Hegel and Schopenhauer but since Derrida himself hardly refers to them we should concentrate on those who seem to have provoked his reactions. No one since Descartes has advanced new Theological claims. Indeed it may be argued that Descartes himself had hardly advanced on Thomas Aquinas!

Immanuel Kant (1724-1804)

Kant tried to reconcile the entirely 'intelligible' methods of Descartes and his Rationalism with the search for the sense-based knowledge based of John Locke, George Berkeley, David Hume and other British Empiricists (see chart).

Kant explored the limits of 'intelligible' knowledge – he called it 'a priori' with a view to building an entire Transcendental Philoso-phy. Kant had no doubt that all our knowledge arises from sensory experience – he called it 'Empirical' – but still there are things we seem to know, such as mathematical propositions, quite independently of that. As he says, take away from a (solid) body 'everything that is empirical . . . such as colour, hardness . . . weight (etc) . . . and there still remains the space which the body . . . had occupied'. What's more we can imagine such a space by a 'pure intuition' of 'extension and form'. We have such 'intuitions' not only of objects extending in space but also of objects existing in time. So concepts of 'space' and 'time' exist within us and we project them on to the world around us. That must be so since we whilst we have senses, such as eyes for seeing, we have no organs specifically for sensing 'space' or 'time', so: 'Space . . . is the subjective condition of our sensibility, without which no external intuition is possible for us' and 'the representation of time itself is an intuition.'

Auguste Comte (1798-1859)

The 'Positivism' of Comte was a somewhat violent reaction to the 'fictions' of Ontology and indeed of Theology.

Comte held that human thinking had passed through its Theological and Metaphysical stages and whilst real questions arose in both of these, no means are available for man with which to answer them. Science, and especially the Empirical science of Locke, Hume and Berkeley, can answer questions on which basis human thought would move to a more Positive phase. For Hume there is a place for pure logic and mathematics, as 'relations of ideas'. But our knowledge of facts must be based, as the Empiricists suggested, on the 'positive' data of our sensory experience.

As for religion, whilst that may be in decay, there is such a thing as a religious impulse. This should be given some objective: Humanity itself; so Comte envisages a religion based on the worship of man with its churches, its calendar and its hierarchy.

Friedrich Nietzsche (1844-1900)

Nietzsche, too, believed that modern science had destroyed the bases of Metaphysics and, even more, Theology. He denies, absolutely, the idea of 'binary oppositions', as he says in *Human, All Too Human* (1878): 'how can something originate in its opposite . . . rationality in irrationality, the sentient in the dead, . . . living for others in egoism, truth in errors'?

Metaphysics has argued each case for the more highly valued of the two: 'a miraculous source in the very kernel and being of the "thing in itself"'. But historical philosophy can no longer be separated from Natural Science which, increasingly, was proving that 'there are no opposites . . . and that a mistake in reasoning lies at the bottom of this antithesis . . .' There is some 'basic element' behind each pair which can be detected by patient observation. So all attempts to explain the nature of existence in religious or philosophical terms were rendered obsolete by science, indeed by Positivism, which of course led Nietzsche towards the notorious claim, in *The Gay Science,* that 'God is dead', and which of course induced in believers states of acute disorientation and distress. Yet Nietzsche took the view that great harm had been done by placing so much credence in God, and especially the Christian God. The great men of Classical Antiquity had no concept of 'thinking of others' which the Christian Church imbues: each strove mightily to further his own ends. Christ had subverted 'the attributes of mastery' into equal and opposite vices. If the 'good' were the powerful then: 'the meek shall inherit the earth'; pride itself became a sin and so on. Nietzsche despises this 'ascetic' ideal; he calls it 'Nihilism'. Religion and Philosophy had both been driven by a powerful 'motivating assumption': that existence, by its very nature, needs explaining. Both denigrate the world of appearance in favour of some other, 'true' world of the Spirit, suggesting that both are concerned with life in decline or at least in some state of acute distress.

Although 'God is dead', certain replacements are available such as nationalism, but Nietzsche prefers that 'Will to Power' which 'Nihilism' had denied. Nietzsche describes it in *Daybreak* (1881) as: 'the demon of men . . . striving for distinction . . . for domination over the next man . . .' So what kind of man will exercise this 'Will to Power'? Well of course there is the 'Superman' whom Nietzsche describes in *Thus Spake Zarathustra*. If his 'Will to Power' is our fundamental driving force; if, as Nietzsche puts it in *Beyond Good and Evil* (1886) 'nothing is "given" except our world of desires and passions', then might we not question: 'whether this which is given does not suffice for an understanding even of the so-called mechanical (or 'material') world? So the world seen from within, described according to its 'intelligible character', would be 'Will to Power' and nothing else. It is hardly surprising that Nietzsche's 'Will to Power' should appeal to the Nazis. Indeed it was seen by some as the force behind Nazism. There are Nietzsche disciples who wish it were not so, who claim that Nietzsche was misrepresented and so on. Yet it was an obscure essay of Nietzsche's, untranslated into English, that had the greatest effect on Derrida's thinking. For in 'Über Wahreit und Lüge im aussermoralishen Sinne', Nietzsche had complained that, since all language is metaphorical, it is quite unable to convey truth.

20th-Century Ontology

Despite the attacks by Comte and Nietzsche on those who spend their time explaining the nature of 'being' and their view that 19th-century Positivism had removed the need for such studies, there have been those who attempted to continue with such things as the only aspect of Metaphysics that could conceivably be brought to new conclusions.

Of course they had to compete with 20th-century science, which, continued by Einstein, Bohr, Heisenberg and others in the spirit of Galileo, with his combination of 'intelligible, sensible' and 'pragmatic' thinking, was leading (see charts) to the zany surrealism of Relativity, Quantum Mechanics and a science-based Cosmology that were so much more interesting, so much more fun than anything Ontology could offer, one wonders why anyone thought it worthwhile to continue.

But Husserl, Heidegger and others did so with dogged perseverance producing ponderous stuff indeed compared with the insights of Empirical Science. There was no way of 'proving' anything they wrote. Or, for that matter, of 'disproving' it. One simply 'believes' them or one does not. The crucial point being that if anyone were to take them seriously, they had to make their Ontology seem more complicated than Science, so difficult to understand, so impenetrable, that people really would not know if it were sense or nonsense.

Edmund Husserl (1859-1938)

The idea of 'absolute knowledge' had been pursued by Franz Brentano (1838-1917) who, starting from a purely Empiricist viewpoint studied, in his 'descriptive psychology', relationships between ideas and judgements, love and hatred. Studies of mental phenomena were to be taken very much further by Edmund Husserl (1859-1938) who looked not so much for 'essence' of being as for the 'roots' of human knowledge. Thus in *The Philosophy of Arithmetic* (1887) he explores Plato's ideas that numbers, somehow, give us clues to 'intelligible' thinking which we should be able to apply in other fields. They are by no means to be found in nature 'ready made' but result, rather, from psychological processes within the brain. Then, after savage criticism by Frege, he decided that the 'objects' of mathematics and logic, not to mention philosophy, are abstract 'essences' present to the mind but by no means states of it. They were quite independent of sensory experience.

Husserl sets out his programme, his search for the foundations of meaning in *Ideas . . .* (1913) starting rather like Descartes with his 'Method of Doubt'. But Descartes had been alone with his consciousness: 'I think therefore I am' whilst for Husserl (p 100) 'nothing essential is altered if, instead of a single Ego a plurality of Egos is taken into consideration'. His own consciousness will be enriched by 'possible mutual understanding' if the world of his experience 'can . . . become identified with that of others . . . enriched by their more extensive (because collective) experience'.

It's a bit like perception for Berkeley: if Husserl isn't actually perceiving something then somebody else might, for: 'a transcendency which lacked the above-described connection by harmonious motivational concatenations with my current sphere of actually present perceptions would be a completely groundless assumption.' Indeed a transcendency which lacked any 'such a concatenation essentially would be nonsensical'.

This 'transcendental consciousness' belongs in the first place to Nature (p 125). But then some organism, human or other, begins to experience part of it. Thus a connection is formed joining that 'consciousness' with a particular organism. It's only because they share this 'transcendental consciousness' that organisms can have any communication or mutual understanding with each other; only thus can a 'cognising subject' know that there is a complete world beyond him: 'common to him and to all other subjects'.

So, enquires Husserl (p 63), 'what can remain' 'if the whole world, including ourselves with all our cogitare, is excluded'? But for Husserl, of course: 'the exclusion of the world does not signify the exclusion of the world'! Such things remain as 'the number series or arithmetic relating to it'. Of course he is looking (p 65) for 'pure mental processes', for 'pure consciousness'. So he starts with 'the Ego, the consciousness, and the mental processes' as they are given to us. In his pursuit (p 65) of 'that consciousness (which) has, in itself, a being of its own which in its absolute essence, is not touched by (his) phenomenological exclusion'.

What's more (p 66) he calls this 'pure' consciousness he seeks 'transcendental consciousness' and he hopes to reach it by transcendental 'reduction'. So what, precisely, is his 'reduction' about? Husserl wants to study his own perceptions; recording, clearly and directly, what happens, during his actual perceiving, describing their relationships and structures. Such structures will be 'universal', that is common to all humans, quite independent of Husserl himself, so of course he believes that his analyses will get to the heart of the matter.

So Husserl hopes to grasp the 'universal' and 'unchangeable structures'; the essences of the things which lie behind his acts of consciousness, and by further 'reduction' to discover his own 'transcendental ego' which will be 'pure consciousness'.

Derrida discusses Husserl's 'theory' of meaning in various writings, but especially in his Introduction (1962) to Husserl's *Origin of Geometry* and in *Speech and Phenomena* (1967) which is actually subtitled: *And Other Essays on Husserl's Theory of Signs*. He analyses the Logical Investigations especially the Fifth and the Sixth of these, the Ideas, the Formal and Transcendental Logic, taking great exception to the idea of being as a 'living presence'. As Derrida says: 'To think of presence as a universal form of transcendental life is to open myself to the knowledge that in my absence, beyond my empirical existence, before my birth and after my death, the present is.'

Martin Heidegger (1889-1976)

Again despite Nietzsche and yet like many others before him, Heidegger set himself the fruitless task of penetrating the roots, the very meaning of existence. He looks for Being 'as such' rather than the 'being' embodied in anyone's particular existence. Heidegger maintains that the human 'way of being' is different in kind from any other and calls it 'Da-sein' ('there-being').

Heidegger pursues this aim in a number of texts such as *Being and Time* (1927); *What is Metaphysics* (1929); *An Introduction to Metaphysics* (a 1935 lecture published in 1953); *The Question of Being* (1955) and, relating directly to architecture: *Dwelling, Building, Thinking* (1954).

Being and Time is an unreadable book, even in German. Heidegger invents 'new' Greek words, 'new' Latin words, 'new' German words; he invents multiple new meanings for existing words. Indeed one of his English translators, Maquerie, says in his Introduction (1952):

Adverbs, prepositions, pronouns, conjunctions are made to do service as nouns; words which have undergone a long history of semantical change are used afresh in their older senses; specialised modern idioms are generalised far beyond the limits within which they would ordinarily be applicable. Puns are by no means uncommon and frequently a key-word may be used in several senses, successively or simultaneously.

Maquerie and his co-translator list some 70 Greek terms, 95 Latin and no less that 750 German ones for which they had struggled to find equivalents. Some 100 of the 'German' words seem to be variations on the idea of 'Being', which clearly fuels Derrida's idea that words need not mean anything very much!

Heidegger's 'Dasein' consists of 'being-there' both as a state of mind and as a physical presence. Being-there, 'thrown' into the world is, to say the least, disorientating. We overcome this, says Heidegger, because we have a potential, an *Entwurf* for understanding why the *Dasein* is there. We 'project' ourselves into the world.

We have two ways of doing this: we can let the world around us determine our understanding by the 'care' of social and other pressures – this leads to an 'inauthentic' existence; or we can identify the purpose of our 'Dasein' – what it is there 'for the sake of', and 'project' ourselves into this by which means we attain 'authentic' existence.

The Dasein however, can be directed towards this major task – of taking its 'fate' into its own hands – by *Angst* or 'dread'. But what do we dread? According to Heidegger: 'Nothing'. We know that we shall die one day and this fills us with angst. The Dasein cannot control this; Death does the calling! Which can trigger in the Dasein it's innermost potential, to grasp its infinite possibilities, make decisions which reveal its full potential.

Eventually, however, Heidegger finds that language itself actually prevents our thinking of such things as the 'Essence of Being'. He took to writing 'Being' as B̶e̶i̶n̶g̶, suggesting that the lines do not represent a 'crossing out'. They mark, rather, the four areas of a quadrangle and their gathering together at the point of intersection.

So Being represents the relation of a being to its B̶e̶i̶n̶g̶. And the crossing out indicates that whilst Being and 'being' exist, the B̶e̶i̶n̶g̶ between them is neither the one nor the other. And indeed as Spivak suggests that (1976) Heidegger pushes language well beyond the limits of any kind of sense when he says: 'Man in his essence is the memory of Being, but of Being'.

For reasons which are difficult to fathom Heidegger has acquired a reputation, especially amongst those who have never tried to read him, of 'standing for' human values in the face of Positivism.

Nothing could be further from the truth, as his recent biographers testify. For in 1933 he became Rector of Freiburg University and in his Rectorial Address he sought some kind of fusion between his philosophical 'language' and the language of National Socialism. Indeed he saw Hitler's seizure of power as the positive grasping of Germany's 'fate'. As Heidegger said: 'Do not let doctrines and ideas be the rules of your Being. The Führer himself, and he alone, is the present and future of Germany reality and its rule.' Later that year he signed a Leipzig Declaration to the effect that voting for Hitler was a 'primal demand of Being'. And even though Heidegger was shortly to resign as Rector he retained his membership of the Nazi Party until the end of World War II.

All this and more is documented by Victor Farias (1987) and Hugo Ott (1989). Derrida considers it, too, in *De l'Esprit* (1987) where he asks whether these personal errors mean that we should condemn the philosophy as well? His answer is that whilst Heidegger left 'traces' of his thinking, there is no philosophy 'as such'. So there is nothing to criticise! But as Roberts points out (1989) Derrida's position is dangerously close to what Husserl calls 'the comfortable and impressive role of academic sceptic'. If the teaching has nothing much to offer, one is seduced by the charismatic teacher. Roberts prefers, as do I, the modesty of John Locke, founding-father of Empiricism, who declares himself 'an under-labourer in the garden of knowledge'. Locke wishes to lay things open for anyone to use, quite indifferent to the leaving of personal 'traces'. For as Roberts puts it, concerning the 'Heidegger case' and with appropriate force: 'a philosophy that rests too heavily on charisma and personality is an irresponsible vanity at best, and at worst is helpless against confusion and terror'.

Yet Heidegger's later essay on: *Building, Dwelling, Thinking* (1951) has acquired a cult status among certain architects. As in *Being and Time* he is concerned with humans and their objects, in this case buildings or, rather 'dwellings' – those which enclose 'locations' that 'make space and a site for the fourfold', the 'fourfold' being Heidegger's mystic union of 'earth and sky, of divinities and mortals'. Earth is 'the serving bearer, blossoming and fruiting, spreading out in rock and water, rising up into plants and animals'; whilst Sky is the 'vaulting path of the sun, the course of the changing moon . . . the . . . glitter of the stars, the . . . seasons . . . the light and dusk of day . . . the gloom and glow of night, . . . Buildings, of course, 'stand there' on the Earth under the sky.

Heidegger's Divinities are 'beckoning messengers of the god-head' whilst his Mortals are mere human beings, 'called mortals because they die'. As for the nature of a building which has these properties, Heidegger describes a bridge over a stream. It does more than merely connecting banks which are there already: 'The banks emerge as banks only as the bridge crosses the stream . . . One side is set off against the other by the bridge.' But surely the banks were there before the bridge was built; it had to be for bridge-building to be possible and even necessary in the first place! But for Heidegger the bridge 'gathers to itself in its own way earth and sky, divinities and mortals'.

Credulity is stretched further when Heidegger argues that whilst we think of 'man' and 'space' as two things standing side by side, space 'is neither an external object nor an inner experience . . . for when I say "a man", and . . . think of a being who exists in the human manner – dwells – then by the name "man" I already name the stay within the fourfold among things.' The crucial point for him being that: 'when we relate . . . to . . . things that are not in our immediate reach, *we are staying with the things themselves* [my italics]. We do not represent distant things merely in our minds . . . so that only mental representations . . . run through our minds . . .'

No, he says: 'If all of us now think . . . right here, [he was lecturing in Darmstadt] of the old bridge in Heidelberg . . . this thinking . . . is not a mere experience inside the persons present here . . . thinking gets through . . . that bridge in itself, persists through . . . the distance to that location. From this spot right here, we are there at the bridge . . . by no means at some representational content in our consciousness.' Indeed they may be nearer to it here 'than someone who uses it [every day] as [a] river crossing [to which they are] indifferent'. One is tempted to suggest that if you believe that you'll believe anything, or nothing!

Derrida on Ontology

Derrida, as we shall see, considers Heidegger a worthy opponent but in principle is opposed to the idea of absolute truths, a 'centre' to human existence of the kind which Heidegger pursues. Indeed in *Spurs* he sends up Nietzsche, Husserl, Heidegger and the whole Hermeneutic tradition; even, it must be said – himself.

Derrida points out in *De l'Esprit* (1987) that despite his search for 'ultimate truths' Heidegger avoids discussion of anything to do with the 'mind' or 'spirit'. Even his Being has nothing to do with them, yet without at least a 'mind', there can be no memory and hence no knowledge that one has been and continues to be!

Metaphysics gives us an intellectual structure which on its own simply cannot penetrate the 'essence' of anything – except the results of pure, unmediated thinking. It is, by definition, out of contact with the world. Plato, as we have seen, tried to suppress the 'sensible' world, and the world of pragmatic 'mechanics'. He trusted only thinking in his intelligible world, as a result of which his *Republic* was an austere and thoroughly art-less place. Nietzsche's 'sensible' world gave inspiration to the Nazis. Heidegger's Phenomenology, literally, gave him so little understanding of human affairs that he saw Hitler as the 'saviour' of Germany. It is no coincidence that this 'Fascist' thread – however slender – runs through the history of Metaphysics. Since there are no substantial truths behind its complex speculations, some backing has to be found and the totalitarian 'We have ways of making you believe' seems at least to ensure a hearing for such things. Tested against our other ways of thinking it proves to have been a signally pointless enterprise. We have seen already that the Cosmology of Metaphysics collapsed completely in the face of Galileo's multi-pronged attack: 'intelligible' thinking informed by 'sensible' observations, using his telescopes and 'pragmatic' experiments, with balls rolling down inclined planes.

Pragmatism

Pragmatics had no real philosophical basis until late in the 19th century when Charles Sanders Peirce developed his Pragmatism which was developed further by William James and John Dewey (see chart). The 'truth' of any proposition for Peirce lies entirely in it's practical effects. Thus if one says: 'This is hard' it actually means: 'If you tried to scratch it, you would not succeed.' Apply this principle of 'practical effects', say, to Husserl's proposition that all meaning resides in some 'Transcendental Consciousness', to Heidegger's 'Being', and all one can say is, 'Oh really,' or, 'So what?' Apply it, as John Dewey did, to religious belief and as he says, there really are people who live better lives because of such beliefs. Their beliefs therefore must be 'true'. Apply it to Nietzsche's idea of the 'Superman', to Heidegger's belief that voting for Hitler was 'the primal demand of Being' and one begins to sense that these were 'true' in some rather monstrous way!

There are further intriguing pragmatic tests. Try buying any of the Ontological texts in your high street bookshop or even your campus bookstore. No doubt you will find a little Plato and Aristotle, Descartes, Rousseau and Nietzsche. You are unlikely to find any Husserl and you will need a rather specialised shop to find Heidegger or even Derrida. You may find a general book on Pragmatism but it's almost certain that you will find, say, Steven Hawking on *A Brief History of Time;* the present state, as it were, of scientific Cosmology.

For architects, of course, Pragmatism has particular significance. Buildings are judged by their practical effects. What is more, as I shall be suggesting, for every 'intellectual' 'Deconstructionist' there have been several Pragmatists. Pragmatic 'Deconstruction' can be just as valid, just as interesting, as the more earnest, intellectual kind but before we go further into either of these we should look further into Derrida and his working methods.

Derrida's Working Methods

The clearest account of Derrida's working methods – in so far as clarity has been achieved – is to be found in Barbara Johnson's Introduction (1981), as translator, to *Dissemination*. As she points out, Derrida attacks not just formal Philosophy but also everyday thought and language, too, as seem to take their values from it. She also points out that Derrida is extremely difficult to read and vastly more difficult to translate, for reasons which she lists such as Syntax: 'Ambiguity is rampant. Parentheses go on for pages. A sentence beginning on p 319 does not end until p 323' – having taken in pages of quotation on the way! Then there are allusions – multiple references to unnamed sources. Derrida does not tell us that his frequent use of words such as 'castration, lack, talking truth . . . letters not reaching their destination' all derive from Lacan. Certain essays seem to fade 'in and out' from nothing to nothing, and of course there are Derrida's multiple games with language. Johnson calls them 'Multiple Coherences' and they range from say the use of a tense, such as future perfect, to a 'theme' of some kind, such as 'stones, columns, folds, caves, beds, textiles, seeds' and so on. There are games with letters: 'd' or 'i' and there are what she calls Anagrammatical Plays such as 'graft/graft, semen/semantics, *lit/lire*' and so on. Above all, as we have seen, there is Derrida's dislike of 'binary oppositions'. She lists good/evil, being/nothingness, presence/absence, truth/error, identity/difference, mind/matter, man/woman, soul/body, life/death, nature/culture, speech/writing.

What is more, in each of these pairs the second element is seen somehow as inferior to the first, a negative, 'corrupt and undesirable', version of it. As Johnson puts it: 'absence is the lack of presence'; 'evil is the fall from good'; 'error is a distortion of truth'. It's not just that the terms are opposed; they are placed into a hierarchy in which one is preferred to the other, considered 'better', comes 'before' it in every sense. So 'in general . . . these hierarchical oppositions . . . privilege, unity, identity, immediacy . . . presentness over distance, difference, dissimulation, and deferment'.

Unlike Derrida, however, we shall not denigrate binary thinking. It is basic, after all, to digital computing. Everything that can be processed: words, numbers, drawings, half-tone pictures, music and so on is reduced, within the machine, to sequences of on/off – that is binary – switching. But it is by no means the only way of thinking. Charles Sanders Peirce founded the 'Theory of Signs' that rivals Saussure's. His 'Semiotic', habitually thought in threes such as Icon, Index and Symbol by which, as we shall see, he and his disciples could solve certain problems which simply were beyond Saussure – and Derrida. However, neither can all human affairs be reduced to three. We miss many valuable nuances, if we forget that in between black and white there is an infinite number of shades of grey. You cannot describe a rainbow in terms of binary oppositions although you might, just, get away with a triad of red, yellow and blue – on the grounds that all the other colours can be mixed from them. But of course you'd do better to adopt what Miller so memorably calls 'The magic number seven, plus or minus one'.

So where does this take us with Derrida? Let us look again at the agenda he set himself in the 'Exergue' to *On Grammatology*. Many of his targets are versions of 'Centrism' with prefixes such as 'Anthro-', 'Logo-' and 'Phono-'. Not that he ever defines them but we can piece together from many fragments something of what he seems to have in mind.

Ethnocentrism

Let us start, as Derrida does in *Of Grammatology* (p 3) with Ethnocentrism which he says: 'everywhere and always has controlled the concept of writing', which seems to him important because in his view his other 'Centrisms' follow directly from that. His 'Phonocentrism' indeed is that in Western tradition – as he sees it – speech has been 'privileged' over writing. The villain of the piece in his view, the grand purveyor of this 'Ethnocentrism' was none other than Ferdinand de Saussure, 'the moralist or preacher from Geneva, who, as we have seen deplored the fact that speech had been 'contaminated' by writing. Which of course as we have seen is not quite what Saussure had said.

So what does Derrida mean by 'Ethnocentrism' in this context? Not that one expects him to define it! Let's take more of Webster's definitions: 'a gentle insistence on the good qualities of one's own group with a concommitant tendency toward viewing alien cultures with disfavour and a resulting sense of inherent superiority . . .' Which is why as Saussure said Western linguists traditionally have regarded cultures which used writing, such as their own, as inherently superior to those that just used speech and concentrated on analyses of written texts.

So, as Ellis says (1989), far from subscribing to such 'Ethnocentrism', Saussure specifically deplored it; attacking those philologists who, restricting themselves to written sources, 'were largely concerned with their own corner of the world' (Ellis p 20). Saussure's specific intention, and his achievement, was to 'turn linguistics away from this prevailing ethnocentric concern with the written word towards the spoken languages of . . . the world outside the Western tradition'.

The Western tradition had been profoundly pro-writing before Saussure; he drew attention to the importance of speech as a way of correcting this ethnocentric view. So, far from continuing a view which had been traditional in the West Saussure turned decisively against it. As Ellis suggests, far from 'correcting' Saussure's supposed ethnocentrism, Derrida reinstates exactly the kind which had prevailed before Saussure drew attention to its major problem: 'the primacy of the written word – the "bookishness" – that is so typical of the Western intellectual tradition'.

Phonocentrism

As for Derrida's 'Phonocentrism'; his 'privileging' of speech over writing, Derrida suggests in *Of Grammatology* that many key philosophers have simply assumed that speech came first, came before writing and is superior to it. Apart from Saussure these have included Claude Lévi-Strauss, Jean-Jacques Rousseau, even Aristotle and Plato.

Aristotle wrote in *De Interpretatione* (1 16a 3) that: 'spoken words . . . are the symbols of mental experience . . . and written words are the symbols of spoken words'. That was so, as Derrida points out (p 30), because in Aristotle's view the voice has an immediate relationship with the mind. It is the 'first signifier' of our thoughts, presenting our 'mental experiences' directly with nothing at all to distort them.

And Derrida (p 27) quotes a fragment from Rousseau's Essay on the *Origins of Language* (1817) to the effect that: 'Writing is nothing but the representation of speech . . .', which is interesting in view of the fact that Rousseau found speaking painful! He describes himself in the *Confessions* (1:41) as 'shy and timid by nature'. Sometimes, aroused by passion, he can find the right words, but (p 44), 'in ordinary conversation I can find none . . . I find conversation unbearable owing to the . . . fact that I am obliged to speak'. He finds it difficult enough to put his thoughts together in writing (p 113), but, (p 116): 'The role I have chosen in writing and remaining in the background is precisely the one that suits me. If I had been present, people would not have known my value. They would not even have suspected it.' So, says Derrida (p 144):

Languages are made to be spoken, writing serves only as a supplement to speech . . . Speech represents by conventional signs, and writing represents the same with regard to speech. Thus the art of writing is . . . a mediated representation of speech.

And of course for Saussure (1857-1913): 'language and writing are two different systems of signs; the second exists for the sole purpose of representing the first'. Writing is merely a 'trace' of what the writer would have spoken if he had been there with you in the first place, speaking his thoughts directly. Given our two ways of using language it's quite obvious that speech comes first in every way. Primitive humans spoke before they could write; children learn to speak before they learn to write and many people who speak quite fluently cannot even write their names.

Plato's *Phaedrus*

The fullest statement of this preference for speech, however, is to be found in Plato's *Phaedrus* on which Derrida wrote critical essays for *Tel Quel* (1968 reprinted 1972). In this particular Dialogue, Phaedrus has an essay, written by Lysis in which the latter argues his preference for partners (male – this being ancient Greece) driven by physical desire rather than by love with all its painful complications! Socrates agrees to listen to the speech provided he and Phaedrus can find a pleasant place to sit. Which they do on a river bank outside the City. Plato describes the speech as a 'pharmakon' – normally a 'drug' – Phaedrus' device for tempting Socrates out and he uses 'pharmakon' later in the Dialogue too. As we shall see Derrida makes (too) much of its very different meanings; these indeed are central to his 'theory' of language.

When they get to their chosen spot, Phaedrus offers to summarise Lysis' speech, but Socrates insists that he read it word by word, which is crucial for Derrida who argues that (p 71):

A spoken speech . . . a speech proffered in the present, in the presence of Socrates, would not have had the same effect. Only words in written form . . . words that are deferred, reserved, enveloped, rolled up, words that force one to wait for them . . . can thus get Socrates moving.

So it's important for Derrida that their walk from the city has delayed, 'deferred' the moment when Phaedrus starts his reading. If Lysis himself had been there, actually speaking, 'speech could be purely present, unveiled, naked, offered up in person in its truth, without the detours of a (written) signifier . . .'

Socrates then presents speeches, both much better than Lysis' Essay, after which he traces the origins of writing to the Egyptian god Thoth – who Derrida sometimes calls 'Theuth'. Thoth indeed was a most remarkable figure even by ancient Egyptian standards; according to the *Encyclopaedia Britannica* he was:

> originally . . . god of the moon, (who) later became the god of reckoning, and of learning in general. He also was held to be the inventor of writing . . . founder of the social order . . . creator of languages, the scribe, interpreter, and adviser of the gods . . . representative of the sun god, Ra, on earth . . . He weighed the hearts of the deceased . . . and reported the result to the presiding god, Osiris and his fellow judges . . .

Plato records a more modest list of achievements: 'It was he who first invented numbers and calculation, geometry and astronomy, not to speak of draughts and dice, and above all writing.'

Having invented it, Thoth presented his writing to the Egyptian God/King Thamus, arguing that it 'will make the Egyptians wiser and will improve their memories, my invention is a pharmakon for both memory and wisdom'. But Thamus is by no means convinced; indeed he rejects Thoth's writing out of hand on the grounds that:

> this invention will produce forgetfulness in the soul of those who have learned it because they will not need to exercise their memories, being able to rely on . . . written . . . marks . . . alien to themselves . . . rather than (their) powers to call things to mind . . . What you have discovered is a pharmakon for recollection, not for memory.

Thus Thamus, the 'Father' of Egypt, rejects this pharmakon of writing and Derrida makes much, as one might expect, of the binary opposition 'father/son'.

But Socrates says that words, too, need their 'father'; they really cannot stand on their own. They are like paintings which look like real people but, when you question them, simply remain there mute; so it is with written words. You'd expect the words themselves to know what they mean, but if you ask them 'they simply return the same answer over and over again'.

Anything committed to writing circulates indifferently, even promiscuously, going quite indiscriminately to those who understand and those who do not. 'Writing cannot distinguish between suitable and unsuitable readers.' So, says Derrida, the reader will have noticed that according to Socrates, words committed to writing will be defenceless, in a state of misery. Speech, of living words, has a far happier time; its living 'father', the speaker, is standing there to support it.

Derrida says in *Positions* (p 22): 'the voice is consciousness itself.' When I speak: 'I am conscious of being "present for what I think . . . of keeping as close as possible to my thought". Each word becomes a signifier "that I hear as soon as I emit".'

All of which makes speech a very special case. In writing, the 'signifiers' are out there on the page, physical things that we can see, with not a 'signified' in sight. The writer is not present with his thoughts, so as Derrida says in *Of Grammatology* writing cannot be transparent to our thoughts in the way that speaking can.

So how does Derrida set about his 'rehabilitation' of writing? In several ways. If writing were merely a 'trace' of speech there could be no such thing as standard spelling. We should each spell words as we pronounce them, record our hesitations, our constant breakings-off in mid-sentence, our frequent repetitions and so on. So writing has structures of its own, often quite different from those of speech. The act of writing may change what we think by imposing its own conventions! Sometimes words which look different are pronounced the same and vice-versa, which leads Derrida to insist that there can be no 'phonetic' writing. Writing only functions because of its non-phonetic 'signs' of punctuation, word-spacing and so on. 'Extras' over speech are by no means 'signs' of the kind words themselves are.

As Derrida says in *Of Grammatology* (p 7): 'Writing is no longer seen as a . . . derivative, auxiliary form of language . . . It is . . . more than an extension of language; writing comprehends language.' So, (p 6): 'Slowly but surely "everything . . . gathered under the name of language is beginning to let itself be . . . summarised under the name of writing.' Nor is writing the only 'non-transparent' kind of signifying. Diagrams, drawings, paintings and works of architecture are 'non-transparent' in this way. So if language is to be taken as a model for these other kinds of signifying, then writing provides a better model than speaking."

So how much sense does all this make? As Welsh points out Derrida is quite wrong in suggesting that writing somehow has been, indeed could be 'repressed', needs 'liberating' and so on. For (p 26): 'All over the world enormous quantities of writing are turned out every day: books, newspapers, journals, reports, pamphlets, advertisements, magazines, etc. In the face of this truly prodigious production and consumption of writing, can we possibly think of it as 'repressed'? And surely if writing and speech give different views on how language works then as Saussure says we need them both? But then Welsh explains (p 29) that Derrida actually needs his extraordinary and intemperate 'moral crusade' against speech because language must take on the qualities he identifies in writing if it is to play the role Derrida needs of it in developing his ideas on the relationship between 'language' and 'reality'. Speech, as we shall see, can be seen to possess far too close a relationship to the speakers thoughts as he speaks them.

Supplément

Derrida uses Thoth to develop his idea of *supplément*. As he says *(Of Grammatology)*, he had found it in Rousseau's *Confessions* (p 108)

– Rousseau had gone to Italy and come back quite 'a different person':

> I had preserved my physical but not my moral virginity . . . my restless temperament at last had made itself felt . . . indeed had caused me some alarm about my health . . . Soon, however, I was reassured and learned that dangerous means of cheating Nature, *(ce dangereux supplément),* which leads young men of my temperament to various kinds of excesses . . . This vice, which shame and timidity find so convenient, has a particular attraction for lively imaginations. It allows them to dispose, so to speak, of the whole female sex . . .

It's his 'supplementary' way of making love – to himself! This of course appeals to Derrida. He sees other *suppléments* in Rousseau; the *Confessions* themselves form a *supplément* to his actual life; writing is a *supplément* to speech, and so on. So of course Derrida is equally delighted when he finds Thoth himself becoming a *supplément* too! For the greater God Ra had instructed him to 'Be in my place, while I shine over the blessed of the lower regions . . . you will be . . . my replacement . . . called . . . Thoth, he who replaces Ra.'

Derrida says: 'The God of writing . . . (takes) the place of Ra, supplementing . . . and supplanting him . . . Such is the origin of the moon as a supplement to the sun, of night light as a supplement to daylight. And (of) writing as the supplement to speech.'

Despite Thoth's role as the 'founder of the social order' he abuses his role as a substitute 'capable of doubling for the king, the father, the sun, and the word', given to 'representing, repeating, and masquerading' for them and even of 'totally supplanting them and appropriating all their attributes'. In all this 'supplementing and supplanting', Thoth is (p 93): 'Sly, slippery, and masked, an intriguer and a card'; in which role he is 'neither king nor jack, but rather a sort of joker, a floating signifier, a wild card; one who puts play into play'. Which pleases Derrida immensely, since he thinks of words, too, as jokers of this kind, 'floating signifiers' which cannot be pinned down; for him, preferably, they are 'undecidable'.

Undecidables: Plato's *Pharmakon*

Derrida likes to find Greek and Latin words with multiple meanings, especially if some of them contradict. And of course Derrida finds one – or so he thinks – in Plato's *Pharmakon*. He uses it first of the speech by Lysis, as a 'device' for getting Socrates out of town. And then both Thoth and Thamus apply it to writing which, for Derrida, is where there are contradictions.

Now 'pharmakon' indeed has many meanings which, according to the vastly authoritative *Dictionary of Ancient Greek* by Liddel and Scott can include:

I 1 *Drug,* whether healing or noxious.

2 (a) *Healing remedy, medicine,* mostly of those applied outwardly.

(b) *A medicine for it, remedy against it . . . a medicine to restore or maintain health.*

3 *Enchanted potion, philtre:* hence *charm, spell.*

4 *Poison* (Pl *Phd.*57a).

5 *Lye* for laundering.

II 1 Generally, *remedy,* cure.

2 Gen. also, *a means of producing* something, (Pl *Phdr.*27 4e); *of the oil applied to wrestlers.*

3 *Remedy* or *consolation* in his own virtue.

III *Dye, paint, colour.*

IV *Chemical reagent . . . used by tanners.*

So Lysis' speech can be a 'charm', or 'spell', for enticing Socrates out of the City. Then later, as we have seen, Thoth describes his invention of writing as: 'a pharmakon for memory and wisdom'. By this he clearly means 'a remedy, a cure', if not an 'enchanted potion, a philtre'. Whilst Thamus in rejecting writing describes it as: 'a pharmakon for recollection, not for memory'.

The great 'contradiction' for Derrida is the pharmakon of writing as 'remedy' or 'poison' – a 'poison', that is, for memory. But Plato by no means calls it that! He calls it, in fact, a 'remedy, a cure', for recollection. Indeed nowhere in *Phaedrus* does Plato use pharmakon as a 'poison' although, as Liddell and Scott show, he uses it as such in his *Phaedo*. And elsewhere in *Pharmakon* where Plato wants a 'drug' or a 'remedy' he uses quite different words! Faced with a word like 'pharmakon', ancient Greek writers such as Plato selected one meaning for any particular text and used it consistently throughout it!

But if his views on words are to mean much at all, Derrida needs his 'undecidables'. He sees them as his most potent means of attacking the 'binary oppositions' he dislikes: 'good/evil, presence/absence, identity/difference, man/woman, speech/writing' and so on. Nothing could be more opposed to these than a word, a single word, which means two opposing things simultaneously. Derrida himself seems to have missed the point that he is setting up another 'binary opposition'; of word as 'opposition' or 'undecidable'! If Plato's pharmakon were such an 'undecidable', at the same time 'remedy' and 'poison', then Derrida would have a crucial point. But as we've seen, it isn't, so he doesn't. The pharmakon indeed is a very tenuous thread for suspending such a load of Derrida's barely intelligible 'theory'.

Memory

But before we dismiss him altogether, let us see what else Derrida extracts from Plato. Using Thamus, via Socrates, as the vehicle for his thoughts, Plato sees writing as a threat to memory. He seems to want memory to 'contain' everything that has happened in our past. But as Derrida suggests (p 109) if we remembered everything then that would be more than memory: it would be, indeed, an 'infinite self presence'. What's more, Socrates seems to want a memory that exists entirely within itself; with no 'signifieds', no 'signifiers', no 'supplements' of any kind. But where within the student can memory actually be? As Derrida points out, it is for Socrates an inscription of 'truth' in the soul, which makes it no more 'live' than writing. Socrates had defended the 'living discourse' of speech, yet his memory, too, is dead; an inscription in the 'soul'. Since writing is 'inscribing', it becomes a 'metaphor' for the very thing that Socrates has been trying to exclude! This, Derrida points out, is an amazing reversal, since: 'While presenting writing as a false brother . . . Socrates is . . . left to envision the (legitimate) brother of this brother . . . as another sort of writing: not merely . . . a (speech-like) knowing, living, animate discourse, but (that) . . . inscription . . . in the soul.' These 'inscriptions' in the soul are 'signifieds' of some kind, however immaterial, which help us recall whatever is not present. But if the soul, or the memory, has 'signifieds' like this then it can be no 'purer' than speech or even writing. Memory, like them, will be 'contaminated' by its own 'substitutes' or 'supplements,' however unwritten or unspoken. We cannot know what forms they take but we can think through the problems they might raise by analogy with words. These are 'substitutes' or 'supplements' standing for something else. The 'thing' may or may not be a 'Being' of Heidegger's kind, but whatever form it takes, no 'substitute' or 'supplement' can ever be the 'thing-in-itself'.

Every time we use a 'supplement' – such as a word – the 'supplement' itself is one of a 'type'. Each time we print a word it looks like that word in every other printing. So of course we can 'substitute' any one printing for any other.

Like Barthes with his 'signs' we have an endless 'chain' within which each 'supplement' can 'substitute' for every other. The word we actually wrote, the first 'supplement', was by no means the 'thing-in-itself'; the actual 'Being', and these endless 'substitutes', take us even further from it. But neither is a 'substitute' a 'non-being' either. For Derrida, as one might expect, each 'slides' between the two states, of 'Being' and 'not-being', much like Thoth – and these mercurial 'slidings slip it out of (any) simple alternative (between) presence/absence'. Which, says Derrida, is 'the danger' of such 'supplements': '. . . that is what enables the type always to pass for the original. As soon as the supplementary outside is opened, its structure implies that the supplement itself can be "typed", replaced by its double . . .' By another occurrence of the same word as: 'supplement to the supplement'. Once this chain of 'supplements' has been started, who can tell where – if anywhere – it is going to end? Not once has it been allowed that this 'supplement' of writing merely stay there, external to us. We read it and of course it insinuates its way into our minds, where as Derrida says in *Pharmakon* (p 110), it 'infects' what lies deepest 'inside' there. Once 'inside', the mind, however, the 'supplement' changes 'lest itself at once be breached, roughed up, fulfilled, and replaced' by a further chain of 'supplements'. If there is such a thing as a 'present' in the mind then each word of the writing is absorbed as soon we read it, augments the present, and changes it, 'in the (very) act of disappearing'.

By these thoughts Derrida is attacking yet another of Plato's 'binary oppositions': that of 'memory/writing'. This 'opposition' represents for Derrida (p 111) 'something like the major decision of philosophy, the one through which it institutes itself, maintains itself, and contains its adverse deeps'.

Plato as Writer

And of course there are some even more obvious points (*Pharmakon* p 159). Plato often uses letters of the alphabet to clarify arguments, to 'come to grips with a problem'. Yet curiously enough Plato never 'comes to grips' with the fact that in doing so, he is actually writing. The Sophists – such as Lysis – says Derrida (p 112) 'are indisputedly men of writing at the moment they are protesting they are not. But isn't Plato one too . . . ?' There is no way we could know what Socrates might have said if Plato had not written it down. Whilst Plato is actually a writer; he attacks writing through the very medium itself. Derrida thinks this a 'banal' argument, yet it is in many ways the essence of 'Deconstruction'.

Elsewhere, in *The Laws,* in a dialogue between Socrates and Clinias, Plato presents a spirited defence of writing, since writing is crucial for *The Laws* to be maintained: 'writing is not simply added . . . like a mute, stupid simulacrum: it assures the law's permanence and identity with the vigilance of a guardian'.

Indeed as Clinias says: 'legal prescriptions, once put into writing, remain always on record, as though to challenge the question of time to come . . . even the dullest student may return to them for reiterated scrutiny . . .'

So it is that Derrida works his major themes into his analysis of Plato's *Phaedrus:* his Phono-centrism, Logo-centrism, Onto-Theology and so on.

Logocentrism

As for Derrida's 'Logocentrism', we have seen already that 'Logos' is the Greek for 'word'. It also means a 'reason' or a 'plan' and the Greeks applied it to the 'Divine Reason' for which Heraelitus instituted the Cosmos itself; ordered it, gave it form and meaning by processes much like human reasoning. Such ideas are found also in Egyptian, Indian and Persian myths of the Creation. But most Westerners learn of Logos from the Gospel of St John the Divine which opens with: 'In the beginning was the Word, and the Word was with God, and the Word was God.' So the Logos, as 'Word' was actually 'God'!

As for 'Deconstructionist' explanations, Ellis points out (p 30) that these usually amount to some statement about the 'metaphysics of presence' with the rider to the effect that belief in this is a 'philosophical error'.

Welsh cites 'explanations' of 'Logocentrism' by Culler (1977), Leitch (1983), Derrida himself (*Of Grammatology),* Culler *(On Deconstruction),* and Norris *(Deconstruction),* with further citations from Lentricchia (1980), Hawkes (1977) and Jameson (1972).

None of these are particularly coherent and some – indeed,

Culler's first and Derrida's own – are barely intelligible. 'The logocentric system', according to Leitch 'always assigns the origin of truth to the logos – to the spoken word, to the voice of reason or to the voice of God', whilst Culler, in his second definition writes of: 'the orientation of philosophy towards an order of meaning – thought, truth, reason, logic, the Word – conceived as existing in itself, as foundation'.

Culler confuses the issue further in that same definition when he writes of 'a direct and natural relationship' between speech and meaning in the Logocentric view since as Saussure points out the sounds of speech themselves are arbitrary and so, once they have been formed into words, are their relationships with meanings.

It all sounds rather like Husserl's 'Transcendental Consciousness' but Derrida refers in several places to Medieval Theology as the basis of such ideas. As he says in *Of Grammatology* (p 13), such Theology assumes the idea of an 'authorising presence': God, and the 'absolute logos' as an 'infinite creative subjectivity . . . turned towards the word and face of God'.

And in *Writing and Difference* (p 146) Derrida draws on Meister Eckhart's the ideas to the effect that: 'transcendence toward Being, permits . . . an understanding of the word God . . . even if this understanding is but the ether in which dissonances can resonate. This transcendence inhabits and founds language . . .'

So 'presence' indeed 'reality' are embedded in this infinite Logos. They exist – as Berkely thought they should – in this purest 'intellect' of all. The best we can hope to do as humans is to approach them from outside, from our 'sensible' world. Which is why we have our two-part 'signs' in which a term 'outside' the Logos, the 'signifier' is coupled with a term within it: the 'signified'. The 'signifier' of course is part of a particular language; a word in English, French or whatever. So each 'signified' is but a tiny part of the 'infinite Logos' within which it has to be 'marked out' before it can be expressed as 'signifier' to the 'sensible' world outside. To which end, says Derrida, we need 'a signified able to "take place" in its intelligibility, before its "fall", before any expulsion into the exteriority of the sensible here below'. And that outer 'signifier', by definition, cannot in itself be the 'inner' signified.

But, Ellis points out, beliefs of that kind in ultimate 'thought, truth, reason, logic, the Word – conceived as existing in itself, as foundation' have formed for centuries the stuff of traditional Essentialism. Plato had his 'universals' that for every kind of physical object there was an 'Ideal Form' existing only in the mind of God whilst for Locke things had 'essences;' qualities inherent within objects quite different from their physical, observable properties, by which 'essences' we identify them for what they actually are. Berkeley too held the view that things can only exist in some kind of mind; that if I am observing something then it exists for me. But if I am not, and nobody else is either, it continues to exist under the watchful eye of God.

In a broader context 'Logocentrism' is Derrida's private name for an age-old philosophical concern over the relationships of words to their referents. So lets assemble from such views the best patchwork we can – with Ellis' help, of what 'Logocentrism' might contain:

1) A belief that things exist in some kind of 'reality'.
2) Which 'reality' amounts to their being signified within some transcendental 'order' of meaning – the Logos – which itself is independent of any human language.
3) That the Logos is the foundation of all possible thinking and meaning.
4) That within it the various 'signifieds' group themselves 'naturally' into clear, distinct, unambiguous and unchanging categories.
5) That the words of specific languages are simply 'signifiers' for these 'signifieds' within the Logos.
6) Thus the 'signifiers' of language enable us to extract 'signifieds' out of the Logos and bring them directly into our minds.
7) Since speech gives us direct access to the speaker's mind it gives us access too directly to the 'signifieds' as they exist within the Logos.

So, as Ellis summarises (p 36): 'Logocentrism is the illusion that the meaning of a word has its origin in the structure of reality itself and hence makes the truth about that structure seem directly present to the mind.'

But as we have seen already from our 'sheep/mutton' example, different languages 'carve up' the world around us in different ways and, as Welsh points out, generations of philosophers, philologists and linguists have known there is no such thing as an absolute structure of 'the Truth' to which every language gives us direct and unmediated access. He cites Wittgenstein, Firth, Sapir, Whorf as only recent examples. Wittgenstein, for instance, in attacking the 'theory of meaning' embodied in Logical Positivism made it sound remarkably like 'Logocentrism'.

So why, in attacking 'Logocentrism', should Derrida believe he is saying something new anyway? Because, says Ellis (p 40), instead of reading 'serious' authors such as these he has drawn on marginal figures – in this particular debate – such as Heidegger, Freud, Nietzsche and Lévi-Strauss. But what does he really say?

Presence

Well those who seek 'the truth' of anything can only reach it's outer representation – its 'signifier' – which is by no means the presence the thing itself. The 'signifiers' of our knowledge can never actually be that knowledge. Derrida suggests (*Of Grammatology* p 19) that of all his predecessors, Nietzsche contributed most to the liberation of the 'signifier' from the Logos and the related concept of truth: the 'primary signified.' Reading and therefore writing were for Nietzsche 'originary' operations. He did not have to 'discover' something in the Logos and then transcribe it. Since God was dead anyway there was no need for Nietzsche to seek any kind of 'divine understanding' in the Logos as a prelude to his writing.

Saussure by contrast, or so Derrida claims in *Positions* (p 19-20) accedes to the idea of a 'transcendental signified'. It's by no means clear what this might be: a 'signified' perhaps within Husserl's 'Transcendental Consciousness'. But more likely he means the Logos itself for this consisted of signifieds within some grand 'Consciousness' of the kind which Husserl had called 'Transcendental'. Which makes some kind of sense of what he says (*Writing and Difference* (p 280): 'in the absence of a centre or origin . . . the original or transcendental signified, is never absolutely present outside a system of differences'. Hardly surprising since according to Saussure neither 'signifiers' nor 'signifieds' can ever be present 'outside a system of differences'. But the 'absence of the transcendental signified extends the domain and the play of signification indefinitely'.

As he says in *Positions* (p 19-20) if there were such a thing as a 'transcendental signified' of course then it would: 'refer to no signifier, would exceed the chain of signs, and would no longer itself function as a signifier. On the contrary . . . from the moment that one questions the possibility of such a transcendental signified, and that one recognises that every signified is also in the position of a signifier, the distinction between signifier and signified becomes problematical at its root.'

Derrida's editor refers us at this point to *Of Grammatology* for light to be thrown on his extraordinary claim that 'every signified is also in the position of a signifier'. But there in *Of Grammatology* Derrida is concerned with the 'Chain of Supplements' from Rousseau. We have seen already that Rousseau came back from Italy with his 'supplementary' way of making love and in Book XII of the *Confessions* a sequence of women who were 'supplements' to his mother. Which triggers in Derrida the thought in *Of Grammatology* (p 157): 'Through this sequence of supplements a necessity is announced: that of an infinite chain, ineluctably multiplying their supplementary mediations that produce the sense of the very thing they defer: the mirage of the thing itself, of immediate presence, of originary perception. Immediacy is derived.'

Barthes had such a 'problem' in 1957 and solved it by having his 'signifier' and 'signified' fuse to form a 'sign' which becomes the 'signifier' of another 'sign' in his 'chain'.

But for Derrida the 'signified' becomes a 'signifier' – or vice versa. So like Barthes he has a 'chain' of meanings which reminds him (*Speech and Phenomena* p 5) of Husserl's description in *Ideas* of paintings in the Dresden Gallery, of which, says Husserl: 'A name on being mentioned reminds us . . . and of our last visit there: we wander through the rooms, and stand before a picture of Tenier's which represents a picture gallery . . . the pictures of the latter . . . in turn portray pictures which on their part exhibit . . . readable inscriptions and so forth . . . .'

A 'chain' of pictures, 'nesting' within each other much as Barthes' 'signs' form a 'chain' of 'nesting' signs! So whatever meaning we think we are going to grasp will be dissipated, always, along a chain of 'Signifiers' and 'Signifieds'. As Sarup suggests

(1988) we shall never 'nail it down'. We cannot find a meaning in a single sign; we shall experience, rather, a 'constant flickering of presence and absence together'. We cannot compare the reading of a printed text, say, to the step-by-step process of 'counting the beads on a necklace'. It will be, rather, a matter of 'tracing this . . . constant flickering'. Each 'signifier' will offer us a 'trace' of some kind and 'trace' in French, according to Harrap's *Dictionary,* has connotations of 'trail, track, spoor, foot-print, trail' – of the 'signified' which will be forever absent.

But, enquires Ellis (p 57) what can it mean to say that a signifier is also a signified. For in Saussure a 'signifier' is the physical manifestation of the sign, the 'distinctive sound' of a word in speech whereas the 'signified' is the thought as part of a sign; the 'idea content' of the word. And since a sound is by no means an idea so the one, literally, cannot become the other. Yet whilst Derrida keeps confusing 'signifier' and 'signified' he nowhere explains how the one actually can become the other.

More generally too he tries to make Saussure's 'Semiology' into a branch of Metaphysics: *Positions* p 19 'he accedes to the classical exigency of what I have . . . call(ed) the "transcendental signified"'. Yet curiously enough, he actually points out that Saussure saw his 'Semiology' as a branch of Social Psychology; nothing at all to do with Metaphysics, still less with Husserl's 'Transcendental Consciousness' or the Logos, the Logos the infinite mind and presence of God! Saussure describes his 'signifier' and 'signified' as two sides of the same leaf and you can't have one side of a leaf within some infinite Logos and the other in the 'sensible' world 'outside'. Leaves just don't grow like that! But Derrida persists in confusing Saussure's 'sign' from social psychology with the 'signs' of Metaphysics thus presenting an absolute travesty of it!

The trouble is, as Ellis suggests, that even if Derrida were right he would by no means have gone far enough. It is easy enough to question Logocentrism, question it, challenge it, stand it on its head. It is no intellectual achievement to say that something is 'problematical' and leave it at that. Stating a problem is the start of an intellectual process, a mere beginning of the hard work that will lead to conclusion of some kind; alternatives to what one finds inadequate, suggestions as to which is best, and why.

As for human 'presence' of the kind which Husserl and Heidegger struggled so hard to find, Derrida presents his views in *Ousia and Gramme*. He cites the Heidegger of *Being and Time* as treating the meaning of Being as 'parousia or ousia', which signifies . . . 'presence'. Indeed as Derrida suggests in *Of Grammatology* (p 12), if there is such a thing as 'presence' then it should exist in many forms. He lists them and they are almost as extensive as Aristotle's ways of 'being'.

But we use signs in the first place because the thing that really concerns us at this moment isn't actually present to our senses: 'When we cannot grasp or show the thing, state the present, the being-present, when the present cannot be presented, we signify, we go through the detour of the sign.' So the sign for Derrida is a 'deferred presence': 'the circulation of signs defers the moment at which we encounter the thing itself, make it ours, consume or expend it, touch it, see it, intuit its presence'.

We are moving towards it but we haven't got there yet; the sign 'defers' the moment when we shall. This is why Derrida is suspicious of extreme attempts, such as Husserl's, to search for the absolutely pure, un-compromised, unmediated foundation of human knowledge. Which indeed would be 'absolute presence', pure and unsullied, a totally certain 'now' which cannot exist for Derrida!

Difference

So what purpose, if any, do 'signifiers' and 'signifieds' really serve? For Saussure as we have seen they give us the very means without which our thinking would be a 'blurred and indistinct mass'. But how can they do this? By differences according to Saussure. We recognise a certain signifier, rather than another, by the differences between them. Which mark, for Saussure, corresponding differences in the 'signifieds' within our brains. So in language 'there are only differences'. Derrida naturally pounces on this with the greatest glee, in *Writing and Difference,* (1967), in *Speech and Phenomena* (also 1967) and, a different translation, in *Margins of Philosophy* (1982).

For Derrida there's more to 'difference' than merely lacking 'positive terms'; he notices that a Classical word – in this case a Latin one – has different if not contradictory meanings. It's the word 'differo' – which according to Lewis and Clarke has a multiplicity of meanings:

differo, differe:

I A *Act, to carry different ways, to spread abroad, scatter, disperse, separate, to plant apart in separate rows.*

B 1. *To distract, disquiet, disturb, to confound.*

2. *To spread abroad, publish, divulge, to cry down, defame . . . to bring into disrepute with them.*

With reference to time:

3. *To defer, put off, protract, delay . . . to reserve for . . . to preserve alive . . . i.e. to postpone her death.*

II   Neut. *to differ, be different,* (esp. frequent since Ciceron period . . .)

Differens . . . different, superior . . . a more excellent name . . . a difference.

Derrida chooses to 'distract, disquiet, disturb and to confound' us by taking two of these meanings, Lewis and Clarke's I.3 and their II, and elaborating on them in his own idiosyncratic way. So they become:

1) The action of putting off until later, of taking into account, of taking account of time. (Time) . . . that implies an economic calculation, a detour, a delay, a relay, a reserve, a representation.

All of which, says Derrida, amounts to various kinds of temporisation; to take recourse, consciously or not, in temporising and the temporal; to suspend accomplishment, fulfilment of 'desire' or 'will'; and:

2) To be not identical, to be other, discernible etc . . . dissimilar otherness, otherness . . . an interval, a distance, spacing. He uses a nice speech-sound difference to illustrate his point, between the French 'differents', which are different 'things' and 'differends' which are 'differences of opinion, grounds for dispute'.

On this basis Derrida coins the term *différance* to combine, in a single French word, the two meanings he has taken from the Latin; by which sleight of mind he uses these two meanings simultaneously. Thus his *différance* means 'to differ' and 'to defer' at one and the same time. Like pharmakon it's another of his 'undecidables' – his reaction to 'binary oppositions'. These 'undecidables,' in his view, can 'no longer be included within philosophical opposition, resisting and disorganising it, without ever constituting a third term'. His *différance* 'suspends itself' between 'differing' and 'deferring', which means that given, say, the *différance* between 'cat' and 'mat', it collapses as soon as we have thought it. What was the 'now' of our thoughts a moment ago become a 'then' already.

Therefore there is no stable 'present' to our thoughts. However hard we try to stabilise them, stability will constantly and forever be deferred. We shall never achieve it if 'difference' and 'deferment' are the same. If we cannot stabilise our thoughts then, of course, that gives Derrida the ultimate 'evidence' he needs for his attack on the 'ultimate truths' of 'Logocentrism' and 'Onto-theology'.

Nor can we ever get to the 'bottom' of things. If we look up a word in the dictionary, we shall find it defined in terms of other words. So if we want to know what the first word 'really' means, we shall have to look up all the other words, and the words used in defining them in some never ending consultation. And even if we could get to the end of that process, we should still be no nearer to knowing what our first word 'really' meant. Especially if like 'pharmakon' or *differo* it has conflicting meanings anyway!

So a single, fascinating word has taken over Derrida's mind and encouraged flights of fantasy which by no means ring true. There's no need for the rest of us to follow! For taken to their 'logical' conclusions Derrida's arguments mean that we cannot communicate at all. Yet struggle as he might to make it hard for us the fact that Derrida words anything, means that something of his thoughts get through.

Of course like the rest of us Derrida is free to use words in any way he pleases – provided he does not wish to communicate. As Lewis Carroll put it in *Through the Looking Glass:* "'When I use a word," Humpty Dumpty said in a rather scornful tone, "it means just what I choose it to mean, neither more nor less."' It can for Humpty Dumpty; so it can for Derrida. And so it can for us if we wish to isolate ourselves from the rest of the world. As Saussure insists, language is a social institution, used by an entire population. It 'blends with the life of society' and, since 'society' . . . by its nature is inert, acts as a 'prime conservative force'; this induces a 'collective inertia'. So, of all our social institutions, language is the least amenable to change. We can conceive of changes in language, as Saussure says (p 73), 'but only through the intervention of specialist grammarians, logicians, etc'. He then goes on to say: 'experience has shown us that all such meddlings have failed'; including, one must say, Derrida's! The rest of the world has by no means consented to merge 'differ' and 'defer' in his ambiguous, 'undecidable' word! Saussure provides good enough reasons for this, and Husserl gives us others when he distinguishes, in *The Logical Investigations*, between 'expression' – the 'pure' meaning of the sign as intended by the speaker, and 'indication' – the 'pointing' function of the sign which occurs whether the speaker intends it or not.

Semiotic

These distinctions had been taken very much further by Charles Sanders Peirce, an American philosopher, whose 'Semiotic' rivals Saussure's 'Semiologie' as *the* 'Theory of Signs' especially now that it has been translated into French! Whilst Saussure thinks habitually in twos: 'binary oppositions', Peirce tends to think in threes. Several of Peirce's 'triads' help us to retrieve consistent meaning after Derrida's attempts to subvert it, and in many ways the most helpful is his: Icon, Index and Symbol in which:

An *Icon* is a sign which is like some other object, draws our attention to it because they look alike (one Gothic church looks much 'like' any other), shares some underlying structure (many of Wright's Prairie Houses, however unlike in appearances, share similar planning arrangements) and so on;

An *Index* draws our attention to 'its object' by some physical relationship. Openings indicate 'going in or out', stairs indicate 'going up or down', corridors indicate 'going along' and so on. All human beings understand such things; so do cats and dogs. Indices are completely cross-cultural;

A *Symbol,* for Peirce, is a sign whose meaning has to be learned. His ideal example is as a word for which Signifier and Signified are learned within a particular culture. The crown is a symbol of the Monarchy, a bank note symbolises a certain amount of wealth, a theatre ticket symbolises the fact that we have paid and so on. Certain building forms are symbols too, learned within a certain culture, such as a Gothic church, a mosque, a glass office tower, the Sydney Opera House.

Now the meanings of Icons – 'likeness' can 'flicker'. One thinks of Wittgenstein's 'duck/rabbit' which looks like one or the other according to how you decide to see it.

But Wittgenstein needed a very special drawing to make his point; most Icons are less 'undecideable' than that. Once you've seen a 'likeness' it usually sticks. Our Icon of a church depends on our remembering how the first one looked, to recognise its 'likeness' in the next. But the 'likeness' will still be there even if we personally forget it. Indices, too, stay constant in their meanings. Not even a Derrida can keep walking horizontally when he comes

to a staircase. And since a great deal of meaning in architecture derives from Icons and Indices its meanings do not 'flicker' as Derrida seems to think they should.

Since Symbols have to be learned in the first place, then they may well have to be re-learned. We re-learn every day the symbolic values of say the Pound Stirling against the Deutschmark against the Dollar. But these values are socially determined so our having to re-learn simply reinforces Saussure's point. But only Peirce's Symbols could be subject to Derrida's 'flickering' Signifieds, and even so, whilst a great Church like Hagia Sophia may be converted first into a Mosque and then into a Museum, its meaning does not 'flicker' between them. It has been socially-determined as one or the other in any particular era.

One has to ask why Derrida does not wish to be 'present'; wants his thoughts to collapse into endless, incoherent, unintelligible 'chains'; wants words and presumably buildings literally to have no meanings. Clearly it is some psychological state which prompts Derrida to want to reduce our thoughts to that 'shapeless and indistinct mass', that 'vague, uncharted nebula' which Saussure thought they would be unless we had the benefit of language to give them shape. Language gives us structures which enable us to think and it is these which Derrida tries so hard to subvert!

One is reminded of other writers from the 1960's such as R D Laing and his *The Divided Self* (1960). As Laing says in a chapter significantly entitled 'Ontological Insecurity':

A man may have a sense of his presence in the world as a real, alive, whole . . . continuous person. As such he can live out into the world and meet others: a world and others experienced as equally real, alive, whole, and continuous.

Such a basically ontologically secure person will encounter all the hazards of life – social, ethical, spiritual and biological – from a centrally firm sense of his own and other people's reality . . .

But there are people who do not feel like this. As Laing says there are people lacking these 'unquestionable self-validating certainties'. There are those who 'in the ordinary circumstances of living may feel more unreal than real'. Such a person may feel:

. . . precariously differentiated from the rest of the world, so that his identity and autonomy are always in question. He may lack the experience of his own temporal continuity. He may not possess an overriding sense of personal consistency or cohesiveness. He may feel more insubstantial than substantial. There will be no 'stable present' to his thoughts. Laing calls such a person 'schizoid' or 'schizophrenic' and he is at pains to point out that this apparently distressing state may offer creative insights of a kind which are quite inaccessible to the 'normal' mind. And one remembers that Derrida's illustrious if un-analysed predecessor, Jean-Paul Sartre, indeed had written of *Being and Nothingness*.

There are, however, more profound reasons for rejecting Derrida's 'flickering indices'. The more we try to probe artificial intelligence the clearer it becomes that whilst computers may be good at some things they are very bad at others. John Searle points out (1989) that these days computers can 'read' syntax much as humans can: Saussure's 'Syntagmatic' relations. But they cannot even begin to comprehend 'Semantics'; the meanings which words and other 'signifiers' represent. That is why translation has eluded them. Understanding meaning is an achievement unique to human beings. Yet this is what Derrida wants to take away from us by extremely dubious processes. Ellis, for instance, cites some brave attempts by Barbara Johnson to explain what Derrida's new form of logic might be (1980, 1981). Johnson cites the Derridas of *Dissemination* and *Positions;* quoting from the former Derrida's view that: 'It is . . . not simply false to say that Mallarmé is a Platonist or a Hegelian. But it is above all not true. And vice-versa.' So, claims Johnson, 'Instead of a simple either/or structure, (of traditional logic, Derrida) attempts to elaborate a discourse that says neither "either/or", nor "both/and" nor even "neither/nor", while at the same time not totally abandoning these logics either.'

It is not just a question of wanting it both ways but of wanting it every-which-way and then some! Now clearly, says Ellis, Mallarmé wasn't Plato and no one in his right mind could think them identical. It would be pointless, indeed absurd, to try and prove that they were. But neither were they absolutely different; they were both human beings after all. So it might be interesting to see what they had in common; where they differed, how much, and so on. Commonalities and differences would both emerge somewhere in the mid-ground between Derrida's impossible extremes. So Derrida's original proposition: 'It is not simply false . . .' is so trite as to be, literally, meaningless, which makes his 'vice versa' totally redundant. So why does he write such nonsense? His aim, of course, is to give the impression: 'of a daring leap from one position to another and back again'. However, since his leaps are bound to start, and finish, somewhere in that middle ground they are hardly very daring anyway. So Derrida gives us an empty 'appearance of sophistication and logic' without the substance. But why? To produce an impression of 'profundity and skill' with no exercise whatever of any intellectual skill and certainly no attempt to make any 'substantial contribution to . . . understanding'. On the contrary . . .

Ellis sees it as mystification of the kind which Ghose identifies in his entry on religious 'Mysticism' for the Encyclopaedia Britannica.

Ghose cites a typical example: 'What is below is like what is above; what is above is like what is below' – quite as meaningless and unhelpful a paradox as Derrida's! The claim (p 9) that 'logic, reason, and analysis are insufficient to discuss Derrida', has also been claimed for their esoteric views by mystics throughout the ages.

As for the Post-Structuralist position from which Derrida emerged, that too is under increasing attack. Umberto Eco, no less, had in the 1960s advocated the active participation of the interpreter 'in the reading of texts endowed with some aesthetic value' (*Opera Aperta* 1962). But as he says (1990) he had begun to think by the time this was translated into English, as The Open Work (1989) that the 'open' side of such reading had been taken far too far. Even the most 'open' of readings depends on the fact that there is a text in the first place before somebody actually reads it, indeed which elicits the reading. So he had studied the dialectics 'between the rights of the text and the rights of the interpreters'. And the 'rights' of the interpreter had been greatly over-stressed.

Of course it may be difficult to penetrate an author's 'real' intentions; they may indeed be quite irrelevant to the reading one wishes to impose. One may want to 'beat' the text into a form which serves own purposes But, says Eco, between the two extremes of author's intentions and reader's intention there are matters we ignore at our peril: 'the intention of the text'. He cites a story by Wilkins of an Indian slave sent to deliver a basket of figs and a letter. There was no way, he thought, that the addressee could know how many figs there had been. So he ate most of them on the way. But the letter 'told' the addressee and the slave was duly admonished. So next time he ate the figs and hid the letter!

Now says Eco suppose the slave had been killed, the killers ate the figs and sealed the letter in a bottle which they then threw into the sea, and the bottle was cast up some 70 years later on Robinson Crusoe's island. Crusoe as an 'active' reader might have looked for metaphors in the references to figs: evocations of expressions such as 'to be in good fig', 'to be in full fig' and so on. Or he might have imposed an allegorical reading, thought the letter to have been written by a poet in some private code known only to him and the addressee.

All much less likely, says Eco, than that Crusoe would assume real figs 'indexally pointing' to a real sender, a real addressee and indeed a real slave. However 'creative' Crusoe's readings he could not convert the figs to 'apples or unicorns' although he might indulge in endless speculation as to who were the sender, the slave and the addressee, why one was sending figs to the other and so on. But, says Eco, Crusoe 'would not be entitled to say that the message can mean everything'. Of course it can mean many things, some of them 'preposterous to suggest'. It says, unequivocally, that 'once upon a time there was a basket of figs' and no reader-orientated theory can take away that constraint on any reading.

But why such 'poetic' readings anyway? Eco points out that whilst 'mathematics, logic, science and computer programming' are still modelled on Greek and Latin rationalism, it is by no means our whole legacy from Antiquity. Aristotle was a Greek 'but so were the Eleusinian mysteries'. The Greek God Hermes was 'volatile and ambiguous'. And in the myth of Hermes, says Eco, 'causal chains wind back on themselves in spirals, the after precedes the before, the god knows no spatial limits and may, in different shapes, be in different places at the same time'.

So he traces the after-life of such ideas to Second century Hermeticism, the thinking of the alchemists, the Jewish Cabbalists, to 'timid medieval Neoplatonism'. And then to the more robust Neoplatonisms of the Renaissance and Christian Cabbalism. Eco describes the legendary Caliph who, since he knew the truth, ordered the destruction of the great Alexandria Library with all the irreplaceable collection of Classical texts on the grounds that if books said the same as the Koran, they were superfluous, and if they said something different, they were wrong and harmful.

Eco contrasts this with Second-century Hermeticism 'looking for a truth it does not know'. It seeks this truth in books, imagining or hoping that each book 'will contain a spark of truth and that they will serve to confirm each other'. Different things may be true at the same time even if they seem to contradict each other. But if the books are telling the truth, whilst contradicting each other, 'then their each and every word must be an allusion, an allegory'. They must be saying things which are quite different from what they seem to be saying. So: 'In order to . . . understand the mysterious messages contained in the books it was necessary to look for a revelation beyond human utterances, one would come announced by the divinity itself, using the vehicle of vision, dream, or oracle.' This revelation would have to 'speak' of some 'as-yet unknown god' of some 'still secret truth'. Secret knowledge, by its nature, must be deep since only that which lies under the surface can remain hidden for long. 'Thus truth becomes identified with what is not said or what is said obscurely and must be understood beyond or beneath the surface of the text.'

And in 'Some paranoid readings' Eco analyses spurious connections of exactly the kind we have seen Derrida making. For if one really pushes such things everything bears some kind of relationship to everything else: by analogy, by contiguity or similarity. He cites an extreme example: 'there is a relationship between the adverb while and the noun crocodile because, in addition to rhyming, they both appear . . . in the sentence . . . I have just uttered.' The 'sane' interpreter sees a minimal connection whilst the 'paranoid' interpreter wonders 'about the mysterious motive that induced me to bring these two words together'. The paranoiac is looking for the 'secret' beyond the words. He brings to his reading an 'excess of wonder' which leads him to overestimate in importance: 'coincidences . . . explicable in other ways'.

Eco finds such things in Rosetti's search for Rosicrucian symbols in Dante's *Divine Comedy*: rose, cross and pelican which he actually finds by, for instance, pressing other birds to serve as 'honorary'

pelicans. He finds similar absurdities in Geoffrey Hartman's 'Deconstructionist' reading of Wordsworth's 'Lucy' poems, including Derrida-like cheating. Hartman, for instance sees 'tears' as an anagram for 'trees.' And of course Eco makes much of the 'secret' intentions others attributed to him as author of *The Name of the Rose*. Schizophrenia? Paranoia? Both, it seems can lie 'behind' Deconstructionist intentions!

Spurs

Before we go on to explore various applications of Derrida's 'Deconstruction' into architecture let us look at one final and perhaps even more absurd example of his working methods: his immensely laboured analysis – 20 pages each in French and English – of a simple five-word sentence from Nietzsche.

This analysis occurs in *Spurs* (1978), Derrida's discussion of Nietzsche's writing styles, most of which is given over to analyses of Nietzsche's anti-feminist stance with side-swipes, from time to time, at Heidegger's reading of Nietzsche. Derrida is clearly unsympathetic to Heidegger's complex hermeneutic and offers, as an alternative, his own zany, speculative reading of Nietzsche. Or rather of that cryptic, marginal note in the manuscript of *The Gay Science* where Nietzsche writes, totally out of context and in quotation marks: 'I have forgotten my umbrella.'

Derrida suggests (p 123) that we have 'no infallible way of knowing the occasion for this sample or what it could later have been grafted on to. We will never know for sure what Nietzsche wanted to say or do . . . nor even that he actually wanted anything.' He wonders if, one day, we might reconstruct the context in which Nietzsche's note was written. But detached as it is from the milieu which produced it, it may always have been detached 'from any intention or meaning on Nietzsche's part', in which case it should remain 'whole and intact, once and for all, without any other context'. Its inaccessibility, however, by no means indicates 'some hidden secret'; it might just as well have been an inconsistency, or even of 'no significance at all': 'What if Nietzsche himself meant to say nothing, or at least not much of anything, or anything whatever?' Or suppose he was only pretending to say something? It may not actually be Nietzsche's sentence, or even written by his hand. Was there, perhaps a secret code which enabled Nietzsche, or even an accomplice, to make sense of his sentence? We shall never know or, at least, as Derrida puts it: 'It is possible that we will never know and that powerlessness must somehow be taken into account. Much as a trace which has been marked in what remains of this non-fragment, such an account would withdraw it from any assured horizon of a hermeneutic question.' And then a typical Derrida play on words: 'And as far as the unpublished piece goes, it is indeed still a matter of reading it, its what for, or why, like a woman or like writing, it passes itself off for what it passes itself off for.'

Now everyone knows what it means to say 'I have forgotten my umbrella':

It is mine. But I forgot it. I can describe it. But now I don't have it any more. At hand. I must have forgotten it somewhere, etc . . . An umbrella is that sort of thing that, just when it is really needed, one might either have or not have any more . . . Or else one still has it when it is no longer needed.

This 'stratum of readability' allows all kinds of operations, such as translation, a 'psychoanalytic' decoding, a 'hermeneutic' decoding and so on. The analyst might make obvious phallic connections with an umbrella as a long pointed object or he might be interested, too, in the 'forgetting'. In which case, although 'somewhat less naive' than the 'impulsive reader or the hermeneut ontologist', he or she would be sharing their belief that the unpublished piece 'is an aphorism of some significance'. But, 'Assured that it must mean something, they look for it to come from the most intimate reaches of this author's thought. But in order to be so assured, one must have forgotten that it is a text that is in question, the remains of a text, indeed a forgotten text.' Which seems to Derrida to be over-earnest. Indeed as he points out in an analysis which comes close to the heart of his method:

> . . . it is quite possible that the unpublished piece, precisely because it is readable as a piece of writing, should remain forever secret . . . not because it withholds some secret. Its secret is rather the possibility that indeed it might have no secret, that it might only be pretending to be simulating some hidden truth within its folds.

And of course the hermeneut – such as Heidegger – 'cannot but be provoked and disconcerted by its play'. Perhaps Nietzsche was exploring the limits of some 'will to meaning' analogous to his 'Will to Power'. Perhaps the whole of the text in which it was found, *The Gay Science,* represents, 'in some monstrous way', writing of the type which Derrida has located in this simple: 'I have forgotten my umbrella'!

But then says Derrida we should take a further step. Suppose his own text were like that too; that he, Derrida, were using quotations from Nietzsche to make the latter say things which he, Derrida actually wants to say? Supposing it's all Derrida's code, shared only by 'me and myself'. But like Nietzsche, Derrida too is going to die. Their relation 'is one of a structurally posthumous necessity'. And even if he had accomplices, they too would die.

And still the text will remain, if it is really cryptic and parodying (and I tell you that it is, through and through). I might as well tell you since it won't be any help . . . (even my admission can very well be a lie because there is dissimulation only if one tells the truth, only if one tells that one is telling the truth), the text will remain indefinitely open, cryptic and parodying: open and closed, folded/ unfolded like Nietzsche's umbrella; a suitable 'undecidable' on which to leave Derrida's working methods.

So what is or was the point of reading Derrida? Intellectual enlightenment? Not much! Convincing 'theories' of language, meaning, truth? Hardly. Challenges to our received opinions? Certainly. Worthwhile challenges? Despite Welsh, I think that some of them are. Derrida's attack on binary oppositions is well worth having; I too often find them mere, restrictive 'substitutes for thinking'. And his 'undecidables' could be marvellous antidotes to 'binality' if he'd chosen his examples more honestly. So on the whole Derrida's analysis of *Phaedrus* seems well worthwhile, especially his banal conclusion that Plato attacks writing through the very medium of his attack: writing itself! As for Derrida's treatment of Saussure, that seems less fair, indeed less honest. But it serves to confirm what a towering figure Saussure was in the analysis of language. Ellis clearly enjoyed performing his hatchet-job on Derrida but clearly he emerged with his own methodology strengthened. There is great value in taking the received wisdom of a discipline – such as Philosophy or Architecture – and questioning its basic premises.

So there is great value in taking influential texts, as Derrida and Ellis both do, and rooting out their inconsistencies, in showing that the author himself, if he were true to the concepts he uses, would have to modify his views. The fact that others before Derrida had done this, to great effect, by no means diminishes the fact that Derrida did it too. And the wilful obscurantism of much writing by the 'Deconstructionists' surely encourages those of us who care about clarity to analyse what makes their writing so obscure, so impenetrable, so as to make ours' even clearer! In other words the sheer wrong-headedness of much of what Derrida does, of what 'De-constructionists' do in general, at least encourages the rest of us to try to be sensible! Ellis suggests that literary critics have been influenced by Derrida in two ways. A few have taken literally his views on signification; that it is a 'limitless, infinite, indeterminate play of signifiers' and used this in their analyses. Rather more have tried to emulate his temperament, his 'habits of thought and style' his 'habit of . . . denouncing unexamined assumptions' and such terms from Derrida's vocabulary as 'putting into question' and 'problematising'. So it has been in architecture too and it's time now to look at how these have been applied in this very different field.

THEOLOGY

It was, of course, Saint Paul (died c AD 67) who first brought Greek philosophy into the Christian Church and others, such as Saint Augustine of Hippo (345-430 AD) justify their Christian Faith by the application of Aristotle's reasoning.

ST THOMAS AQUINAS (1225-1274)

St Thomas Aquinas goes further. He takes from Aristotle such notions as Matter and Form, Actuality and Potentiality, not to mention the idea of a Prime Mover, and applies them to the Christian God using, indeed, precisely Aristotle's argument for the existence of his 'Prime Mover'. Hence his Five Proofs for the Existence of God; based, Aristotle-like, on the fact that things come into existence, flourish, die and decay. His Proofs are much like Aristotle's for a 'Prime Mover' but Thomas also argues that in day to day life we judge some things as better than others. If degrees of perfection are possible then their source must lie in a Supreme Being which is perfection itself.

JOHN DUNS SCOTUS (c 1265-1308)

But others, such as John Duns Scotus by no means accept Thomas' 'Five Proofs'. Belief in God is entirely a matter of Faith and Faith is not susceptible to reason. Belief is entirely a matter of Will; it has nothing to do with the intellect. Duns Scotus separates 'Reason' from 'Revelation' and therefore distinguishes, sharply, between Philosophy and Theology.

Theology is a study of God and his attributes; his existence cannot be 'proved' by the evidence of the senses. Philosophy and Metaphysics, however, are concerned with being and its various attributes.

WILLIAM OF OCKHAM (c 1285-1349)

William of Ockham too argues that Theological truth cannot be attained by reason. The only 'realities' are the objects of our sensory experience. These are material things contingent on the Mind of God but by no means existing within it. Each must be studied for its own sake and not merely as an example of a certain category, on which basis he develops his famous intellectual Razor: 'What can be explained by the assumption of fewer things is vainly explained by the assumption of more things.'

SCHOLASTICISM

Early Christian Fathers such as Saint Augustine believed that the teachings of Christ could be reconciled with those of Plato and particularly Aristotle. As Boethius put it (early 6th century): 'As far as you are able, join faith to reason' against which the probably contemporary, 'Pseudo-Dionysius', as 'Denis the Areopagite' proclaimed the mysteries of faith by 'negative theology'. We cannot, with our finite understanding, begin to comprehend the nature of God.

EMPIRICISM

A view that knowledge can only be gained by experience ('empeiria') based on the evidence of our senses but may grow by further introspection. A reaction to the 'intellectual' approach so favoured by Plato who believed that everything could be thought through, from self-evident principles, by logical argument. The Stoics saw the mind at birth as a 'clean slate' to be stocked by ideas occurring as the external world 'impinged' on the senses. The Epicurians believed all our concepts to be 'memory images'. These ideas began to flourish in the Middle Ages:

ST THOMAS AQUINAS (c 1224-74)

Believed that body and soul would both participate in perception and that all our ideas are abstracted by the intellect from what is 'given' by the senses. We derive our ideas of unseen things, such as God and the angels, by analogy with things we have seen.

ROGER BACON (13th CENTURY)

Emphasised the empirical nature of our knowledge.

WILLIAM OF OCKHAM (c 1285-1349)

All our knowledge of nature comes from the senses and from this we can attain to the 'abstractive knowledge' of necessary truths. Especially if we apply his famous intellectual 'razor'.

FRANCIS BACON (1561-1626)

Argued that the only knowledge worth having on any subject is to be gained from systematic observations both of 'instances' and 'contrary instances' (thus in considering heat one would look also for its absence in cold things); careful plotting of these in tables and the derivation from them, by processes of induction the nature of the concept in question.

THOMAS HOBBES (1588-1679)

True knowledge is *a priori* – that is prior to experience – but the senses provide 'ideas' resulting largely from the 'impact' on them of external events. They help us form definitions on which we act by 'reckoning', that is, rigorous deduction of a kind for which geometry gives us models.

JOHN LOCKE (1632-1704)

The mind, at birth, is 'white paper, void of all marking' which 'comes to be furnished' by the experience of our senses. This gives us simple ideas on which we can act, by 'reflection', to develop complex ideas. Concepts such as existence and unity derive from sensation and reflection whilst the notion of 'substance' may indeed be *a priori*.

GEORGE BERKELEY (1685-1753)

Nothing is 'real' unless someone is perceiving it. Since there may be things which, at any one time, no man is perceiving their 'reality' continues thanks to the ever present, never sleeping, watching mind of God.

DAVID HUME (1711-76)
We gain our 'impressions' directly from our sense experiences, passions and emotions but we also have 'ideas', which are 'faint images' of our 'impressions' recalled during the processes of thinking and reasoning. We can deal with 'Relations' between 'Ideas' by geometry, algebra etc but we cannot endow 'Facts' with equal confidence. Whilst we may learn from experience that one thing, habitually, follows from another, such as that day follows night, our senses do not show us any process of 'cause' and 'effect'. So we have no logical reason for accepting the process of 'induction': that because a certain thing has always followed another it will do so next time. However, to live our day-to-day lives, we may have good psychological reasons for believing in inductions of this kind. Nor, since our knowledge derives entirely from sensory experience, can we know anything of God, the human soul, absolute moral values, and so on.

EXISTENTIALISM
From the earliest times, man has wanted to know what he is. Socrates had commanded 'Know thyself' and Aristotle had seen the heart of his Metaphysics as the problem of 'Being qua being'. Descartes thought he had solved the problem with 'I think, therefore I am' but Montaigne was not so sure with 'If my mind could gain a foothold . . . I would make decisions . . .' Pascal too was preoccupied with the problem of 'Being' and 'Nothingness'. Early in the 19th century de Biran wrote that even in infancy she: 'marvelled at the sense of my own existence'. This instinct led her 'to look within myself' so she could know 'how it was possible that I could be alive and be myself'. Of course, there are many ways of approaching this.

SOREN KIERKEGAARD (1813-1855)
Described himself as 'a lonely pine tree, egoistically shut off, pointing to the skies'. It seemed to him important that passion and feeling should be just as esteemed as reason and intellect. Kierkegaard seems to have inherited from his father a general melancholy, despair, a sense of 'dread'. He objected, in particular, to the abstract concepts of Hegel, the idea that each of us is simply some expression of the dialectical process in its current state. He saw as morally wrong to disregard the nature of human will and the facts of personal choice. Not so much choice based on pre-formed criteria but made out of doubt and uncertainty. It is a 'leap of faith' based on one's total, individual separateness,

taking responsibility for oneself.

KARL JASPERS (1883-1969)
Much influenced by his early training in medicine and psychiatry, Jaspers was rather more involved than, say, Heidegger, in contemporary social and political problems.

MARTIN HEIDEGGER (1889-1976)
Since Heidegger was concerned with Being 'as such' rather than with mere human existence, he objected to being lumped with the Existentialists. But he has much in common with them. Unlike other living creatures, humans are aware of their existence; able to reflect on it. He sees the human way of 'being' as Da-sein, there-being and it gives us choices; simply to go along with 'being' in the world, which he calls 'inattention existence' or to take charge of our own affairs and live 'authentic' lives. We can face this because of the 'angst' we feel in the face of death. This encourages us to take responsibility. Many see him as the epitome of a philosopher who 'redeems' civilisation from the onslaught of science, technology and calculating 'rationality'.

JEAN-PAUL SARTRE (1905-1980)
Describes *Being and Nothingness* (1943) as 'an essay on phenomenological ontology'! In this sense 'ontology' is the study of 'consciousness' and its contents; 'ontology' of what is actually there in the universe. So Sartre asks: 'What is it like to be a human being?' And in his view it is both things: 'being', as an object or a thing, and also consciousness which is not that thing. Since consciousness can, and wants to be, involved in a future world it forms the nature of our human freedom. It makes us conscious of what we are not with the possibility of choosing what we will be in the future. So we contemplate the world which does not exist and project into the 'emptiness' the self we want to be. We do not choose to exist, we have that already. We choose the way we *want* to be.

GABRIEL MARCEL (1889-1973)
Also wrote on *The Mystery of Being* but from a Christian (Catholic) rather than an atheist or Marxist point of view.

POST-KANTIAN PHILOSOPHERS
Kant himself had attempted a reconciliation between the strongly empirical view of philosophers such as David Hume and the idea that certain kinds of knowledge are inborn.

GEORG WILHELM FRIEDRICH HEGEL (1770-1831)
Hegel developed Aristotle's syllogisms in his 'Dialectic' of Thesis, Antithesis and Synthesis.

ARTHUR SCHOPENHAUER (1788-1860)
Schopenhauer's Fourfold Root of the Principle of Sufficient Reason (1813) is based on causality, logical connections between concepts, mathematical truths and our knowledge of ourselves as subjects who exercise will by reference to the laws of motivation. For as a knowing subject one is also a subject who wills and what one wills of course is determined by one's motivations. The will has to be recognised as an objective 'thing' just as the body is. For the human will has parallels elsewhere, in: 'the force that shoots and vegetates in the plant . . . by which the crystal is formed . . . that turns the magnet to the North Pole . . . all these he will recognise as different only in phenomenon, but the same according to their inner nature'.

As Schopenhauer puts it: 'every man is what he is through his will, and his character is original, for willing is the basis of his inner being.'

WILL TO POWER
Friedrich Nietzsche by contrast (1844-1900) had no time for religion. He, like Berkeley, was suspicious of the belief that the world has an objective structure, 'out there' independent of human apprehension. Nor are there absolute values or meanings for us to discover. We have to distinguish ourselves from the 'meaningless flux of things' and do so by creating for ourselves new values and new ideals. The great men of Classical Antiquity never thought of morals in our sense. They had no concept of that 'thinking of others' which, say, the Christian Church advocates; each strove mightily to further his own selfish ends.

But in Christianity 'charity, humility, and obedience' replaced the basic pagan virtues of 'competition, pride and autonomy'. Nietzsche despised this 'ascetic' ideal; he called it 'Nihilism', seeing such ideals expressed whenever 'soul' is preferred over 'body'; 'mind' over 'sense'; 'duty' over 'desire'; 'reality' over 'appearance' and so on. Religion and Philosophy were both driven by a powerful 'motivating assumption': that existence, by its very nature, needs some kind of explanation. Both denigrate the world of appearance in favour of some other, 'true' world of the Spirit, Thus both are concerned with life in decline, in some acute state of distress.

But in Nietzsche's view both had been superseded by Positivism, which of course leads Nietzsche towards his most notorious claim; the 'death' of God. Certain replacements were available for God, such as nationalism, but Nietzsche preferred that 'Will to Power' which 'Nihilism' had denied. The 'Will to Power' had been there all the time, masked and even negated by traditional Philosophy, Religion and Morality.

Our actions reveal our personal 'authenticity' and those with Nietzsche's 'will to power' might challenge the 'received truths' of Christian belief but such people, ahead of their time will be lonely, abused and misunderstood.

What was this 'Will to Power'? As Nietzsche says in Daybreak (1881): 'the love of power is the demon of men'. It is a 'striving for distinction . . . for domination over the next man . . .' So what kind of man will exercise it? Well, of course the 'Superman' whom Nietzsche describes in Thus Spake Zarathustra, is constantly mastering adversity; forging, continually, a new and higher destiny for himself, affirming life joyously. That is the essence of human existence, the source of all our aspirations, all our strivings but also of that cruelty, the need to trample on others, which is a necessary, if regrettable part of our existence.

This prompts a fundamental question: 'whether this which is given does not suffice for an understanding even of the so-called mechanical (or 'material') world?' May not that too be driven by the 'Will to Power'? In which case the world seen from within, described according to its 'intelligible character' – would be the 'Will to Power' and nothing else.

Despite this ardent advocacy of power, Nietzsche himself was a gentle, even ineffectual individual and not without his perversions. In Thus Spake Zarathustra for instance he says of 'Women' (1883): 'Everything about woman is a riddle, and everything about woman has one solution: it is called pregnancy'; 'The true man wants two things: danger and play. For that reason he wants woman, as the most dangerous plaything'; 'Man should be trained for war and woman for the reception of the warrior: all else is folly . . .'; 'Are you visiting a woman? Do not forget your whip!'

So perhaps it is hardly surprising that in 1889 he became insane. His sister took charge of his affairs, deciding what would be published and when. It was she who assembled Ecce Homo after his death and, in her old age, she believed Adolph Hitler to be the personal embodiment of Nietzsche's 'Superman'. Indeed, it is hardly surprising that Nietzsche's 'Will to Power' appealed to the Nazis and was seen by some as the force behind Nazism. There are Nietzsche disciples who wish it were not so, who claim that Nietzsche was misrepresented by his sister. But he did indeed write those things!

PHENOMENOLOGY
First used by Lambert in the 18th century to distinguish truth from error in his theory of knowledge and used also by Hegel in the Phenomenology of Mind in tracing the development of the human spirit from mere sensory experience to 'absolute knowledge'. Bernard Bolzano (1837) argued that pure logic could be founded in psychology. Phenomenology embraces sensory experience as the basis of knowledge; Husserl himself – see below – declared (1913) 'We are the true positivists' but admits as of equal value non-sensory, 'categorical' data such as relations and values provided that these are acquired by 'pure intuition' and not by processes of logic and reasoning.

FRANZ BRENTANO (1838-1917)
Started from a purely Empiricist viewpoint his 'descriptive psychology', studying relationships between ideas and judgements, love and hatred, from which he developed his 'theory of truth' based on 'evidence' in the sense of what is evident. He also developed the concept of 'intentionality' – the 'directedness' of consciousness towards some particular object. His studies of mental phenomena were to be taken very much further by his pupil, Edmund Husserl who argued (1887) that numbers are by no means to be found 'ready made' in nature; they result from mental activity but Gottlob Frege accused him of confusing psychology and logic. Husserl therefore concentrated on the structure of his psychological acts, especially their logical structures. He concentrated on his own conscious acts, examining the relationship between consciousness and being. He tried to probe intuition devoid of all interpretation in processes such as perception, representation, imagination, judgement and feeling and developed his ways of 'bracketing out' the world and everything else beyond 'absolute data grasped in pure, immanent intuition'.

PRAGMATISM
A philosophy of action which dates back to ancient Greece. Polybius (died 118 BC) called his writings 'pragmatic' because they were intended to be instructive and useful. The word 'pragma' itself means 'action' from which 'practice' and 'practical' are derived. Kant described as Pragmatisch a kind of empirical, experimental and purpose-directed thought 'based on and applying to experience' whilst Hegel described as 'pragmatical' a reflective kind of history.

CHARLES SANDERS PEIRCE (1839-1914)
Launched 19th century Pragmatism with his classic paper on 'How to make our ideas clear.' For Peirce the 'truth' of any proposition lies entirely in its practical results. To say that a substance is 'hard', for instance, means that few others can be used to scratch it. There is no point in arguing about concepts which do not have equivalent practical results. And where there are disputes of interpretation in science there will be increasing acceptance of the 'true' proposition within the community of scientists and increasing rejection of the false.

WILLIAM JAMES (1842-1910)
Added to Peirce's morally 'neutral' Pragmatism ideas of value, worth and satisfaction. Truth and meaning themselves are aspects of value. And just as in the body, the actual function of an organ gives it meaning, so the 'use' of Mind is defined by the observable effects of its presence. And in a famous essay on 'The Will to Believe' he argued that if belief endows psychological and moral benefits on the believer then it is reasonable actually to hold metaphysical or religious beliefs.

JOHN DEWEY (1859-1952)
Combined in his Instrumentalism Peirce's logical and James' humanist views of Pragmatism. Thus, scientific knowledge was combined with beliefs concerning human values and purposes. Any kind of scientific, moral or social problem may be solved by thinking through by the determination of its future consequences. The closest we can get to 'truth' is 'warranted assertions'.

COSMOLOGY
The ancient astronomers observed that seven 'heavenly bodies' seemed to wander, backwards and forwards, across the night sky within a belt of sky containing the 12 constellations they knew as 'signs of the zodiac'. They gave these planetes, – 'wanderers' – names which are still recognisable in the days of the week: English (Sunday, Monday), French (Mardi, Mercredi, Jeudi, Vendredi) and English again (Saturday).

ARISTOTLE (384-322 BC)
Worked out a totally logical system to explain all this. The whole system must be centred on the Earth, spherical and perfectly static, otherwise we should sense its movements. The planets, including the Sun, must move round it in celestial spheres and since movement slows down and stops without some force to impel it, the planetary spheres must be kept in constant motion by some external Prime Mover. There were spheres according to how many were needed to explain the motion of the Sun and the Moon. Aristotle also thought that falling bodies were attracted to their 'natural home' – the centre of the Earth – and that heavier objects, naturally, would fall faster than lighter ones.

ARISTARCHUS OF SAMOS (c 310-230 BC)
Having observed the Earth's shadow on the Moon during a total eclipse Aristarchus calculated their relative diameters and the distance between them. He established too that the Sun is much

bigger than the Earth which led him to speculate that the Earth rotates around the Sun.

PTOLEMY

Made precise measurements and realised that Aristotle's 'theory' of the 'spheres' could not account for the backward motion observed for instance in Mars. He advanced the 'theory' of 'epicycles'; small backward loops from the surfaces of the spheres which accounted with great accuracy for these apparent backward movements.

NICOLAUS COPERNICUS (1473-1543)

Rejected Ptolemy's extremely complex explanation in favour of Aristarchus' simpler one but continued to think that the planets – including the Earth and the Moon – moved in circular orbits round the Sun. His predictions therefore were less accurate than Ptolemy's.

TYCHO DE BRAHE (1546-1601)

Still held to the Ptolemaic model but observed in 1563 that the available planetary tables were quite inaccurate and resolved to obtain the finest possible, non-telescopic measurements. These were so good that in 1582 they led to reform of the calendar and the introduction of leap years. Forced to move from Denmark to Prague he took as his assistant Johannes Kepler.

GALILEO GALILEI (1564-1642)

Used sensory-observations to override the 'mental sets' of those who relied entirely on logic and intellectual processes. Thus his observations of pendulums in action led him to quite different conclusions from Aristotle's about momentum. He used 'vulgar handicraft' to make inclined planes down which he could roll balls to refute Aristotle's views on gravity 'For I know that one concludent experiment doth batter to the ground a thousand probable arguments.' And he used his telescope to show that the illumination of Venus varies with its position in relation, not to the Earth but to the Sun; that Jupiter has moons so the Earth too might have a Moon; that the Sun was by no means Aristotle's perfect sphere; it had spots.

This combination of Sensory observation, Pragmatic experiment and intensive logical deduction lead Galileo to conclude that the Sun is the centre of the solar system, that freed from air resistance, friction or other interference two bodies dropped, of different weights, will fall at the same speed. He realised also that under similar, interference-free conditions a body, once in motion, will continue in a straight line at uniform speed.

RENE DESCARTES (1596-1650)

Refined this into the First Law of Mechanics.

JOHANNES KEPLER (1571-1630)

Tycho de Brahe's assistant promised to continue his work yet, despite Copernicus and Galileo, still believed in Pythagoras and the 'music of the spheres'. He tried to work out their notes, and also to nest the planetary system into Plato's five geometric solids. But they did not fit; nor, given Tycho's figures, could the planets be moving in circular orbits. He took Tycho's measurements for the most 'eccentric' of them: Mars and tried to fit them to various curves allowing for the fact that Tycho's observations had been made from a moving Earth. The best 'fit' proved to be an ellipse, with the Sun at one focus and ellipses too fit Tycho's measurements for the other planets. Kepler realised too that the closer in its orbit to the Sun, the faster a planet moves.

ISAAC NEWTON (1642-1727)

Like his great predecessors Newton combined three major ways of thinking: Plato's purely intellectual kind and the two which Plato despised; sensory observation and the Pragmatic methods of 'vulgar handicraft'. Thus he showed by experiments with his prism that Descartes was quite wrong in his entirely intellectual speculations as to the nature of light.

And of course it was a falling apple – Pragmatic if not 'vulgar handicraft' – which lead Newton to speculate that the force which pulled it downwards was also that which held the Moon in orbit, which led him, eventually, to codify Galileo's findings into three great 'Laws of Motion': 1) That in the absence of external forces the inertia of a body at rest causes it to remain at rest and that of a body in motion causes it to remain in motion in a straight line. 2) Given the difference between the weight of a body – its gravitational attraction to some other body such as the Earth – and its mass – the quantity of inertia or resistance to acceleration it possesses – then force is a product of its mass and its acceleration. 3) For every action there is an equal and opposite reaction. From this collectively, Newton deduced that the motions of the heavenly bodies could be explained by gravitation.

RELATIVITY

Newton's ideas held sway for over 200 years until further combinations of 'intellectual', 'sensory' and 'pragmatic' – thinking caused Albert Einstein (1879-1955) to believe that certain revisions would be needed. Newton had thought that light consists of particles: photons but in 1803 Thomas Young had shown that it also had wave-like properties, to which gravitation would not apply in quite the same way. And between 1864 and 1873 James Clerk Maxwell had worked out a series of equations from which he calculated that electromagnetic waves travel at 300,000 kilometres, or 186,300 miles per second; Heinrich Hertz measured this in 1888 and already in 1882 Albert Michelson had measured it also as the speed of light. He and Edward Morley showed in 1887 that this was constant irrespective of whether the light travelled with or at right Angles to the Earth's rotation. This constant speed, 'c' stimulated Einstein, by the sheer application of intellect, to some quite extraordinary conclusions – as did his application of principles from electrodynamics to the rest of physics.

ALBERT EINSTEIN (1879-1955)

It takes some time – however infinitesimal – for light to travel from, say my watch to my eye; a little longer from the Moon to the Earth (12.25 seconds) and longer still from the Sun (9 minutes). And of course for intergalactic distances the time might be tens, hundreds, thousands and even millions of years. So how can we ever know if two things happened simultaneously even, say, on the Earth and the Moon?

If we were in a spacecraft midway between the two we might see simultaneous events but if our spacecraft were moving from one to the other we should see the event we were approaching before the one we were leaving. And time in our moving spacecraft would move more slowly than time in a static craft! There is no space here even to catalogue other amazing predictions which Einstein made to such things as the constant speed of light, the loss of mass by radioactive materials as they emit energy in the form of light, the way in which mass – dependent on gravity – and acceleration produce equivalent effects, the implication of locating, say an atomic particle, not just in the three dimensions of length, breadth and height but in the fourth dimension of time.

Einstein's 'General Theory of Relativity' (1915) enabled him to make an extraordinary series of predictions with numerical values attached. For instance he explained the curious fact that Mercury, far from returning to the same points on each of its orbits round the sun, shifts orbit every century by some 43 seconds of arc.

Einstein also presented the very strange idea that light rays can be bent by gravity. Thus the light rays from a star will be bent by the gravity as they pass by the sun. This of course sounds quite absurd but as Einstein points out this 'Theory' can be tested as it was in 1919 when Sir Arthur Eddington observed light rays bent during a total eclipse of the Sun.

Einstein predicted that the stronger the gravitational field in which it is emitted the more the light from a star will be shifted in wavelength towards red. Such shifts were actually measured in the 1960s.

He also predicted that in order to escape the Earth's gravity an object would need a speed of 4.7 miles or 7.5 kilometres per second. His prediction of this 'escape velocity' of course was 'confirmed' in 1958 when the Russians launched their 'Sputnik', as it has been by every space launch ever since.

How much more interesting, how much more exciting these 'speculations' of Einstein's which have been confirmed, not only by 'sensible' observations, such as Eddington's, but by extraordinarily dramatic actions, such as the explosion of the Bomb, the launching of space vehicles, the generation of nuclear power.

EDWARD POWELL HUBBLE (1889-1953)
In 1924 observed Nebulae outside our galaxy which Shapley suggested were other galaxies. Hubble realised that not only were they receding from us but the further away they were the faster the speed of their receding and that this could be measured by the degree to which light from them was shifted towards the red end of the spectrum.

ABBE GEORGES EDUARD LEMAITRE (1894-1966)
Realised in 1927 that if one calculated backwards the positions of Hubble's expanding galaxies they must have exploded from some central 'Cosmic Egg' or 'Superatom' in the 'Big Bang' some two billion years ago. Baade realised in 1952 that this must have occurred at least six billion years ago.

GEORGE GAMOW (1904-1968)
Worked out how the debris from Lemaitre's 'Cosmic Egg' could 'condense' to form the elements of the universe and popularised the 'Big Bang' Theory.

ROGER PENROSE
Showed mathematically in 1965 that the surface of a star, collapsing under its gravity, would sink to zero. Which meant that its volume too would shrink to zero; its density would become infinite. It would be a 'singularity' within the space-time of the universe: a 'black hole'.

STEVEN HAWKING
In the same year Steven Hawking realised that if time were reversed in Penrose's equation then it could be applied to a universe expanding from a 'Cosmic Egg'.

ATOMIC STRUCTURE
The idea that matter is composed of atoms seems to have originated with Leucippus of Miletus and his disciple, Democritus, extended to idea much further (c 430 BC). Democritus thought them hard, uniform, indivisible and indestructible. There were atoms not just for matter and its properties: sweetness, whiteness and so on but for perceptions, and even for the human soul.

These ideas were dismissed by Plato as not abstract enough and Aristotle on the grounds that for there to be atoms there would also have to be voids.

But Galileo believed that a void could exist in the form of a vacuum and experimenters such as Robert Boyle, showed that this could be so. So atoms are accepted as the basis of matter by revolutionary scientists such as Boyle, Mariotte, Gassendi and Newton himself.

John Dalton, Gay-Lussac, Mendeleyev, Bernoulli and many others explored further implications but it was not until 1897 that J J Thompson realised that the atom is not a homogenous mass. It consists, rather, of a nucleus and orbiting electrons. These were investigated by Millikan, Wien and Thomson whilst Becquerel, Rontgen, the Curies and Rutherford investigated the radioactivity which certain kinds of atom, apparently, emitted. Pragmatic research resulted in much intellectual work on the structure of the atom:

LORD KELVIN (1824-1907)
Conceived a 'plum pudding' model in which the atom is a sphere in which atoms are embedded like raisins in a pudding. If disturbed they will return to their original position.

MAX PLANCK (1858-1937)
Replaced this in 1911 with a model in which the atom has a tiny, positively charged nucleus at the centre containing virtually all its mass with tiny, incredibly light, negatively charged electrons orbiting around it.

NIELS BOHR (1885-1962)
Rutherford's electron would lose energy and spiral down into the nucleus so Bohr conceived his concentric 'shell' model. The shells were somewhat like Aristotle's 'spheres': each electron would be locked into a shell and might emit radioactivity if it jumped from one orbit to another in quanta of the kind which Planck had described.

LOUIS-VICTOR PIERRE RAYMOND DE BROGLIE (1892-)
Others objected that Bohr's atom was a hybrid of Newtonian mechanics for the orbits of the electrons and a little quantum mechanics for keeping them in their orbits. De Broglie therefore reinforced the idea that like light, electrons had both wave-like and particle-like forms.

ERWIN SCHRÖDINGER (1887-1961)
Schrödinger suggested (1926) that electrons within an atom should be seen as waves of energy on the basis of De Broglie's idea. The orbit they took within a Bohr-like atom would depend on the energy within them.

WERNER HEISENBERG (1901-)
All this, of course, was intellectual stuff and Werner Heisenberg established, by 'thought-experiment' the limits to what kind of sensory observation might be possible. He concluded (1927) that in observing the smallest particles of matter the apparatus itself might interfere with, and change, what was being observed. The 'Uncertainty Principle' which he derived from this, of course has been extended, metaphorically, as the indeterminate which can affect many aspects of human behaviour.

PAUL ADRIEN MAURICE DIRAC (1902-)
Schrödinger's equations too can only describe particles moving slower than the speed of light. They cannot satisfy the principles of Relativity; Dirac therefore described not one but four wave-functions for the electron. They might spin clockwise or anti-clockwise; and they might have a positive or a negative charge. Which meant that since electrons have negative charges there could exist forms of 'anti-matter', which Anderson found in 1932.

Research into the structure of the atom has consisted of firing particles at each other: positive/positive or positive/negative, to see what other forms of energy are released.

There is a zany Surrealism about recent physics which makes it far more fun, whilst also being more challenging, intellectually, than anything that recent Metaphysics has produced.

PSYCHOANALYSIS

SIGMUND FREUD (1856-1939)
In his early research Sigmund Freud looked for the causes of hysteria in the physical structures of the brain, but in 1885 J M Charcot introduced him to psychological studies. He learned to hypnotise patients and persuade them to recount their most painful memories or desires that normally were suppressed, which led him to believe that the mind has 'conscious' and 'unconscious' states. He began to find 'free association' more effective in revealing what had been suppressed since it helped the patient understand deep-seated motives and avoid its more destructive effects. And in 1900 he suggested that *The Interpretation of Dreams* in particular reveals the contents of the unconscious mind. In 1905 he published his views on infant sexuality and the energy deriving from it (the 'libido')

which persists, often suppressed, in adult life. Later he derived a three-part structure for personality: the *id*, an unconscious reservoir of drives; the *ego*, responsible for perception, cognition and action; the *superego*, the ideals, values, moral standards which 'censor' the actions of the *ego*.

ADOLPH ADLER (1870-1937)

Adler was one of Freud's first disciples and one of the first to secede. He disagreed with the primacy Freud gave to the sex impulse believing instead that the 'aggressive drive' towards power is our primary motivating force. The child is powerless in a world of adults and develops an 'inferiority complex'. So the rest of one's life is given over to attaining some kind of 'compensation' by the exercise of 'masculine protest' against 'feminine weakness'. Sexual relations themselves are attempts by pairs of people to dominate each other. So far from causing mental disturbance sexual abnormality itself was caused by such disturbances. Adler spent less time trying to probe the unconscious and tried to go instead directly to the patient's problems.

CARL GUSTAV JUNG (1875-1961)

Having read Freud's early work Jung developed his method of 'word association' which, by forcing quick responses, tapped the unconscious before the conscious mind could intervene. Having been a disciple of Freud, Jung broke from him on the question of infant sexuality on the grounds that whilst this may explain hysteria in adult life it was no help in more deep-seated disorders such as schizophrenia. He developed his 'analytic psychology' with its emphasis on attitudes: extrovert (outward-looking) and introvert (inward-looking) also the functions of the mind: thinking, feeling, sensing, intuition. Jung's early interest in archaeology lead him to develop the idea of a 'collective unconscious'; traces of the most primitive cultures imprinted in the mind of the child. These had led in early times to the formation of myths which meant that deeper levels of the subconscious could be interpreted in terms of mythology.

JACQUES LACAN (1901-1981)

Lacan's psychoanalysis was based on Freud interpreted against Saussure's Semiology and Lévi-Strauss' Structuralism. The unconscious itself is structured 'like' a language with its own signifies organised by Saussure-like associations, especially metaphors and metonymies. The child in developing a sense of 'self' goes through the Oedipal phase, identifying with 'mother' and seeing 'father' as a rival. This and the structure of language itself will help the child enter the 'symbolic order'; giving a name to a thing means one has distinguished it as something other than self. So one can think of oneself as 'I' and this marks full entry into the symbolic order, which in turn fashions us according to the structures of that order. Increasingly there will be a split between what is lived and what is spoken. Relationships between things; self and other, parent and child are determined, not directly, but by the symbolic order which 'distances' us from the 'truth' as we live it directly.

POST-STRUCTURALISTS

MICHAEL FOUCAULT

Like Barthes – and Derrida – Foucault too despises 'clarity'. As White says (1979):

> . . . the thorniness of Foucault's style is . . . ideologically motivated. His interminable sentences, parentheses, repetitions, neologisms, paradoxes, oxymorons, alternations of analytical with lyrical passages, his combinations of scientific with mythic terminology – all this appears to be consciously designed to render his discourse impenetrable . . .

He writes 'discourse', based largely on 'catachresis': – the slight misuse of words such as 'anachronism' for 'anomaly' or 'chronic' for 'severe'. But for White it is precisely this style that gives authority to what Foucault has to say! As far as argument is concerned Foucault seems closest to the Nietzsche of *Ecce Homo* with the 'madness' of all 'wisdom' and the 'folly' of 'knowledge' from which point of view he attacks humanism, science, reason and the other great institutions of Western culture!

In *Madness and Civilization* for instance (1961) he was concerned with the way in which the 'official' discourse of psychiatry perceives, classifies and allocates such insubstantial 'things' as 'sanity' and 'madness'. They are defined, at any given time, by those with social power. It is by no means a matter of deriving them from observation and hypothesis or theory and practice – they are the actual basis of theory and practice at any given time. Western man's 'will to knowledge' had been not so much a development toward 'enlightenments' as a product of endless interactions between 'desire' and 'power'.

Thus in the Middle Ages madness was seen as a sign of sanctity; a repository of the divine truth. But in the 16th century it was denied that status and in the 17th it was 'set over against' reason; bestiality against humanity. So the mad were imprisoned with 'outsiders' such as criminals and paupers and then in the 19th century they were seen as 'proper' but sick members of society. And Freud of course actually listened to the insane although he did not free them from the 'tyranny' of the doctors.

Foucault mistrusts every kind of authority; every 'opposition' such as 'permitted/forbidden', 'rational/irrational' or 'true/false'. He sees them as expressions of 'hierarchy' in social practice which, he believes, derives from the 'Fall' of man into language. But there is error in any verbal representation and error arises from our perceptions of 'sameness' and 'difference'. Sameness enables a social group to identify itself as a unity; difference then allows hierarchies to be set up.

Since the time of Kant at least Western culture had concerned itself with 'the theme of origin' which promises some kind of 'return'. But, says Foucault in *The Archaeology of Knowledge* (1974), he aims to 'free' us from this 'circle of the lost origin' – an anthropological idea in which all such questions are 'around the question of man's being'. This means that actual practice is left unanalysed. He is trying instead 'to operate a decentering that leaves no privilege to any centre'.

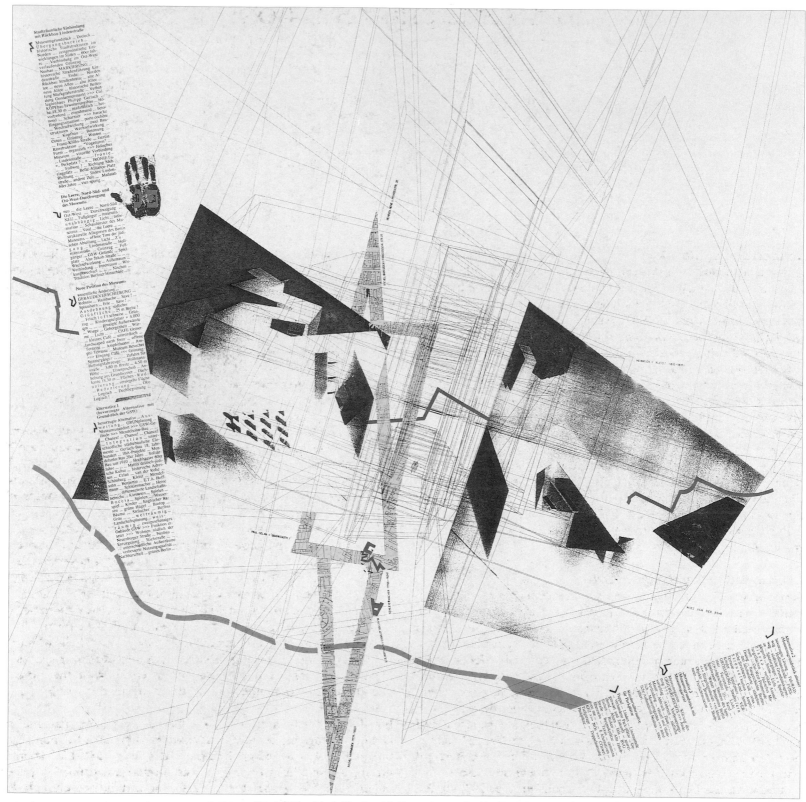

Daniel Libeskind, The Jewish Extension to the Berlin Museum

DECONSTRUCTION IN ACTION

Architectural Applications

We have seen that Derrida's major arguments were published in French in 1967, but it took quite a while for Deconstruction to make much impact on the Anglo-Saxon World, with its strong Empiricist traditions. Those texts of 1967 remained unpublished in English until 1973 *(Speech and Phenomena),* 1976 *(Of Grammatology)* and even 1978 *(Writing and Difference).*

But Derrida had an ardent advocate in Paul de Man, Professor of Humanities at Yale. He was pressing home, as early as 1971, Derrida's point that 'language bears within itself the necessity of its own critique'. Which meant, of course, that a generation of American East Coast University literary critics could justify their very existence as 'writing about writing'!

So Deconstruction replaced Structuralism as the dominant intellectual mode – at least in East Coast Universities of the United States, which may explain why Philip Johnson sought to raise the intellectual stock of architecture by establishing its links with 'Deconstruction'.

But what is there to 'deconstruct' in architecture anyway? And why would anyone want to do it?

Deconstructing Architectural Texts

'Deconstruction', after all, is a literary matter concerned – as Derrida insists – with written texts. So perhaps we should explore the 'deconstruction' of writings on architecture, taking the great books from, say, Vitruvius to Le Corbusier to Robert Venturi onwards, trying to find their internal contradictions. We might 'deconstruct' them against Derrida's 'Enthno-centrism', 'Logo-centrism', 'Phono-centrism', 'Onto-Theology' and so on to see how these permeate the writing. In the process we might go into the finer details: logos; 'binary oppositions' from 'sensible' and 'intelligible'; 'signifier' and 'signified' to 'inside' and 'outside', 'supplement'; 'deferring', 'difference', 'différance', and so on, relating them to basic architectural concepts to see how far these survive Derrida-like processes!

Such work has been done already by non-Derrideans. Take the basic idea, for instance, that architecture consists essentially of internal space. As Van de Venn shows (1978), there is a long tradition of thinking in this way which dates back, long before Vitruvius, to the Chinese philosopher Lao-Tzu, who wrote in the 6th century BC that:

> We make a vessel from a lump of clay:
> It is the empty space within the vessel that makes it useful.
>
> We make doors and windows for a room;
> But it is these empty spaces that make the room livable.

Frank Lloyd Wright, no less, concluded from this that: 'Internal Space is the reality of the building'. Van de Venn assembles some 90 exponents of this view and there is also Bruno Zevi's formidable history (1957) of *Architecture as Space.* Yet Roger Scruton 'deconstructed' this whole historic concept with a single paragraph when he wrote in 1979:

> Taken literally, the theory that the experience of architecture is an experience of space is obviously indefensible. If space were all that interested us, then not only must a large part of the architect's activity seem like so much useless decoration, but it is even difficult to see why he should bother to build at all. If I stand in an open field then I can have a full experience of all the separate spaces that are enclosed in St Peter's in Rome. The only difference is that here the shell which Bramante and Michelangelo constructed around these spaces does not exist, and so does not interfere with the pure unmediated contemplation of the spaces as they are in themselves.

But there's much more to it than that. For Zevi the 'essence' of architecture lies in the 'obstructions which determine the perimeter of possible vision, rather than the "void" in which this vision is given play'. In other words, it is in the surfaces enclosing the spaces rather than the spaces themselves. But that is not enough for Scruton either. A simple building, such as the Treasury of Atreus, may offer nothing more than 'moulded space'. But 'space' alone by no means captures everything that interests us about St Paul's Cathedral. There is much more than 'spatial grandeur' to Wren's deliberate effects of 'light and shade, of ornament, texture and mouldings'. So for Scruton the 'essence' of architecture lies in 'significant detail' including the material from which it is made. For Derrida, of course, there are no such things as 'essences' of this kind anyway. So we could go on to 'deconstruct' Scruton's argument by insisting that in addition to being *of* something: stone – brick, timber, or whatever – his detail must be *on* something too – solid, like a wall, a ceiling, a vault, a pier, a column or a beam. And only when we have all three – solids whose surfaces do the enclosing of spaces – can we say we have architecture whole.

Robert Venturi demonstrated a parallel kind of 'deconstructive' thinking' when, in C*omplexity and Contradiction* (1966), he wrote of 'Both-And' architecture: the closed-yet-open quality of Le Corbusier's Villa Shodan, the symmetrical-yet-asymmetrical quality of the Tudor Barrington Court, the unity-despite-duality of Guarini's Church of the Immaculate Conception. Venturi's 'Both-And's are rather more convincing than Derrida's 'undecidables' since they are real buildings and they have these ambiguities whereas Derrida, as we have seen, rather cheats with the Classical words. And as Geoff Bennington points out, (1987) – Bennington translated Derrida's *The Truth in Painting* – Venturi also mounted in *Complexity and Contradiction* his attack on the 'transparency' which critics such as Pevsner and Giedion saw as crucial to the 'modernity' of the Modern Movement; the essence of what made it different from the architecture of the past. As Giedion puts it in *Space, Time and Architecture* (1941) – he was writing about Gropius' Offices for the Fagus Works and the Bauhaus itself:

> there is the hovering, vertical grouping of planes, which satisfies our feeling for a relational space, and there is the extensive transparency that permits interior and exterior to be seen simultaneously . . . variety of levels of reference, or of points of reference, and simultaneity – the conception of space-time in short.

Thereby making, of course, the Einstein connection: that Space-Time relations are the essence of Relativity, hence the title of his book. But for Venturi, walls are there to hold the building up and to enclose space, to separate the inside *from* the outside. We build a house, for instance, to offer people protection, to give them privacy, both physical and psychological. So it's for Venturi that the inside and the outside are different, that the one is separate from the other. And if the inside expresses the outside, is moulded, as it were, around the internal spaces, there can be no such thing as urban design! Each building turns in on itself and cannot integrate with its neighbours. So, says Bennington, Derrida demonstrates 'the impossibility of conceiving the inside of a sign prior to the outside. Only an outside can define an inside.' Bennington finds other parallels in Venturi with Derrida's attack on 'Phonocentrism' for example, the

'privileging' of speech over writing. As we have seen he prefers writing on the page, with no need for the author's presence. Buildings are like writing in this sense; 'texts' to be 'read' with no hint of direct 'transparency' to the author's thoughts. But, as Bennington points out, Derrida writes in *Grammatologie* (1967) of the inside and the outside of the sign – Saussure's 'signifier' and 'signified'. Indeed he actually writes of 'The Outside and the Inside': 'The Outside Is the Inside' and so on, denying their necessary connection, wanting to separate them, split them apart, as Venturi, a year earlier, had wanted to separate 'The Inside and the Outside' of the building!

Venturi rejects the physical transparency of walls and Derrida rejects the mental 'transparency' of speech. And just as Derrida suggests that in our endless search for what a word 'really' means, each signifier in turn becomes a signified for an endless sequence of others so Venturi pursues the subtleties of spaces 'nesting' inside each other – as in St Basil's Cathedral, Moscow – 'residual' spaces and so on. So it seems in buildings too that the 'inside' of one space becomes the 'outside' of another.

So why do architects need Derrida when such subtle, Derrida-like 'deconstructions' have taken place without him? Venturi gives us certain clues. For quite independently – or so it seems – he and Derrida were thinking on equivalent lines: of 'Both-And' or 'undecidables', of 'transparency' and how undesirable it was. And whilst his approach may seem, and actually is, chaotic, Derrida's 'deconstruction' is at least sustained. He performs it many times of many things and equally sustained 'deconstructions' of architectural writing may plumb greater depths than the brilliant 'one-offs' of a Scruton or a Venturi ever could. There is no space here to suggest more than a pointer or two but we might attempt a couple of Spurs-like analyses, taking sentences as terse as Nietzsche's: 'I have forgotten my umbrella.' Or simply play word-games as Derrida himself does! For whilst much of his writing is turgid indeed he can, when he chooses, word-process language with great glee, using puns, alliterations and other devices to forward his many-stranded arguments. This is a quality which he, Eisenman and Tschumi may even show in their architectural work. Some of Derrida's word-games translate whereas others most certainly do not. In his *Aphorismes,* for instance (1986C) Derrida writes, surprisingly, of building materials 'tous les mots en R: la terre, la matière, la pierre, le verre, le fer' without which there cannot be any stable architecture. But the point is quite lost in translation: 'all the words ending in (the sound) R: the earth, the matter, the stone, the glass, the iron . . .' So of course Derrida is right in describing himself (1968B) as: 'I who write . . . using displacements, withdrawals, fragmentations, play with identities, with persons and their titles, with the integrity of their proper names.' So let us take as an example the first sentence of Vitruvius, Book one paragraph one where he says: 'In all matters, but especially in architecture, there are two things: that which signifies and that which is signified.' Well, we know already what

Derrida says about that!

And now let us 'Deconstruct' that basic Le Corbusier sentence: 'A house is a machine for living in', taking Harrap's French/English Dictionary and Lewis and Short's Latin/English Dictionary:

Among other things a 'machine' can be a 'play with stage effects'. What would Derrida do with that? So obvious, so easy that really it isn't worth doing! Or let us take Mies van der Rohe's: 'Less is more' taking Oxford English Dictionary definitions:

A	HOUSE IS A	MACHINE FOR	LIVING IN
FRENCH (Harrap)	MAISON	MACHINE	HABITER
	house	machine	to inhabit
	business firm	stage effects	to dwell in
	home		to live in
	astrological house	bicycle	
			to occupy
		machine tools	
	family		to live
	dynasty	thing	to reside
		gadget	to dwell
	household	contraption	
		engine	
	especially of	prime mover	
		locomotive	
		dynamo	
LATIN: (Lewis and Short etc)	DOMUS	MACHINA	HABITARE
	house	an engine	inhabit
	home	fabric	live
	native place	frame	dwell
	family	scaffolding	remain
	sect	staging	be always (in)
	any sort of building	easel	
	or abode	warlike engine	
		military machine	
		etc	
		platform on which slaves were exposed for sale	
		painter's easel	
		scaffold	
		device	
		plan	
		contrivance esp	
		a trick	
		artifice	
		strategem	

LESS IS	MORE
Of not so great size, extent or degree (as something mentioned or implied)	greater in size, larger, taller, bigger
of inferior dimensions, bulk, duration, etc	greater in number, quantity or amount
smaller	greater in degree or extent
of smaller quantity or amount	greater or superior
not so much	of two things
of lower station, condition or rank	greater in power or importance
inferior	also having a fuller title to the designation
Of action: not so great, worthy or excellent	having a greater supply of
or (after Latin use) younger	a greater number of elder
Used spec to characterise the smaller, inferior	existing in greater quantity, amount or degree

INTERVIEW WITH BERNARD TSCHUMI

– *You used to speak of Derrida when you were teaching early in the 1970s.*

It was more a matter of the intellectual climate in Paris at the time: Post-Structuralist. My heroes were those who expressed themselves well, the group around *Tel Quel* such as Barthes and Foucault. I delighted in the intellectual climate after 1968. Derrida has been singled out but it was a general condition. There was an extraordinary stimulus in literary criticism that affected history, psychology, psychoanalysis. It gave us new tools and its not surprising that some architects got involved – such as Antoine Grumbach. He wrote about Freud and Lacan in 'The Pure and the Impure'.

French architects generally were violently anti-intellectual. There was a notice at the *École des Beaux-Arts* that said 'Books Forbidden Here'. They were not very cultured, not very verbal, so I was a total oddity. No-one was interested in what I had to say.

– *How did you make contact with Derrida?*

I called him one day, just after we won La Villette. He had lots of misgivings. I wanted to stage a situation that would get other contributions to La Villette. I wanted Jean-François Lyotard to work with Daniel Buren and Jacques Derrida with Peter Eisenman.

– *What did Derrida say?*

He asked why I was interested in Deconstruction. Architecture is a matter of structure, form and hierarchy but I was trying to get away from that.

– *At that time Eisenman was speaking of 'decomposition.'*

But I got him talking to Derrida. With Buren and Lyotard it didn't work but Eisenman and Derrida came up with the 'Choral Work'. It has my greatest respect but I'm not sure it will ever be built. It came out much over budget and the client got frightened. It's a tiny site, 20m by 309m and most of it is underground. It is an actual building with lots of layers.

– *Like Eisenman's scheme for Berlin.*

More like his 'Romeo and Juliet' for the Venice Biennale.

– *How about the rest of La Villette?*

We've built 14 *folies* and the landscape gardens. We are doing the next eight and we will finish in 1992. We lost a year two years ago with a change of government and funds were frozen. But now we have funds to complete and they have to be spent.

– *So your strategy proved correct?*

I like your word 'strategy'!

– *I just want to check a few dates. You came to Portsmouth in 1969.*

I started at the Architectural Association in January 1970 and I was there (AA and Portsmouth) until 1974. I started at the Institute (for Architecture and Urban Studies) in 1975 and I also started at Princeton in January 1976. In 1977 I was commuting between London and New York and in 1979 I finished at the AA. I taught at Princeton and Cooper Union. We won La Villette in 1982 and I stopped teaching in 1983.

– *How did your ideas develop?*

It was a matter of the intellectual climate. Between 1970 and 1976 I didn't draw – not one project. I was interested in theory, in certain positions taken up by Foucault, Sollers and the *Tel Quel* group.

Then in 1976-77 I started to write *The Manhattan Transcripts,* to explore concepts through drawing. The drawings weren't the outcome of those concerns. I developed ideas through the medium of drawing. It was a dialogue. I call it the import-export relationship between drawings, theories and writings. The writings follow the drawings. I wrote the Introduction to *The Manhattan Transcripts* afterwards. It was a post-rationalisation. The drawings were instrumental in developing the ideas.

The one feeds into the other in a way that would have been impossible in Paris. It's impossible in France to have the import of theory into architecture.

The *Manhattan Transcripts* took four years, from 1977-80. They could go on and on, and keep transforming the ideas in a sequence of transformations like the *folies.*

The *Transcripts* contain the ingredients for La Villette. It took us four weeks work to win the Competition then we had to develop our ideas. The *Transcripts* were there as an anchor behind all this.

– *How does that relate to Deconstruction?*

Deconstruction is only one relationship. There was no attempt to bring it completely into Deconstruction. There are more cultural parallels. There is the notion of 'meaning' that you and Charles Jencks explored. These things are always connected. Our memories get separated. There is no one meaning experienced, no fixed meaning.

– *That's in Derrida; do you think he got it from Barthes?*

You could find it in Derrida; I read Barthes less. Although there's the use of fragments, there is structural analysis in Barthes and the idea of sequence relates to Barthes' work in cinema. But a linear sequence is such a constraint.

After my rejection of architecture in the early 1970s I came back to it through the art scene. By first showing 'Transcripts '78' in an art gallery, Artists' Space, I was the first architect to show drawings in a commercial gallery. I got to know the artists very well. That is why I stayed in New York. I never expected to; I thought I'd go back to Paris.

– *What do you think when you see students applying your ideas very badly: Cross-programming; Trans-programming and so on?*

I'm more concerned with the ones who do it better than me. I think: 'Where did I go wrong?' It gives students freedom to explore in new directions. It's not just one thing; there are half a dozen different connections, different discourses.

– *How do you see things developing?*

Competitions are no good; they have to be done too fast. You do a competition to get the job but it's not the best way to develop architecture.

– *What are you working on now?*

You know Flushing Meadows on the way in from the airport where there's the Shea Stadium and the site of the old New York World's Fair? Well, I'm doing a conceptual plan for Flushing Meadows Park: 1250 acres and a billion dollars. I'm the Master Planner and it will take 25 years. The bureaucracy is slower than in Paris.

I'm doing the programming and we have two sets of drawings; those we use to develop the scheme and those we show to the clients. It's like Goya, you know, the *Maja vestida* and the *Maja desnuda.*

That's the largest project I'm doing. The smallest is a disco, well, a display of video clips: Sex/Music/Video for Gröningen in Holland. Peter, Zaha, Prix (Coop Himmelblau) and I are all doing sections. Mine is over-budget but it's got more glass than Mies.

Then we won Lausanne; it's a valley east of the city centre and there are five bridges.

– *With all this work, how far do you automate the office? What use do you make of computer-aided design?*

For the *folies* these days I sketch a plan, section and elevation on to a sheet of A4 and fax it over to Paris. There it goes into the computer and they check it against the rules for designing *folies.* Then the computer draws the details. I was afraid it would freeze things up but it's not computer design; more computer drawing really. But we are doing an exhibition for the Beaubourg on 'Art et Publicité' – posters by Toulouse-Lautrec, Rodchenko; that kind of thing. And we are having the computer design the layout. But that's just a two-dimensional design, as in the *Transcripts,* with overlaps, rifts and shifts.

– *Finally, let me check what Derrida you've actually read?*

Grammatologie, Marges and *Positions.*

So Mies van der Rohe's gnomic utterance – his basic 'binary opposition' – can be made to say everything from 'The not so great in size is superior', or 'Small is beautiful', to a Biblical 'Those of lower station will be of greater importance', or 'The meek shall inherit the earth'! Which are very like some of Derrida's verbal games!

Derrida expresses particular admiration for Peter Eisenman who, he says 'does not only take great pleasure, jubilation, in playing with language, with languages, at the meeting, the crossing of many idioms, welcoming chances, attentive to risk, to transplants, to the slippings and derivations of the letter. He also takes this play seriously . . .' – as we shall see shortly.

But what is there to deconstruct in architecture itself? Let us now look at 'deconstructing' the brief or programme.

Deconstructing the Brief or Programme

This indeed is what Derrida himself attempted to do. Yet when he was asked what could and should be 'deconstructed' in architecture his list of potential targets was remarkably conventional (1988A & B). Derrida had been involved with the *Collège Internationale de Philosophie*, a peripatetic organisation which was aiming to set up a permanent home. Derrida naturally persuaded his colleagues to question the very assumptions on which the *Collège* was based and it is perhaps worth quoting a fragment of the language in which he describes all this (1988A):

> The *Collège* had to be prepared to invent . . . a configuration of places which do not reproduce the philosophical topos (topique) which, quite rightly, was itself being interrogated or deconstructed. This topos reflects the models or reflects itself in them. The socio-academic structure, politico-pedagogic hierarchies, forms of community that preside over the organisation of places or in any case never let themselves be separated from them.

A quotation from Derrida which represents him perhaps, at his most turgid. But it does reveal, albeit reluctantly, that he was encouraging his colleagues not to take anything for granted, to search for a form that their community might take by questioning its hierarchical nature, the kinds of teaching it did, the need – if any – for classrooms, and so on.

Derrida also questioned more general matters, such as the nature of aesthetics in architecture, the relationship of buildings to their functions, the nature of habitation, or rather of 'dwelling' in buildings as Heidegger argues that we do, which all sounds remarkably like the original 'question everything' programme of the Modern Movement, not to mention the student revolution of 1968! Or indeed the earlier work of Chermayeff and Alexander in *Community and Privacy* (1963), of Cedric Price with his 'Fun Palace' project of 1961, his 'Potteries Thinkbelt' of 1964 and his built Interaction Centre of 1975.

Parc de la Villette

The largest demonstration of 'Deconstruction' at work in architecture is certainly Bernard Tschumi's Parc de la Villette. He asks the fundamental question: 'Is the Parc de la Villette a built theory or a theoretical building?' Can the pragmatics of actual building be combined with the abstract rigour of intellectual concepts?' Tschumi seeks to demonstrate that complex architecture can be organised without reference to the traditional rules of 'composition, hierarchy and order'.

Like the Derrida of *Marges* Tschumi sought 'a reversal of the classical oppositions and a general displacement of the system'. For him the basic 'cause-and-effect' oppositions were those between 'form and function, structure and economics or (of course, architectural) form and programme'. The point is to substitute for them 'new concepts of contiguity and superimposition' of 'permutation and substitution'.

Just as Derrida shows by his 'deconstructions' that the writings of various philosophers contain within themselves challenges to the very concepts on which they are based, so Tschumi hopes to show that in architecture 'deconstruction' of the programme challenges the 'very ideology' on which the programme itself is based. This means dismantling the conventions of architecture by using concepts derived from architecture itself, certainly, but also from cinema, literary criticism, philosophy and psychoanalysis. For in the previous 20 years boundaries had been eroded between these different ways of thinking and architecture has 'relations' with them all. Tschumi sees these relations as offering an 'intertextuality' subverting the 'autonomy' of Modernism. But above all 'deconstruction' erodes the historic split between architecture as building and architectural theory.

Tschumi sets out various approaches to deconstructing the brief. Indeed he describes his 'Post-Deconstructivism' methods of programming as follows (*A+U* 89:10):

CROSSPROGRAMMING: Using a given spatial configuration for a programme not intended for it, ie: using a church building for a bowling alley.

Similar to Typological Displacement: a town hall inside the spatial configuration of a prison or a museum inside a car park structure. Reference: crossdressing.

TRANSPROGRAMMING: Combining two programmes, regardless of their incompatibilities together with their respective spatial configurations.

Reference: Planetarium + Roller-coaster.

DISPROGRAMMING: Combining two programmes, so that the required spatial configuration of programme A contaminates programme B and B's possible configuration. The new programme B may be extracted from the inherent contradictions contained in

Bernard Tschumi, Parc de la Villette, Paris

programme A, and B's required spatial configuration may be applied to A.

Elsewhere, in *Cinégramme Folie,* Tschumi sets out his strategies for design. Confronted with an 'urbanistic programme' – such as La Villette – an architect may attempt:

a) to design a masterly construction, an inspired architectural gesture (a traditional composition);

b) to take what exists, fill in the gaps, complete the text, scribble as it were, in the margins (producing a complement to what is there already);

c) to deconstruct what exists by analysing critically the historical layers that preceded it, even adding other layers derived from elsewhere – from other cities, from other parks (a Derrida-like palimpsest);

d) search for an intermediary – an abstract system to *mediate* between the site, the constraints of the programme and some other concept quite beyond the actual city or programme (as a mediator).

The programme for La Villette was complex indeed. It had to

include workshop, gymnasium and bath facilities, playgrounds, places for exhibitions, concerts, scientific experiments, games and competitions. Already on site were the 19th-century cast-iron-and-glass Grande Halle, Fainsilber's Museum of Science and Industry with a new City of Music also to be built. All this could have been organised into one of the largest buildings ever to be constructed but Tschumi saw it as an open-air cultural centre with separate buildings – fragments, as it were, of a single structure designed within 'an integrated policy' which related both to the city's needs and to its current limitations. The 'structure' would overlap certain areas of the city and existing suburbs, in which respect it would offer 'an embryonic model' of what the new programmes for the 21st-century city might be like.

Tschumi rejected both 'composition' and 'complement' at Villette since these evoke ancient architectural myths and impose their own pragmatic limits. Nor did he explore 'palimpsest' here although he had, in some detail, in the *Screenplays* of 1976. But the 'figurative' or 'representational' elements contained in a 'palimpsest' seemed incompatible with the technical and political, not to mention

Bernard Tschumi, City Bridges, Lausanne

Bernard Tschumi, Parc de la Villette, Paris

programming constraints which he saw embodied in the challenge of La Villette. Nor was there any guarantee that if a 'Total Concept' were accepted by the authorities, it would ever be realised; whoever was appointed chief architect would have to improvise, during the process of realisation, according to economic and ideological changes. This would be easier if 'improvisation' itself were the very basis of the concept. Hence Tschumi was concerned, reinforced by recent developments in philosophy, art and literature, that the Park possess a strong conceptual framework containing within itself multiple 'combinations and substitutions'.

Thus the programme can be in constant change, according to need, one part substituted for another, and so on. One of the folies indeed was changed from restaurant to gardening centre to arts workshop; these changes could be accommodated easily, whilst the Park as a whole retained its overall identity.

Tschumi, moreover, acted on 'a strategy of difference'. If other designers were to contribute to his Parc then it would be a 'condition' of their contribution that their projects differ from his Folies or break the continuity of his cinematic promenade. Tschumi

aimed, therefore, to present 'an organising structure that could exist independent of use, a structure without centre or hierarchy (hence the grid), a structure that would negate the simplistic assumption of a causal relationship between a programme and the resulting architecture'. A clear statement indeed of 'Deconstructionist' programming.

As for a 'mediator', Tschumi had used grids on previous occasions such as his Joyce's Garden project with students from the Architectural Association in London in which they had used the grid of the Ordnance Survey to locate various points where London might need 'interventions'. Tschumi saw this grid as a 'mediator' between *Finnegan's Wake,* the literary text he had in mind, and the 'architectural text' his students were proposing for London. The point was to show that there was no necessary link, no 'cause-and-effect relationship between the two terms of programme and architecture'. Nor do grids need, indeed they resist, the 'stamp of individual author'. This anonymity makes the grid 'a paradigmatic 20th-century form', and by its nature also the grid resists any sense of hierarchy; it offers instead 'an incomplete, infinite extension . . .'

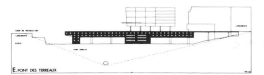
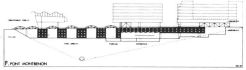

Bernard Tschumi, City Bridges, Lausanne

The grid presents a series of 'dynamic oppositions'; one wonders what Derrida thinks of that. Tschumi and his colleagues were designing a Park but 'the grid was anti-nature'; they had to fulfill a number of functions but 'the grid was anti-functional'; they had to be realists but 'the grid was abstract'; they had to respect the local context but 'the grid was anti-contextual'; they had to be sensitive to site boundaries but 'the grid was infinite'; they had to take into account political and economic indeterminacies but 'the grid was determinate'; they had to acknowledge precedents in garden design but 'the grid had no origin, it opened onto an endless recession into prior images and earlier signs'.

The grid of points is only one of three systems. There are systems of lines and surfaces too: 'Each represents a different and autonomous system (a text), whose superimposition on another makes impossible any "composition", maintaining differences and refusing ascendency of any privileged system or organising element. Although each is determined by the architect as "subject," when one system is superimposed on another, the subject – the architect – is erased.'

One could argue that Tschumi continues to control because he devised the three systems but the Competition conditions required that other designers be involved, any one of whom could bring in other systems. Indeed their work would be successful only in so far 'as they inject discordant notes into the system, hence reinforcing a specific part of the Park theory'.

There are indeed gardens by others in the Parc already, such as Paul Chemetov's 'Garden of Bamboos', Vexlard and Vacherot's 'Garden of Gardening' and Alain Pelissier's 'Water Garden' but the most Derridean of all no doubt will be the 'Choral Work' by Peter Eisenman and Jacques Derrida himself which we shall be analysing shortly.

So, 'The principle of heterogeneity – of multiple, dissociated and inherently confrontational elements – is aimed at disrupting the smooth coherence and reassuring stability of composition, promoting instability and programmatic madness (*la folie*).' What is more, the structures on site already, such as the Museum of Science and Industry and the Grande Halle, add further 'calculated discontinuity'. Instead of conventional 'composition', therefore, Tschumi presents 'montage' at La Villette, which of course had been developed as part of film technique by Eisenstein and others. In 'montage' independent fragments may be juxtaposed thus permitting 'a multiplicity of combinations'. There can be repetitions, inversions, substitutions, insertions and so on 'but in film, each frame (or photogram) is placed (within a) continuous movement. Inscribing movement through the rapid succession of photograms constitutes the cinégram'.

In much of his earlier work, such as the *Manhattan Transcripts,* Tschumi had questioned 'the very idea of structure' which paralleled, he says, research on literary texts. The superimposition of three structures at La Villette, each coherent in itself, could never,

by the nature of those structures produce some 'supercoherent mega-structure'. Collectively they were bound to give an 'undecidable . . . the opposite of a totality'.

The addition of systems, each with its own internal coherence, produces a result which is by no means coherent. The excess of rationality within the systems is by no means rational. So La Villette points to new social and historical conditions; as a built 'reality', it is dispersed and differentiated', which, for Tschumi, marks an end to 'the utopias of unity'.

So there was no way in which his Parc could be 'homogenised' into a totality. The superimposition of his structures prevented any idea of a 'pre-established causality' between the programme, the architecture and its signification thus encouraging the 'intertextuality' he sought and the 'dispersion of meaning'. What's more Tschumi ignored, rejected and even subverted the context, subverted any notion of 'border' to his site. If there is no border there can be no 'context' so the Parc de la Villette is quite unrelated to its surroundings. Unrelated because of course the three geometric systems, of points, lines and surfaces are, as Tschumi would say, 'autonomous'. Neither their dimensions nor their forms derive in any way from the actual site, not even from its boundaries. For as Derrida himself says (1985): 'To establish a grid is to cross through. It is the experience of permeability. Furthermore such crossing does not move through an already existing texture; it weaves this texture . . .'

It is noticeable that in his discussion of La Villette Derrida concentrates, almost exclusively, on Tschumi's *folies* to the virtual exclusion of the geometric systems which for Wigley were the essence of Tschumi being a 'Deconstructionist'. Spaced as they are to Tschumi's 120 metre grid his *folies* quite simply are not big enough in themselves to suggest anything like the familiar kind of urban enclosure defined, say, by four-storey buildings surrounding streets and squares. This of course is entirely his intention: to unsettle 'memory and context' by rejecting both 'contextualist' and 'continualist' approaches in his design, indeed anything which implies that the architect's 'intervention' always refers to some established 'typology', some 'origin', some 'determining signified' of building, urban space or even park design. Tschumi rejects absolutely the idea that his Parc should express in any way some 'pre-existing' content of some kind be it 'subjective, formal or functional'. So, overall, there is: 'conflict over synthesis, fragmentation over unity, madness and play over careful management'.

For Derrida the Parc 'calls into question the fundamental or primary signified of architecture': its tendency is to obey some 'economy of use' to be 'in service, and at the service' of some function or use. Instead of that La Villette offers 'programmatic instability'; each building functions as a *folie* and the *folies* themselves have no fixed and specific uses.

Folies

As with the Parc as a whole so with these *folies*, which, with their bright red paint are the most striking features on site. Each started as a ten metre – 33 foot – cube divided three-by-three-by-three into 27 11-foot cubes, each representing a particular stage in a vast geometric transformation which gives solid walls, curtain walls, trellises combined according to rules of intersection, repetition, qualification, distortion and fragmentation. So any one cube could be left four-square as a frame or skeletal form or it may be tilted diagonally. It may have metal plates filling all exposed sides and thus look like a solid cube or it may have some combination of frame and 'solid'. Some of the 'one-third' cubes may be missing or displaced.

There might be spiral staircases attached to the cube or passing through it, large or small in diameter, vertical or conical in form. There might be 'Constructivist' sculptures attached: an open horizontal cylinder, a water wheel. And then there are solid buildings clustering around some of the *folies*, built of gleaming polished granite; rectangular, circular, or with angles as acute as, say, I M Pei's in his Extension to the National Gallery in Washington DC, capable of housing some function such as information centre, bar, restaurant or exhibition gallery. I say 'capable' of housing these things because of course Tschumi is anxious to break the 'binary oppositions' of 'architecture and programme', of form and function.

Meaning

By these means he subverts the 'functional' ideals of Modernism and, Derrida-like, also denies an 'obsession with presence'. For just as Derrida rejects the idea that meanings are 'immanent' in words – inherent to them – so Tschumi rejects the idea that meanings are 'immanent' in the structures and forms of his buildings, that his architecture has a direct capacity for signifying.

Hence the geometric rule-play of his grids – whether in his site plan or the permutations of his cubes – intended, like Eisenman's in his early house, to give an architecture of pure syntax with no semantic references at all. For in Derrida's 'Deconstruction' – 'postmodernism involves an assault on meaning, a rejection of the idea that "a well-defined signified" . . . guarantees . . . authenticity'!

'Meaning' is never 'transparent'. It is always 'socially produced', the result of others making their readings of what the author has produced. Each of us will interpret this in his own way: 'according to psycho-analytic, sociological or other methodologies'. So there will be no absolute 'truth'; such 'meanings' as the Parc may have will result from our personal interpretation. No 'meaning', as such, will be inherent in the objects themselves, or in the materials of which they are composed.

It is interesting that Tschumi should see 'Deconstruction' as a form of 'Postmodernism' since he goes on to say that 'Postmodernism', in its more ingratiating forms . . . cannot stomach (these alternative readings)'. It offers a more 'palatable' style in place of the Modern Movement, a 'nostalgic pursuit of coherence' which, for Tschumi, 'ignores today's social, political, and cultural dissociations'. So

'Postmodernism' becomes the 'avatar' – the ritual incarnation – of a certain, and particularly conservative, architectural 'milieu'.

In that form 'Postmodernism' is an architecture of symbols which Tschumi rejects as a particular historic 'refuge of humanist thought'.

Like Derrida he wishes to 'dislocate', to 'de-regulate' the idea of meaning. Words such as 'park', 'architecture', 'science', 'literature' and so on, have lost their universal meanings. No longer do they refer to any kind of 'fixed absolute', any kind of 'ideal'.

Since, by its nature, La Villette is in a state of constant production and constant change, its meanings also will be constantly changing. So Tschumi sees whatever meanings it may have, Derrida like, as constantly 'deferred, differed, rendered irresolute'. The architecture, literally, 'means' nothing. It is an architecture of signifiers with no signifieds as pure 'trace' or play of language.

Tschumi refuses to 'express' himself in the Parc and the Parc 'negates' any 'immanent dialectic' of form. Whatever meanings begin to emerge will be displaced by 'superimpositions and transformations' to the elements from which the Parc is formed and these, in their turn, will always exceed 'any given formal configuration'. So, in Tschumi's language: 'Presence is postponed and closure deferred as each permutation or combination of form shifts the image one step ahead.'

Much of this reads in terms which permeated the Portsmouth School of Architecture when Tschumi was teaching there in the early 1970s: Laurie Fricker's insistence that neither garden nor landscape can be bounded; Barry Russell's explorations in General Systems Theory with its 'Open', 'Closed' and superimposed Systems (see Bertalanffy 1950; Emery, 1969) and my own insistence that some 70 percent of functions could be housed in 70 percent of forms (see *Design in Architecture* 1973, 1988).

But on one thing, certainly, we parted company then and we part company now: the 'immanence' of meaning. For like any other sign-system, the Parc and its *folies* 'carry' their meanings in various ways.

Tschumi argues that the 'truth' of his red *folies* is by no means the 'truth' of Constructivism. But some of his *folies* actually take Constructivist forms. They look like them, are like them, remind us of them, are 'Iconic' with them. If we've seen Constructivist forms then of course we are reminded: Tschumi cannot take that from us.

And many of them are inviting. They 'ask' us to walk up their ramps and staircases, to go through their portals and so on. So in Peirce's terms they are 'Indices' and Tschumi's pious hoping that they won't communicate by no means diminishes their qualities as such.

As for their symbolism, well of course that has to be learned and everyone, world-wide, in the world of architecture has seen La Villette in journals, has learned within the culture of architecture that La Villette symbolises, more than anything else, more than any other building complex in the world, the application into architecture of Derrida's 'Deconstruction'!

Bernard Tschumi, National Theatre of Japan, Tokyo

La Villette and *Learning from Las Vegas*

There is a further irony: Tschumi's *folies* give rhythm to, and therefore articulate the space between them. They differ in shape and size – within his 10-metre cube – but their regular spacing, their bright red colour, and the family resemblances of their Constructivist forms, mean that one reads them as 'punctuation marks' within the space of the Parc.

If one has to find parallels for Tschumi's 'space', especially before the walkways were constructed then, more than anything, it was 'like' those spaces on the Urban American Strip which Denise Scott Brown found so intriguing, which indeed inspired *Learning from Las Vegas* (1973). That space was defined by signs rather than by buildings and Tschumi's *folies* seem to be placed at 'sign' rather than at 'building' distances. This may sound quite blasphemous in this 'Deconstructivist' context but, as we shall see, the Venturis had other insights of a kind which make some of their thinking parallel, to say the least, to some of Derrida's!

So much for a 'theory' of 'deconstruction' in architecture but what about the practice? Whilst Mark Wigley with his 'Deconstructivism' was concerned entirely with 'deconstructing' form, the form itself may be generated from other things starting with the building brief or programme.

As I suggest in my *Design in Architecture* (1973,1988), form may be generated in several ways which I call: Pragmatic: finding out by trial-and-error what the materials etc will do; Typologic: in which an established type or form is repeated; Analogic: in which one draws visual or other analogies with existing forms, often from outside architecture, such as plant or animal forms, painting or sculpture. And my fourth 'type of design', Syntactic, is a matter of using some geometric syntax.

National Theatre of Japan

As for Tschumi, he uses a different 'coding' device to 'deconstruct' the programme of his project for the New National Theatre of Japan (1987). He starts with music-like 'Notations' – much favoured by his contemporary in Portsmouth, the sculptor Malcolm Carder – and these help him to 'deconstruct' traditional relationships between the various parts of the theatre building. As he says (*AD, A+U*): 'No more artful articulations between auditorium, stage, foyer, grand staircase; instead a new pleasure through the parallel juxtaposition of

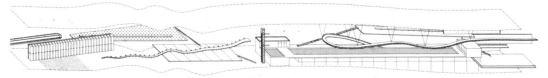

Bernard Tschumi, Kansai International Airport

Bernard Tschumi, National Library of France, Paris

intermediate cultural meanings as opposed to fixed historical practices.'

So he drew music-like eight-line 'staves' as bases for his notations and on to these he strung symbols representing 'auditoria', 'stages' and so on. His 'staves' of course had parallel lines and spaces which gave him plans 'banded' inwards from the facade to give a glazed avenue of entrance lobbies, multi-storey foyers, auditoria, a service strip, stages, backstage areas and a multi-storey artists' concourse with dressing rooms.

And then as Tschumi says the: 'deconstructed elements can be manipulated independently, according to conceptual, narrative, or programmatic concerns'.

It has to be said that the resulting organisation is much like Edward Stone's Kennedy Centre for the Performing Arts in Washington DC with its vast, building-length foyer giving access to various auditoria planned side by side. But whilst Stone's design is excessively monumental, Tschumi's is not at all monumental; indeed the glazed vault of his entrance lobbies curves down to a single-storey facade thus under rather than over-playing the celebration of 'entrance'.

Kansai International Airport

Tschumi, naturally, develops other ways of 'deconstructing' later programmes. In the case of Kansai Airport he, like other competition finalists, took the basic concept developed by Paul Andreu and the *Aéroports de Paris* for a site on an artificial island off Osaka. There was a large central block of administration, hotel and other facilities with, on the runway side of all that, domestic arrivals and departures. At either end were massively long 'wings' for international arrivals and departures, which gave a very linear building. This could, of course, be 'expressed' in many ways from Bofill's concrete and glass neo-Classicism, the High Tech of Piano (the winner), Foster and Pelli, to Tschumi's 'Deconstruction'.

Tschumi extends Andreu's concept, seeing the airport itself as a destination unto itself: (*A+U*) 'an event, a spectacle, a new city of interchange and exchange, a city of business, commerce and culture – a 24-hour-a-day continuous invention that acts as an extraordinary counterpoint to the city of Osaka . . . a new urban segment for culture and recreation, superstores and great hotels'. Indeed he sees it as being extended along the length of Japan, around the Pacific rim and, eventually, around the entire Globe! To

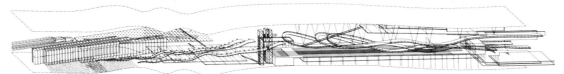

Bernard Tschumi, Kansai International Airport

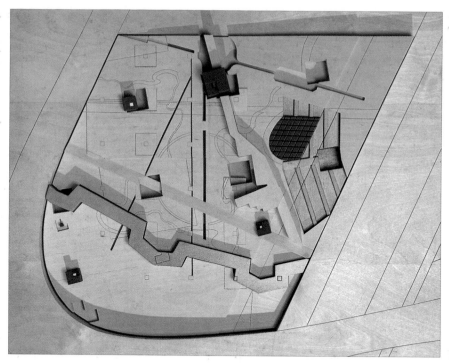

Peter Eisenman, Parc de la Villette, Paris

this end Tschumi designed a two-part Airport consisting of a Deck and the Linear City.

The Deck contains the actual terminal facilities: check-in counters, immigration offices and related functions. But Tschumi sees it also as a 'functional landscape' containing offices for trade and commerce, places for art and culture. To this end he designed a simple four-storey structure with curtain walling to be adapted, modified or extended as necessary.

The Linear City is a much more complex structure to be built in phases for the Airport to a total length of one mile. Like other Tschumi projects it is divided into parallel 'strips'. The runway-side, 'transfer functions of the airport' – gates and connections – take up a single-storey strip, behind and parallel to which is the 'slab': a four-storey solid structure, eight metres deep, containing bedrooms for two hotels, offices on hourly rental and so on. Access to these is by Tschumi's 'sine-mover', small cabins on rails which undulate up and down the storeys thus combining 'the functions of elevator and teleferic'.

Parallel again there is another long, thin block: the 'wave', which Tschumi sees as an 'entertainment/cultural/sports centre' some 12 metres wide containing cinemas, exhibition spaces, swimming pools, golf courses, shooting galleries and so on. Access to these is by travelators which follow the curves of the actual wave. And since the wave-form undulates in plan-form too it 'questions gravity', stimulates vertigo in the way that flying itself used to do. The plane of the ground ceases to be a datum; 'datum' instead becomes 'a new

conceptual or technological parameter'. And, as at La Villette, the masts supporting the 'wave' become all important since they act as 'the last remaining link between earth and air. For slab and wave already belong to the realm of the sky, as the wave begins to hover above the new airport city'.

Parallel yet again and beyond the 'wave' is another lengthwise, single-storey transfer strip. So, as Tschumi points out, there are extraordinary spaces between his four 'bands': transfer strips, slab, 'wave' and also his deck, the spaces, architecturally, being as significant as the constructable bands themselves. They 'challenge traditional architecture', no less, with their 'spectacular . . . disjunctions . . . stunning visual rifts'. Such linear 'negative spaces' are 'non-classifiable'.

We have no previous experience of spaces anything like these; there are no precedents in architectural history and no established 'repetitive typologies' against which we can judge them. Thus they raise fundamental questions as to the very nature of architectural composition.

National Library of France

Tschumi sensed the ever growing conflict between (A + U) 'the traditional institution of the past and the computerised library of the future, the book and the electronic image, the contemporary crowd and timeless scholarship'.

He saw this almost in those Classical terms by which, say, Plato's Academy was both a school of philosophy and a wrestling school,

Peter Eisenman, Cannaregio, Venice

or perhaps it occurred to him that the High (Electronic) Tech of library systems these days seems to be matched by the High (Electronic) Tech of circuit training in the gym! At least he envisaged 'the concept of the open circuit, where the endless pursuit of knowledge is matched by the pleasure of physical effort'. So the Library has a running track on its roof, to embody 'the library's complex role as the generator of a new urban strategy (the open circuit)'; the Library Circuit opens on to the River Seine to articulate a new quarter of the City whilst other (electronic) circuits 'induce a new Library Transmitter Tower' which indicates the presence of the Library to the rest of Paris.

The entrance from the river frontage is by an oval 'great hall', containing reception/information facilities, multi-media exhibitions, a café, a bookshop, meeting rooms, a conference room and banks of escalators. Around the top of this is an upper circuit with video displays, temporary exhibitions and a small café whilst the roof forms a sloping terrace overlooking the Seine. Above this again is the running track 'for energetic scholars and intelligent athletes, supported by splayed, trussed, cigar-shaped columns. The main reading room wraps around some three-fifths of the great hall extending some three storeys above it with the readers, as it were, stacked on 'trays'. Beyond the reading room are book stacks, administrative offices and so on. There are further 'circuits' in the detailed planning, for the public, the administrators, the books; there are electronic circuits and mechanical circuits and these various circuits meet for interaction at strategic points.

Deconstructing the Programme: Eisenman

Eisenman too has strategies for 'deconstructing' the programme. As he says (*A+U* August Extra 1988) the proportions of the human body have provided a 'datum' for architecture over the past five centuries. But recent developments in technology, philosophy and psychoanalysis render this no longer relevant. So 'the grand abstraction of man as the measure of all things, as an originary presence, can no longer be sustained', yet it persists in architecture.

Romeo and Juliet

In his 'Romeo and Juliet' project for the Venice Biennale of 1986 Eisenman develops a different strategy: 'he employs another discourse, founded in a process which he calls scaling. He uses in this 'scaling' three different 'destabilising concepts': 'discontinuity, which confronts the metaphysics of presence; recursibility, which confronts origin; and self-similarity, which confronts representation of the aesthetic object'. He sees 'presence, origin, and the aesthetic object' as 'confronting' three aspects of architecture: the site, the programme, and the problem of representation.

The site, after all, is a 'given'; a 'privileged presence, as a context that is knowable and whole', but Eisenman, like Tschumi, fights the constraints of this. He treats the site as more than a mere 'presence': it is for him a 'palimpsest and a quarry' in which capacities it contains 'traces' both of memory and potential or, as he says: 'immanence'. The site can be thought of as 'non-static', and that is how Eisenman prefers to think of it.

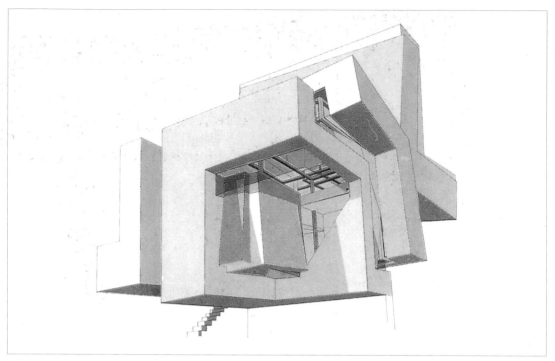

Peter Eisenman, Guardiola House, Santa Maria del Mar

As for the second of his 'destabilising concepts', the programme for the Biennale was drawn from Shakespeare's *Romeo and Juliet*. In it, Eisenman sees certain 'structural' relationships between Romeo and Juliet, of division, union and a dialectic for which he finds parallels in the geography of Verona, where the play is set. This he reads as a Derrida-like 'palimpsest' so: 'The project's superimpositions of scale and place address the dominant themes. In overlaps and coincidences of registration arise interrelated elements of present conditions, memory and immanence, revealing aspects of the structure of the textual narrative.'

Choral Work

Eisenman continued his experiments with 'scaling' and 'dislocation' in the Garden which he designed with Jacques Derrida for Bernard Tschumi's Parc de la Villette. For Eisenman, the garden is 'an attempt to dislocate the notions of metaphor and metonymy through dislocation so that actual time, place and scale are replaced by analogies of these conditions.' Thus the site 'will be an actual place but also will have another time, scale and another place in it. The site will contain its own presence as well as the absence of its own presence in the set of superpositions.

In previous projects, such as his Housing for Checkpoint Charlie in Berlin (1982-86) and the University Art Museum for Long Beach in California (1986 onwards) Eisenman had employed the process of 'palimpsest'. A 'palimpsest', of course, is an ancient manuscript, possibly Greek, which has been 'rubbed out' so that, say, a

Medieval text can be written over it. For Eisenman the process consists of rooting down to earlier developments on the site: ancient foundations and so on and displaying *on the site itself* these traces of its own history. And if, as in Berlin, he could not find the full sequence of the history he needed, he would design and build foundations that *ought* to have been there.

Such layers at La Villette should have included the Paris city wall of 1848 or earlier, the *abattoir* of 1867 and of course Bernard Tschumi's project of 1982 including, specifically, its grid. For, by an extraordinary coincidence, Eisenman himself, in 1978, had designed Cannaregio Town Square for Venice on the grid of Le Corbusier's Venice Hospital Design. Here, too, there was an *abattoir* on the site which of course was bounded by a canal. Thus Cannaregio and La Villette had three 'likenesses' to each other: abattoir, canal and grid which Eisenman thinks of as 'analogies'.

Thus: 'Canal to canal, *abattoir* to *abattoir*, grid to grid, Tschumi to Eisenman = creating an analogic space. So *that's* what he means by 'an actual place' which also has 'another time, scale, and another place in it'.

Eisenman's grid differs from Tschumi's in orientation – their main axes are at 90 degrees to each other – and in scale. The grid for La Villette 'coincides with that for Cannaregio at a ratio of two to one'. Thus 'Analogous material at differing scales is used for several reasons', one of which, of course, is to subvert the notion of human body as the source-authority of scale'. And by presenting the same 'analogous' material at different scales within the same project: 'we

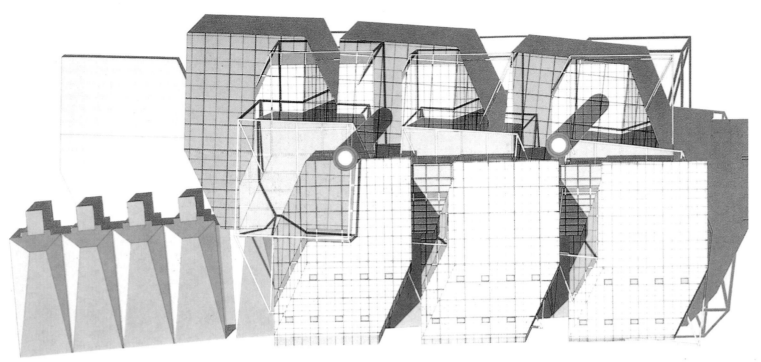

Peter Eisenman, Carnegie-Mellon Research Institute, Pittsburgh

subvert the value of the thing itself, the privilege of a specific object at a specific scale.

One notable example of this is the form which Jacques Derrida himself drew as part of their collaboration. It's a curious form with two straight lines connected by an obtuse angle, their outer 'open' ends connected by a curve which is used within the project at two quite different scales: as a sculptural 'feature' contained within it and as the site-boundary for the whole.

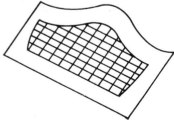

Derrida looked to Plato for their programme, especially to the Timaeus in which Plato, for the first time in any philosophy – describes the Creation of the World as entirely a work of Reason. The universe had been in 'discordant and inharmonious motion' (Book I, paraphrased from Cornford 1937). God thought that intelligent beings would be better than unintelligent ones, 'and, moreover, that intelligence is quite impossible unless it has a soul. So in framing the universe he fashioned reason within the soul and soul within the body . . . so the work he accomplished, by nature, would be as excellent and perfect as he could make it.'

But then he realised (Book II) that if things were to be brought into being, there would have to be somewhere for this to happen. So '. . . we must try to bring to light and describe a form which is difficult and obscure. What nature should we conceive it to possess and what part does it play? More than anything else, it is the Receptacle, or as it were the nurse, of all, Becoming.' But this 'Receptacle', or *chora* seems to take many forms: like a mass of plastic material – possibly gold – which may be moulded and remoulded in different ways. The *chora* from which all bodies take their forms must be as malleable as this. So Plato concludes that for each object there must be an ideal 'Form', which of course exists 'intelligibly' only in the mind of God; and then there are the 'sensible', physical copies which take their place, spatially, within the *chora*. And to play this role the *chora* must be 'Space, which is everlasting, by no means admitting destruction, providing a situation for all things that come into being, apprehended in itself without the senses by some kind of bastard reasoning and hardly, in itself, an object of belief.' Naturally Derrida and Eisenman are delighted to have a word even more ambiguous than *pharmakon*, something between 'container' and 'contained'. As Eisenman says (1988): 'For Plato the receptacle is like the sand on the beach, it is not an object or a place, but merely the record of the movement of the water, which leaves traces of high-tide lines and scores imprints – erosions – with each successive wave receding to the water.' So he and Derrida have great fun deriving further meanings for *chora*. It is, says Derrida 'carried over into song (choral) and even into

FRANK GEHRY

Gehry for a long time now: those of Chardin and of course Morandi, but also perhaps those of the Dutch Masters where crystal glasses, the moisture of oysters and the silver skin of fish sparkle (more on the question of zoomorphism later). Did you say chance? Let's be quite clear on this point, there is no more chance in the juxtaposition of the 'quiet little boxes' that founded most of Gehry's projects in the early 80s than in the shapes that were considered unlikely during the preceding decade: here again reasons of orientation linked to light and landscape are primordial. Added to them are the questions linked to the architect's familiarity with art. The appearance of new materials (Finnwood, a sort of dark red plywood, galvanised iron, stone) and the exploration of research themes aroused by Gehry's attention to the works of artists like Michael Heizer or Gordon Matta Clark (after all, Heizer's *Adjacent, Against, Upon* or Matta Clark's *Splitting* are both architectural subjects).

Gehry's position as regards art and architecture, which has been judged ambiguous, has earned him criticism on both sides: architects attempting to recompose the profession by wallowing in his references approach him with wary perplexity; artists judge him harshly, jealous as they are of their domain and perhaps secretly envious of the scale of his realisations.

Says Gehry: 'Unlike most architects, all these guys that I know (the artists) call my work into question. Just think . . . for God's sake! Think of Gordon Matta Clark! He called everything into question, didn't he? And architects have never done that! What's interesting is that his ideas well up little by little through culture. He's dead, gone, *fini*. And what he did and said is so strong that it comes through anyway (or rather in another way) while the others (the architects) only get a third-hand version, that of the advertising agencies or the media. A version they pick up without knowing anything at all about the original. Something similar is happening to Warhol: lots of lousy architects are designing Pop architecture without really knowing its origins nor how it came to them, Gehry has no complexes in speaking of the influences of his heroes, the taste they instilled in him for crude materials (Judd's galvanised iron, Andre's lead), for relationships between materials without transition (which sets him miles apart from modern academics who camouflage their connections with pretty cosmetic details, applied where the project's cost is inscribed). In the final analysis, materials and forms are there only for what they are: their grain, texture, line, colour and physical presence. To be caught in their nudity and their first truth. And devoid as much as possible of any residual signification. On this point, the appearance of the fish and serpent shapes in Gehry's vocabulary has given rise to various commentaries. Was it a gag? A distant reference to a Jewish childhood? A Christian symbol? An astrological quotation? Gehry himself gave an explanation one day in the form of a retort: since the post-modernists sought their references in history, he intended to go back even further, to prehistory, even before the appearance of man. This pirouette might just be more meaningful than it looks. In use, we see that the fish has been taken for what it is: only a supple shape, a scaled skin that reflects light. Gehry uses its primordial physical presence without loading it with mythical images or weighty notions, in a frank and primitive way. This is not very far removed from Michael Heizer's approach, whose work has something in common with Carnac, Chichen Itza and Ayer's Rock. Or that of Richard Serra raising an orthogonal steel menhir right in front of the church at Tournus, and of which Gehry, staggered, spoke recently without making it clear what he himself would have liked to have been the author of: Serra's sculpture or the Romanesque church. In this way Gehry might be both archaic and modern. Above and beyond attitudes as regards matter and its transformation by the hand of man, what he has in common with his heroes – Brancusi and Andre, Serra and Heizer – is the endless quest for the origins of the world and the tacit ambition to give it a form.

Olivier Boissière

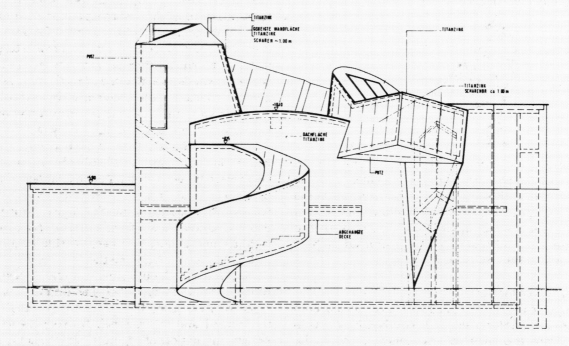

Frank Gehry, Vitra Design Museum, Weil am Rhein

choreography. With the final l, choral: *chora* becomes more liquid or more aerial.' These word games unfortunately involve a mispronunciation of *'chora'* which should have soft 'ch' as in 'loch', and this invalidated much that followed.

Once it had inspired Eisenman to call their joint venture 'Choral Work' Derrida played further word games. The name itself, he says: 'imposes from within a new dimension: choreographic, musical and vocal'. Thus 'the work becomes musical, an architecture for many voices . . . a gift as precious as it is petrified, a coral *(corail)'* – an even harder 'ch'! Quite specifically it becomes a 'garden' of water and stone. Derrida sees Eisenman's 'two words, so close to silence' as 'created . . . with a wave of the magic wand . . . the magic wand (which also) is the baton of an orchestral conductor'. He sees Eisenman's gesture as 'like the masterpiece of a maker of fireworks . . .' which reminds him of Handel's *Music for the Royal Fireworks* and therefore of Handel's 'architectural sense'. He muses further on chorale, on Corelli, and so on.

But Plato goes on to describe the chora as somewhat like a 'plokanon', a 'winnowing basket'. Cornford is quite clear that it is not a 'seive' but Derrida takes the traditional misreading and says:

I propose therefore the following 'representation', 'materialisation', 'formation' . . . in one or three examples. (If there are three with different scalings) a gilded metallic object (there is gold in the passage in *Timaeus* on chora and in your Venetian project) would be planted obliquely in the ground. Neither vertical nor horizontal, a very solid frame resembling at the same time hatching, a seive, or a grille (grid) and a stringed instrument of music (piano, harp, lyre?, strings, stringed instrument, vocal chord, etc).

Then says Derrida, his grille or grid would have a certain rapport with a telescope or camera filter, a machine having fallen from the sky having photographed, radiographed, filtered from an aerial view. Eisenman duly incorporated Derrida's 'sculpture' – somewhat modified, in which form it is scaled up to make the site plan. The garden itself, of course, is a 'palimpsest' – a 'reconstructed' archaeology of Paris with battlements and other features.

University Museum for Long Beach

Eisenman uses 'palimpsest' also in designing his University Museum for Long Beach, California (1986-present). He overlays incidents in the history of the site from its original role as a ranch, its role in the Gold Rush of 1849, the founding of the University in 1949, and an imagined 'rediscovery' of his Museum in 2049. So the 'traces' which are to be rebuilt on site include an obsolete oil derrick and the (inverted) Rainbow Pier.

All this, he says, because the traditional role of architecture has been not only to realise a sheltering function, but to represent and symbolise it as well. But whilst its function is to shelter art, it does not follow that the Museum as a building must symbolise that fact. It could represent instead the relationship of art to society; it might raise questions about the museum as a social institution; it might even display a new way of representing the solution.

Guardiola House

Eisenman presents a further 'rationale' for 'deconstructing' the programme in his account of the Guardiola House at Santa Maria del Mar near Cadiz. The idea of *topos* or 'place', he says, has been central to man's relationship with his environment. The *topos* might be defined by a clearing in the forest, a bridge over a river, the crossing of the main streets, cardo and decumanus, in a Roman encampment. But today, he says, two things have happened to bring into question such traditional forms of place-making: first, technology has overwhelmed nature – the automobile and the airplane, with their potential for unlimited accessibility, have made the rational grids and radial patterns of the 19th century obsolete; secondly, modern thought has found 'unreasonableness' within traditional reason, and logic has been seen to contain the illogical.

Traditional reason has repressed such 'challenges to order' but new conditions mean that we can no longer repress them. Nor have they been suppressed, of course, from the time of Einstein, of Heisenberg, of Gödel – not to mention David Hume!

One wonders, therefore, why it follows now – as Eisenman seems to think it does – that in architecture we must question whether it is still significant for man to mark his conquest of nature. We acknowledge too that the idea of *topos,* 'place', has always contained the idea of *atopia,* 'no place'. But as traditional ideas of topos break down so there are breakdowns too in the traditional categories of 'figure/ground' and 'frame/object'.

But since Classical times such contradictory states have co-existed in such things as Plato's *chora* 'something between place and object, between container and contained'. The *chora* is not 'an object or a place': it is like sand which records the movements of the waves, footprints and so on. For, 'Much as the foot leaves its imprint in the sand, and the sand remains as a trace of the foot, each of these residues and actions are (sic) outside of any rational or natural order; they are both and neither.'

So Eisenman's House is a *chora*-like 'Receptacle' in which 'traces' of logic and irrationality become 'intrinsic components' of 'object/place' or, as he says, the 'arabesque'. So the House exists ' between the natural and the rational, between logic and chaos'. Thus it breaks any notion of 'figure/frame' because it is, simultaneously, figure and frame. The L-shapes of which it is composed are

Rem Koolhaas and OMA, The National Dance Theatre, The Hague

constantly interweaving, penetrating each other in the three planes.

Non-Derridean Deconstruction

Tschumi and Eisenman of course are committed to Derrida and his 'Deconstruction' but that is by no means true, as we have seen, of Frank Gehry. He argues that by its very nature architecture is real, hard, solid and concrete. Gehry has no use for word games. Despite this, he too, of course, 'deconstructs' the programme, as one sees, for instance, in the Winton Guest House with its separate pavilions for different functions. And, says Gehry, 'Unlike most architects, all these guys (his artist friends) call my work into question. Just think .. . . for God's sake. Think of Gordon Matta Clark! He called everything into question didn't he? And architects have never done that!'

Well, some clearly have, most recently under the banner of 'Deconstruction'. There's no reason why Gehry should even try to read Derrida when he 'deconstructs' so splendidly anyway. But neither he nor his apologists can deny others the right to see parallels between what he does and committed 'deconstructors' do.

As for Coop Himmelblau, whilst their advocate Frank Werner points out (1988) that they, Eisenman, Tschumi, Hadid, Gehry, Koolhaas had all been 'deconstructing' long before anyone made the Derrida connection, they themselves are somewhat less sceptical. Their work had been called Visionary Architecture which was acceptable too, but the problem, for them, is criticism which is often unable to follow, let alone accept, new developments.

The crucial point for Coop Himmelblau is 'the point of intersection, the moment of such an exhibition' as they had mentioned in an interview with the Viennese journal *UMRISS* when asked about the 'Deconstructivist' Exhibition at MoMA. The time was right because, intellectually, architecture is dead. 'There is no imperative which forces architects to keep on building replicas but if seven who do not are selected for an Exhibition – shown as originators of a (new) direction – the other 400,000 speak against it. Who wants to hear that he's not up to date any more?'

So whilst it is hardly evident from the 'Deconstructivist' Catalogue it seems that 'deconstruction' of the brief or programme is of crucial importance for the 'Deconstructionists', whether committed (Tschumi, Eisenman) or reluctant (Gehry). Wigley's major concern was the 'deconstruction' of building form.

Deconstruction of Architectural Form

Indeed in his Catalogue he does a Derridean 'all the d's' to summarise this approach as:

an architecture of disruption, dislocation, deviation, and distortion, rather than one of demolition, dismantling, decay, decomposition, or disintegration. It displaces structure rather than destroys it, which of course still makes us feel uneasy. It is disquieting, because it challenges our sense of stability, coherence and identity which we associate with pure form.

Wigley seems to be equating architectural form with structure but as far as 'deconstruction' is concerned it seems useful to

Coop Himmelblau, Funder Factory 3, Carinthia

separate the two. For if one takes the simple, geometric forms to which in Wigley's view all architects aspire, they may be constructed very simply of load-bearing walls, timber frames and so on, left perfectly intact as structures even though the form itself may be more or less distorted.

One thinks, say, of Gehry's Winton Guest House in which simple, geometric sculptural forms are displayed, truncated and skewed (in the case of the pyramid), segmented (in the case of the curved wing) and so on. Whilst of course they are constructed there is no kind of structural expression whereas, say, Coop Himmelblau's Roof Space seems to be nothing but a structure expressed which happens to contain accommodation!

Curiously enough Coop Himmelblau and Gehry both represent one of the five basic ways of thinking available from the time of Plato. They are 'mechanics' or Pragmatists as against, say, Eisenman who in his early, geometric houses, thought entirely in Plato's 'intelligible' terms as indeed he does in more recent projects: the Research Institute for Carnegie-Mellon University in Pittsburgh and the Guardiola House at Santa Maria del Mar near Cadiz.

Between them this Intellectual and these Pragmatists represent extremes of the kind which Plato would have recognised: Eisenman inhabits his 'intelligible' world; Coop Himmelblau and Gehry are rude 'mechanics'. It's no wonder that the latter refuses to read Derrida! And indeed many later 'Deconstructionists' use 'mechanics' of the kind that Plato deplored of Archytas and Eudoxus. They use 'mechanical devices' – adjustable set-squares – with much

'vulgar handicraft' to draw their highly complex clashing angles!

For ways of thinking are one thing, practical applications quite another. In my *Design in Architecture* of 1973 (and 1988), I described four ways of thinking which architects employ when they are conceiving three-dimensionally. These gained gratifyingly wide acceptance and they are in their 1988 manifestations:

Pragmatic Design: in which one finds by trial-and-error what one's materials do, the effects of climate and so on.

Typologic Design: in which one tries to find the essence of a type – from the scale of door knob to the scale of a city – and then designs according to the 'type'. Rob Krier extracts such types in his book *Urban Space*.

Analogic Design: in which one draws visual or other analogies into one's design problems: Rietveld's Schröder House is like a Mondrian painting.

Syntactic Design: in which one draws on a set of geometric rules, like the rules of syntax in language, and derives one's forms accordingly. Eisenman's early houses are perfect examples.

All four types apply in 'deconstructionist' design just as they do in any other. Gehry, clearly is a Pragmatist as one sees from his many trial-and-error models, sketches and experiments on site.

Zaha Hadid seems to have a series of 'types': the building as 'bar', the building as glass 'sail' and so on. So do Coop Himmelblau with their buildings as 'eagle', 'insect' or 'Concorde', as bent 'bars' or 'whales' and so on. All of these are also analogies: Hadid's 'bars' and 'sails'; Coop Himmelblau's 'eagle', 'insect', 'Concorde' or 'whale'.

INTERVIEW WITH COOP HIMMELBLAU

- Are your chances of realising the Ronacher project better now? Do you see the possibility of building in Vienna today?

Sorry, but we do not think that we know more than you or the interested public. But in the Austrian press we often read that in Vienna there are plans to build our draft for the Ronacher. This we were told by the mayor and the town councillor for culture at the award ceremony for the prize of architecture of Vienna.[1]

- It seems that the architects of Coop Himmelblau have to compete against the successful musical Cats. *It is said that* Cats *is to be played in the provisional renovated Ronacher until at least 1991, and that only after that is there a possibility of starting on the project for this building. Is it true that you have planning instructions to reduce Vienna's expenses and in which state is this revision?*

Well, concerning *Cats* we were told that this musical is playing in the Ronacher only to make it possible for us to plan longer and more intensively. Until today we have not had planning instructions. Regardless of that, we managed to reduce the expenses and come near to the demanded estimate of the budget. Vienna got this planning modification from the Ronacher AG, so to say within the bounds of the competitive procedure . . .

- . . . the concrete appearances are deceptive. So, as you already said, there are no planning instructions. Now the obvious question is whether you, at a later moment, let's say in ten or 15 years, will be prepared to realise the project won in a competition called Expert Procedure in 1987?

Of course not. There is this famous time-limit in Vienna, too, that plans a completion in 1992. We are astonished about the fact that until now we haven't got official planning instructions. If we were thinking in the Viennese way, we could draw the conclusion that the connection between *Cats* and the Ronacher is the perfect strategy to prevent the realisation of the project. Lately we heard the phrase 'what do we need it for anyway?' One thinks about how to build, respectively renovate only the stage and the auditorium of the Ronacher and to forget about all the other spatial and architectonic elements. If there really are such considerations this would be pure cynicism. It would mean that our project would be brought down. But this is the way it goes in Vienna over and again. The Viennese simply are the biggest tacticians, unwittingly. If the tactical and strategic moment were brought up consciously, Vienna would be different.

- And your tactics against the tacticians?

Tactics are unfamiliar to us. If we are interested in something, then it's strategy. That's the first step to succeed with such a project. But we are afraid we have already missed something. Maybe we let ourselves be deceived, for the opinion in Vienna about our Ronacher project was entirely positive, and it would have been possible to be pushed through with the maximum amount, liked by the media and the public. We were asked and we answered. We were asked again and we answered again. In the meantime, precious time passed.

- In Vienna there seem to be reservations about the contents of the project. The puffed-up possibilities for multiple use, for instance, would bring additional organisational provisions and a much higher budget means into operation.

We know that there are these reservations. But these additional offers are important to us. We do not want just a theatre. Anyway, it's symptomatic that a multifunctional theatre, able to do everything, is now realised in New York.

- It is known that the mayor has this advisory committee that has no official character, but still there are certain decisions made there. And it is well-known that the artists and architects belonging to this advisory committee take a different view from your architectural mentality. Could those exponents feel threatened in their self-image, maybe even in their own work, by your project? Could this be an explanation for the prevailing logic on the one hand, that one has to plead for such a new development in architecture, and on the other hand there are scarcely forces that support a quick tackling of the Coop Himmelblau project?

Concerning this repetition of the competition, the reason may be found there. But we do not think that Hollein and Rainer are against our project. We do not know about the others, but we think that there is nobody who objects vehemently to it. However, this is the very point – everything lies somewhere in between, it is not tangible.

- So everything is still open . . .

. . . of course we hope that there will be a happy ending. We have invested a lot of time and expense in this. But it seems to be a common situation for architects. You win a certificate, you are emotionally involved, you see the project as almost built, and then, of course, you are easily used. The patron can ask for almost everything. To have the cruelty then to say, 'now it is definitely over, I'll do without the job,' is hardly an imaginable effort, even though it would often be more reasonable. But it will take more than one time to throw the Ronacher project away.

- You mentioned a sort of exploitation, but actually this concerns every architect who takes a complicated procedure into consideration, where claiming and dealing with the theme of architecture is not divisible anymore.

Yes, of course. This can be almost perilous, threatening the existence of a group like ours. But this does not happen consciously. And certainly it is connected with the public patron compared to a private building owner. We always stood up for not dividing the architect from his patron, as it isn't possible for the architect to do solely what the patron wants him to do, because he cannot produce quality in substance.

- Your Ronacher project for Vienna is an important point for this city concerning the development of the representation of modern architecture. And you could say that this is putting to the test the responsible politicians who will have to show their hand as to whether this extraordinary definition of the theme, the experiment in architecture, is important to them. Shouldn't the Viennese mayor, as he did with Hollein's building,[2] support it with the power of his position?

Yes, that's the way we see it too. But we want to take up again what you mentioned before. What you said is right, we mean that the contents is not to be divided from the language of forms, it's an inseparable whole. Many people are shocked at our forms, at the visual appearance, but actually they stick to the contents; for instance, our manifold layout of the room, the multifunctionality. The formal is only a pretext to thwart the contents and, by that, our projects.

- Let's change the subject. We've seen the exhibition Deconstructivist Architecture in New York. Since then you have the stigma of deconstruction. What are you going to do now – will you go on bearing the stamp of being deconstructivist or are you going to dissociate yourself from this event?

It's not very hard to refuse, if one isn't invited. More important is the point of intersection, the moment of such an exhibition. The time was chosen correctly, as regards the intellectual dimension, because architecture is dead. You don't have to think about replicas and you don't have to build them anymore. And it's clear that – if seven architects are shown as originators of a direction – the other 400,000 speak against it.

- Media appreciation cannot be seen as a sign of quality in architecture, can it?

There are no excuses allowed. Everybody is responsible for everything he does. Is that clear now? The attitude is important, and that's what it's all about. What we've shown in New York is nothing less than the result of a consistent development. We didn't work out a new project or stand on our head for this exhibition. Of those seven architects, everyone has worked on his own thing independently for about ten years. In contrast to that, the Post-Modern direction in architecture did not succeed in doing justice to the philosophical claim of the same term; the architects simply weren't able to translate that into their own language.

– Vienna is a sort of stronghold of the mistaken term Post-Modern. How did it happen that you got such great attention and even enthusiastic approval here with your Ronacher project?
We are sure that we wouldn't have won the competition, if the jury[3] had consisted solely of Viennese participants. Living here makes you practiced in finding the actual information between the lines – you can find the desperate attempt to put the threatening deconstructivist elements out again.

– Are you talking about Otto Kapfinger[4] and his related species?
Everything's a question of the point of view, of the horizon. We are anxious to see how Otto Kapfinger will push off. This will give us a great pleasure. Vienna never went into this direction – it was always grossly Post-Modern! Vienna wants to take part in everything, even if it's new. If Vienna had a similar relation to the Post-Modern as Paris, there wouldn't be any problems with deconstructivism.

– You mean, the creative act is limited to contemplation, sometimes to admiration?
Yes, of course. Nothing is questioned vehemently, nothing is destroyed. It's harmless.

– What are the plans, the programmes of Coop Himmelblau for the future?
At the moment, two of our projects, neither one very easy to realise, are nearly completed – a factory in Carinthia and an extension of a loft in the Viennese Inner City. At the same time we are working on two new books[5] where we are going to reveal our next steps in architecture. We do not want to repeat our current formal language forever. This would be the way to ruin. It's not likely that we will; and architecture is too big an adventure for that.

– Is it allowed to do what you do? After all there is a sort of strict code of morals in Vienna . . .
It's easy to answer this question. There's this sentence of Hermann Czech that says: 'Architecture is only allowed to speak when it's asked'. Just substitute the word children for architecture, meaning that children are only allowed to speak if you ask them something. And this is the attitude we have fought since 1968 – for our children to speak unasked as well.

1 The presentation of the award took place in the autumn of 1988 by the Viennese mayor Helmut Zilk.
2 *The Haas-Haus,* after an outline by Hans Hollein, is now under construction at the Viennese Stephansplatz. See *UMRISS* 1/87, Peter Noever: 'Is Hollein still among us?'.
3 Participants of the jury were: Egbert Kossak, BRD/Adolf Krischanitz, Wien/Hans Puchhammer, Wien/Peter Schweger. BRD/Wolfgang Windprech- tinger, Wien/Ganther Zamp-Kelp, BRD. Experts: Hans Mayer, Wien/Franz Mrkvicka, Wien/Peter Weck, Wien, among others.
4 Otto Kapfinger is architecture critic for the Austrian newspaper *Die Presse.*
5 Coop Himmelblau, *The Outline and the Model.* Coop Himmelblau *Open Architecture.* Hetje publishers, Stuttgart, Rizzoli, New York, July 1989, December 1989.

Peter Noever and Elisabeth Schweeger interviewed Wolf D. Prix and Helmuth Swiezinsky.

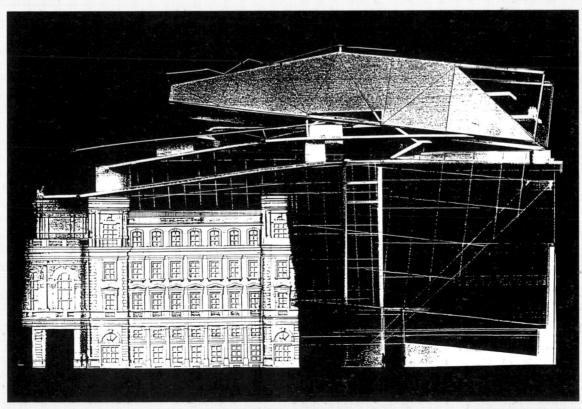

Coop Himmelblau, Ronacher Theatre, Vienna

Syntactic Deconstruction

As for 'deconstructors' of syntax, these include Tschumi with his interlocking systems at La Villette, Eisenman with his complex geometric systems, and so on. So of course one can analyse everything 'deconstructed' in these ways. As indeed one could with any other kind of architecture.

Of the Pragmatists of Form by far the most notable is Gehry. Whilst his forms may appear more or less chaotic if one looks at them from a broader perspective, as Cohen says (1989) we see them to be, more often than not, the result of pure architectural reasoning, resulting from Gehry's search for light, for orientation on the site, framing the view and so on allied, so Cohen says, to Gehry's more personal internal logic, indeed, his aesthetic.

National Theatre of Japan

But form can be derived in other ways and curiously enough Eisenman, in his endless quest to break the 'anthropocentrism' of architectural design, uses what he calls Analogic but which in my terms is Typologic Design. This is in his project for the National Theatre of Japan in which he wants to undermine 'the traditional ideas of human scale, architectural type, and sheltering function as organising design principles'. So he draws on 'architectural analogies' by overlaying forms derived from the history of theatre in Japan, which in itself derived from the shifting balance of power between the Emperor and the Shoguns.

He takes the various forms, differing in scale, function and type, adjusts them to a single scale and overlays them, which reveals coincidences which otherwise would not have been perceived. 'Each such scale change finds new relationships between sites and objects which were formerly seen as static and fixed'. So of course the site 'becomes a palimpsest – the record of a series of registrations and superimpositions of different places and times, seen at the same place and time'.

Research Institute for Carnegie-Mellon

As for Eisenman's Intellectual, entirely Syntactic, Design, he abandons ideas of 'palimpsest' completely in his Research Institute for Carnegie-Mellon, where for the Frankfurt Biocentrum he takes a piece of geometry from science; in this case the 'Boolean Cube', a structure with an infinite number of geometries which, he says, will be useful in Artificial Intelligence. For since his Cube can move in an infinite number of directions it will allow information to be moved along an infinite number of paths 'within the information matrix'.

But since this will take an infinite time it's unlikely that the concept will be applied. Indeed in his 'theoretical' discussion Eisenman reduces his infinite 'N' to a 100-N Cube and when it comes to architectural applications, his 100 is reduced to four or even three! This in practical terms amounts to, say, a cube shifted diagonally to form an eight-sided solid with square top and bottom surfaces, square front and back, hexagonal sides and diagonal rectangles connecting top and front, bottom and back. Of course the original cube can be moved diagonally sideways as well, giving a slightly more complex form; a cube can be solid or made as an open frame. A solid cube can have transparent sides, and so on. As Eisenman says:

> Each building is made up of three pairs of 4-N Boolean cubes. Each pair contains two solid cubes, with 40 and 45 degree members and two frame cubes with 40 and 45 degree members. Each pair can be seen as containing the inverse of the other as solid and void. The 40 degree solid and the 40 degree frame 4-N cubes are places in a 5-0N relationship with each other where their points are 40 degree away from each other in a parallel orientation. The 45 degree solid and the 45 degree frame 4-N cubes are placed in 5-N parallel orientation. This places the project between a reading of 5-N cubes oscillating between and frame and 4-N cubes.

Quite so, but then he has to put the floors in!

Nothing, ever, anywhere could be more 'syntactic' than that and of course Eisenman has much more to say about the nature of his cubes which he sees as lying somewhere between 'the purity of a Platonic form and the infinite and unlimited form of a non-Euclidian structure'. And the purpose of all this? To demonstrate 'the fallibility of man' which is shown, by these elaborate means, as 'undercutting the hyper-rationality of the forms of knowledge systems, leading to a new and complex condition of the beautiful'.

Guardiola House

As for the Guardiola House, this too is formed of interlocking cubes; not Boolean in this case but open on three sides. Eisenman calls them 'quadrants' and they represent the ambiguity which Eisenman and Derrida had found in Plato's use of 'receptacle' or chora as 'place and object' or 'container.

So of course they overlap and penetrate each other as L-shapes in plan and section, skewed against each other too, by up to eight degrees also in plan and section. So there are steel grids, marking the skew around which the concrete floors and walls are cast. The skew relationship appears again 'in the surfaces of two of the quadrants in the form of glazed and unglazed tiles, and the remaining quadrants are treated with coral and white stucco to reiterate the duality of the reading.

Intuitive Deconstruction: Koolhaas and Oma

At the opposite extreme from Eisenman's highly intellectual 'deconstructions' of architectural form are the highly intuitive ones of Rem Koolhaas and OMA – although their Housing for Checkpoint Charlie (1982) was remarkably prescient. They placed five storeys of social housing over the Allied facilities at the border between West Berlin and East. Their roofed concourse has a synthetic night sky with arcs of neon 'describing the turning points for buses' and spotlights in constellations to illuminate the areas of activity on the tarmac. Then hovering over all this is a metal roof, clad in polished alloy, in the form on an aeroplane wing. But they see their programme as self-destructing: 'when the city is no longer divided and the Wall is replaced by a leisure zone, the concourse will be occupied by a supermarket'. The metal wing will remain as 'the only element from the iconography of a once historic point hovering over the street'.

Their National Dance Theatre for The Hague (1984-87) is a rather clumsy assemblage of an inverted, truncated gold cone surrounded by disparate geometric blocks: Modernist – with horizontal windows – and, conceivably, Post-Modernist with unmatching diagonal cladding, sloping roofs, curtain walled areas and so on.

The Town Hall and Library for The Hague (1986) is a Modernist pavilion-on-a-plinth whilst their Office Building for the Churchill Plain in Rotterdam (1988) is a further OMA 'game' with a straight-up-and-down, curtain walled slab and, contiguous with it, a more solidly clad 'wing' with a quite violently angled front elevation.

Their Bio-centrum for Frankfurt (1988) consists of two long rectangular blocks connected by wings between courtyards. All this accommodation is contained beneath a landscape with gardens, containing a tennis court. The wider of the long 'blocks' contains the most 'deconstructed' elements: a curved service road at ground level and a free-form 'blob' of auditoria which rises through it.

In the Netherland Institute for Architecture and Building (1988) OMA's original scheme had a black concrete tower for archives, perpendicular to the (sloping) roof of the podium which contained the entrance, an exhibition gallery and the library. Then over the podium there was an auditorium, a lecture room and a cafeteria. The facades were covered successively with a green glass wall, undulating glass fibre and natural glass. The roof was gold. This project was abandoned but the major elements were retained in their final scheme, including the podium and the (skewed) archive tower. But these were mediated by a (more staid) rectangular block, with courtyards, on the podium and next to the tower.

In Koolhaas' National Library for France he has, as in previous schemes, much of the ancillary accommodation surrounding a courtyard at ground level but the major Deconstructive element in his design is a vast cube with book stacks forming the whole of one (solid) side and nine huge structural columns rising through it. Between these are suspended various 'pods', blocks, bars, containing reading rooms, various specialised libraries, conference rooms and so on only partially hidden by the 'skin' which covers the other three sides.

The Parc Citroën, Cevennes is far more contextual than Tschumi or Eisenman would allow, developed as it is 'from a series of formal relationships with the ugliness of the existing and projected architecture that will (eventually) define the perimeter of the park'. So 'a landscape free of nostalgia . . . can equal the powerful – yet unrecognised – beauty of the late 20th-century urban landscape'.

There is a central 'metropolitan' meadow and, around this, a perimeter zone from which different spaces are cut away. Each is intended to respond to the adjacent architecture thus: 'responding to the programmatic potential of the surrounding quarter(s) . . . and the river Seine on the fourth side'.

There are Urban Renewal schemes, including one for the Bijlermeer in Amsterdam (1988) and Lille (1989) not to mention the Urbanisation of a wooded landscape at Mélun-Sénart; but Deconstructionist Urbanism needs a book of its own.

Koolhaas' office towers for Lille are rather skittish permutations on the more-or-less vertical towers with slabs attached in overlapping layers, tapering in elevation, section or both, and clad in contrasting materials – 'a world of amusement, and variety'. In Koolhaas' view such a combination of 'flexibility of form with a firm integration of road, rail and commerce – might just do the trick!'

Deconstruction of Structure

There's no hint in these formal 'deconstructions' by Gehry, Eisenman and Koolhaas, that the structures of their buildings will be other than conventional. Of course there may be rows of columns at odd angles, as in Eisenman's Guardiola House and no doubt there will be tapering frames within Koolhaas' towers and slabs for Lille. But clearly in schemes like, say, Coop Himmelblau's Roof Space the building as a whole gains its 'deconstructed' form from the twisting, skewing, bending of its actual structure.

So what is it about structures that actually can be deconstructed? I suggested in *Design in Architecture* (1988 edition) that structure can be treated, generally, as a pragmatic matter – as can climate, site form and other physical aspects of the context into which the building will be placed. And that the kinds of structure which can be analysed by the trial-and-error methods of pragmatics are:

Mass Construction: in which solid materials, such as stone, brick or concrete form solid masses containing, perhaps, small chambers as in the Pyramids of Egypt or Mexico.

Plate Construction: in which 'plates' of solid material are used straight to form walls, as in Mies van der Rohe's Brick House designs; or curved, in plan or even in section as in Romanesque vaulting.

Frame Construction: in which timber, steel, concrete or other sections are used to form columns, beams, arches and other linear elements; and

Skin Construction: in which plastic skins are stretched over, or suspended from, frames to form tents, welded into shapes which, sealed as appropriate can be inflated and so on.

Deconstructed Mass Construction

There have been few solid Mass constructions since the Mexican pyramids. The last to be built on any large scale, probably, were the gun-emplacements of World War II. One thinks also of André Bloc's 'Sculpture Habitables' – proto-Deconstructionist buildings of solid

Zaha Hadid, Pavilion, Gröningen

brick with very small internal chambers. Nor in the nature of things, will there be much new 'deconstruction of mass' but there is some: in the 'negative masses' of gardens at La Villette; the 'Water Garden' of Pellisier; the 'Choral Work' of Eisenman and Derrida. These, in a sense, are inverted pyramids, stepping down into the ground. But they are massive, solid underneath and their surfaces are just as solid, just as 'massive' as those of any pyramid rising into the air. And the 'deconstruction' of their visible surfaces is fundamental to their design.

But whilst I had in mind solidity as the essence of 'Mass', there is another aspect of architecture which has similar, visual qualities. Plato would call them 'sensible'. That is the massing of buildings; the visible, external composition of their three-dimensional forms. So whilst 'massing' may be derived pragmatically, typologically, analogically or syntactically, it will help us penetrate 'deconstruction' if we treat the effects of massing as a pragmatic matter. This means that we can take as 'masses' the 'deconstructed' forms of, say, Frank Gehry's houses even though their 'hollowness' is essential to their habitability.

Deconstructed Plate Construction

There has been rather more 'deconstructed' plate construction and this has taken several forms. The early Best Product designs by James Wines and SITE ('Sculpture in the Environment') are obvious examples. In each case SITE took the standard Best shed – a rectangular 'merchandising box' for selling, at discount, household appliances, furniture and jewellery on the typical American commercial strip and gave it specific 'identity', by 'peeling off' the front wall (Richmond, Virginia, 1972), raising the walls to give an irregular silhouette and having bricks 'cascade' on to the canopy (Houston, Texas, 1975) or tilting the front wall upwards and outwards from one corner (Towson, Maryland, 1978). In the most ambitious of these, the Cutler Ridge Showroom for Miami, Florida (1979), SITE slid forward successively from the main block, the whole front wall, a large segment from the lower half of that wall including the canopy, and forward of that again the three doorways making four 'layers' in all. And in the Parking Lot Showroom for Best, Site make the roof into a wave-form 'plate' rising literally out of the car park.

Hiromi Fujii has his own rather special brand of 'deconstructing' and interlocking 'plates' with gay abandon. Examples include his Metamorphologie in Architecture of 1980, his International Arts Festival Centre, Ushimado of 1985, his Mizoe-1 and -2 of 1988-89. Fujii's 'plates' in many cases are large, wide-membered grids which shear into each other at dizzy angles.

Then the 'sails' of Zaha Hadid's schemes for Berlin are curved 'plates' of exactly the kind I had in mind even though they are made of glass. It is clear from her drawings that these qualities depend on the opacity of glass, according to the lighting conditions and when they are transparent, such as at night, then their 'sail' forms will still be traced by the edges of the floor slabs behind them.

Hadid uses such forms again in her Tokyo Forum (1989) 'carving

Zaha Hadid, Tomigaya building, Tokyo

out space' to gain a high site utilisation, through which her main auditorium – contained in a 'beam' – rises through the cantilevers out over the adjacent railway lines. Two other 'beams' stacked above each other, puncture through the 'plate' which forms the roof.

The basement is devoted to a series of 'infinitely flexible' conference rooms which can be seen through a glass 'plate' of a floor. The roof is covered by gardens from which a slit – a 'negative plate' – descends through the building admitting daylight down to ground level. Arquitectonica, too, in their design for the 'Forum' use a Hadid-like 'sail' or 'curved plate' form.

As for more solid 'plates' on a larger scale one can see Koolhaas' office towers for Lille as having 'deconstructed' slabs attached to them. And what is a slab but a very thick plate?

But the most spectacular 'deconstructed plates' by far are to be found in Daniel Libeskind's scheme for his Berlin Museum (1989-). Libeskind's zig-zag plates enclose zig-zag spaces and, like Tschumi in other contexts, Libeskind clearly is concerned with the sensory experience of moving between his 'plates'. The walls offer display space for flat objects, such as paintings, whilst each change of direction in Libeskind's zig-zags will offer a perfect place for 'framing', or at least locating, some three-dimensional object.

Deconstructed Frame Construction

The flood-gates open, however, with Deconstructed Frame Construction which, more than any other, lends itself to the expression of 'Deconstruction'. This has been true from Gehry's very first sketches of, say, the timbers around the windows of his house. Coop Himmelblau's early projects: 'Architecture must Blaze' (1980); the Red Angel (1980-81); the Merz School (1981); the Open House for Malibu (1983) and the Atelier Bauman (1984), all display complex frame constructions with clashing angles, supporting plates or masses of various kinds.

Roof-top Remodelling

The Roof-top Remodelling in Vienna (1983-88) is a light, airy and rather joyous thing; as if an insect has settled on a roof made of leaves, eaten all but the stalks and the veins leaving gossamer spiders' webs between them! It presents a complex interaction of superimposed frame systems: the taut steel bow from which everything else follows, a 'foundation system' in delicate reinforced concrete and steel, a 'primary' steel' system, a secondary supporting steel structure and a glazed canopy.

Of their primary steel system, for instance, Coop Himmelblau say:

> The main truss forms the visual and structural spine of the construction. The spatially slanted and laterally supported 'Gerber Cantilever' truss transgresses the existing roof lines and encloses the conference room by spanning the roof-top. The side trusses define and differentiate the glazed canopy spatially and structurally.

All these are irregular of course. Not for Coop Himmelblau the bay-

INTERVIEW WITH ZAHA HADID

– I'm trying to piece together the story of Deconstruction, and as you can imagine it's quite difficult. Can we start with some of the deconstructionists you know?

If I go back ten years ago, Bernard Tschumi and Daniel Libeskind's work was different, Coop Himmelblau's was beginning to change. Peter Eisenman's work was definitely different; Frank Gehry's I think hasn't changed; and Rem Koolhaas' work has changed slightly but not in a deconstructivist way – it became almost more 'pure'. When I started to study for my student work I became interested in Abstraction and the Russian Suprematists, not the Constructivists, and the whole notion of Abstraction and the effect it has on certain issues of architecture. It has to do with the plan but there are many layers to it. Everybody got to a point from a different thing. There is a difference between my thinking and European thinking. The 'rules' they are supposed to be breaking are European rules; I am not European, and I am not from that kind of background. I have never read Derrida, although I have heard him lecture.

– They are not important rules?

I think it is fundamental. I'm quite intuitive. It's just a very different sensibility. With the idea of 'de-regularisation', if you are talking in a European sense, you have to accept that there's a 'regular' which you have to de-regularise. In the West everyone always maintains that there's one solid system of thinking. Then Structuralists and Deconstructionists begin to break it and dissect or question it. But somehow for me the rules don't always apply – not in terms of language. The Structuralists are very French; the whole issue of chaos and order have become very fashionable. All these things are part of a tendency in the 70s which was to do with the breaking of rules – I think it was a kind of a leftover from the 60s. We rebelled in the early 70s. I always maintain that when I came to live here myself I felt a sense of displacement. You can only really belong to one place, and this displacement can either be liberating or confining. For me the idea is that we have been operating within a particular system and we have to take another leap, test new boundaries. These boundaries have not yet been given.

There were clues from the Suprematists, but things didn't happen in isolation in the 30s. There were big connections between the Russians, the Functionalists and the Americans. They were all interested in minimal moves, making major moves on cities to do with planning and urbanism. It was a new century, a new way of life; the ideology was that we have to improve it.

Ultimately because of advances in technology it became feasible. This idea that it was possible liberated them in the same way that it could liberate us at this point. Forgetting about the labels, the Architectural Association becomes a critical factor; it was the only School in the 70s and the 80s which was not under a Post-Modernist banner. It was also a School which did not want to operate under a strict 'representational' rule. You didn't have to submit a portfolio with a section, an elevation and a plan. You could do it in many different ways. Architecture was not limited to a building; it was a much bigger sphere of activity. People always look to London for ideas, whether it's fashion, music or graphics. For architecture it was an important beginning.

You can't achieve everything on one project. You want it to operate as a plan and you want it to operate as a building. I don't want it to be perfectly detailed like the central Europeans; that's not my idea of detail – every door handle designed. It has to come together, otherwise it doesn't interest me.

Ten years ago people thought it highly unlikely that anyone would come to me as a client – that it was all hot air and would change. Now, seven years later people have accepted my work – not everybody, some people – as an object which is buildable. So we've overcome one major hurdle.

The point for me about the Suprematists was that it's like looking at the Galaxy through a microscope: cosmic. This implied that it could generate a new kind of plan: much more fluid and dynamic. It implied a certain kind of freedom and fluidity, a different kind of spatial organisation. To me that is what's very important. And also that the buildings have a degree of lightness as they are drawn or designed. They are not heavy handed.

Learning is to do with a 'reductivist' quality. Only a few elements are significant. It's done with panache and no decoration. It's absolutely pure. The elements have to represent themselves and that could lead to a very pure structural system. Fundamentally it implied a new kind of plan. When I did the Irish Prime Minister's House ten years ago and my School work, nobody could understand anything. The walls were not at right angles. Of course everybody was very thrilled by it and all that, and for me it was a great thrill because it was the first time I attempted to do what is called a 'chaotic' plan which had a certain logic in a confined space.

A very important lesson was how this idea, this notion of fragmentation, could operate. It's not random, with no logic at all: it's all a kind of order. People move through a building differently and not in a straight line all the time. I think that is the central lesson from all this. And like in culture, it's heavily layered. There are many different potentials, not just one.

– How did you get on to the Suprematists in the first place?

That was almost completely accidental. I was in my third year with Leon Krier who was not as dogmatic as he is today. This was before the Rationalist Show in Oxford. I liked him a lot and thought he was a very good tutor. He made us look at the city when no-one in any school would have done anything like that. But I felt at the end of that year there must be some kind of alternative. One didn't want to accept this defeatist attitude: 'there must be no progress anymore.' I joined Elias Zenghelis and Rem Koolhaas for my fourth year in 1975. They gave two projects in the first term: one of which was the Malevich Tektonik. Each student was to take a piece of it and design it; one would take the top, one the middle and so on. We each had two programmes; mine was the Malevich Tektonik and a 'social condenser' which I was trying to put together. I decided to make the Tektonik horizontal and then place it over London, imposing a finite object on an existing city fabric. It was on a bridge, and was heavily layered. We were given linear pieces and through looking at them, over a year, we realised we couldn't design interiors like a normal building. What began to happen is that the elevator core needed to be broken, so I started with that.

The theme also with this thing – and this made my connection to Elias and Rem very close – was that it was a club. Also the club theme – a night club – was a shipwreck. The angle of a shipwreck is already a disaster, a distress, and the idea of the shipwreck became abstracted. It started as a physical ship, became more and more refined and then began to break. Then a whole bunch of other projects took on some of these issues: a museum of the 19th century was all about juxtaposition, intersections between opposing programmes, different facilities coming together; this idea of lightness, linear, new spatial organisations, new civic zones. I liked to look at various cities like New York, the idea of the major lobbies and what they could imply. The Tektonik implied that you could make a new urban geometry which could then infiltrate the cities. Or you could add another layer like the 19th century museum – another layer added on a historic condition. That's what I think is the difference between the early Modernists and myself. I don't think we're into erosion, taking away; it's more a matter of superimposing different geometries. It is archaeological and geological.

This idea also came into the Peak. The hillside was rock; the idea was you excavate the rock and replace the old geology with a new one. Therefore each layer was slightly different and it was seen like a 'plate'; geological plates stacked up on one another.

– How about the linear planning?

All the buildings have this stretched quality because of the site. There were three sites on the Peak and there were three programmes. The central story of the Peak was about the beams and the central space: a five-storey high void. It was a civic space. We made the programme as a private club and made an extension of the city and opened it up to Hong Kong . . . It didn't have walls around it. The land is being formed like an animation and two programmes come together with the journey of the beams flying over and the geology being made there, being gyrated. Then the building is completed like a movie. I had this idea that the beams would fly across, of the land being formed and the beams flying over frame by frame. They are conceptual drawings; they tell a story. It's a description of an idea rather than a framework.

The forms are signifiers: free, refined, pure and simple. Here is every freedom of movement. The middle zone is public, civic, compressed, settled. It's difficult to retain such laboratory research even in the office where there are so many people trying to spark off ideas

from one another. I was never worried about people ripping me off – I rip myself off. You can't be creative every five minutes.

– What about the curved glass walls of your Berlin and later schemes?

The curved panels started with the Peak, the two top beams of which were bridges with no structure between the spaces – they were free. You can break them by curved planning, using paraboloids, to get plastic space. The breaking can be done in a simple way. There were no jumps in the work and I had only been working since 1976, therefore only six years.

Culturally one is of many layers and history itself is to do with layers. The fact that the Americans have done a neo-classical building to me doesn't mean that they have reincarnated their history. Ideas filter through and become superimposed on one another. What I find interesting is metropolitan life with the constant collision between opposing activities, the fact that your neighbour is so close, and yet there is no relation between you and him/her. Many outcomes of observations and experiences were in the Peak and after I designed it I began to think of it as a geological condition.

The Kurfürstendamm looked very exciting. Despite the smallness of the site you could still relate to free space, and because the site was so

small we had to get the structure within a very specific zone. Peter Rice worked on this project. The project involved the absolute purification of formal elements with the stiffening of walls, the different spaces, and all behind the glass. The Tokyo project however was more severe, being only three metres wide.

– Some of your drawings make the walls look solid and some of them make them look transparent. Which do you intend?

At the Kurfürstendamm the glass is slightly green, the glass being next to concrete and answering from the street. There's no vertical dimension.

– What are you doing now?

The new projects include a new one for Berlin; a project in Hamburg; the Osaka Foundation; a restaurant in Japan and two buildings in Japan. Then there's the immense Düsseldorf project and a video exhibition in Gröningen.

– Tell me what you know of Derrida.

The way Bernard or Peter use Derrida is legitimate, but you don't need to quote directly. I've gone to two lectures of his at Harvard. There was nothing curious about them. Derrida is off-beam with the universe. This awareness of self becomes an ego-issue: you challenge issues. It's very dangerous for creativity, this over-awareness of self.

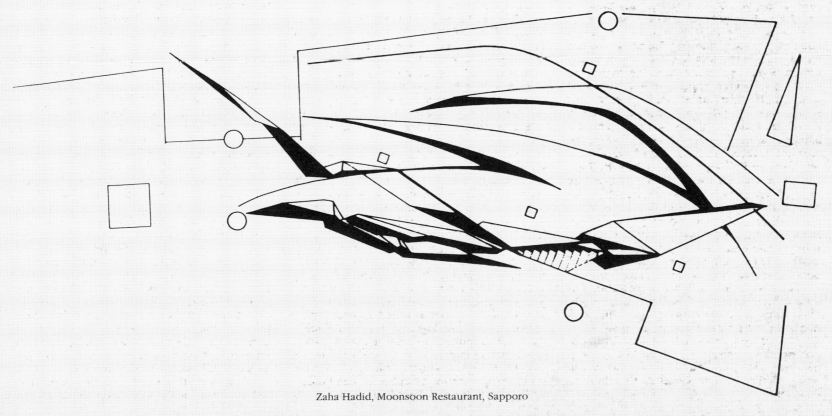

Zaha Hadid, Moonsoon Restaurant, Sapporo

OMA, Checkpoint Charlie Housing, Berlin

by-bay repetitions of High-Tech Architects such as Norman Foster, Richard Rogers, Nick Grimshaw or Michael Hopkins. Indeed, the Funder Factory (1988) was to have been as regular as any of these could have envisaged from Foster's Sainsbury Centre onwards. But Coop Himmelblau were invited to transform it into a much more 'assertive' architecture. So:

> The design concept was based on the idea of destructuring the site into its architectural elements: the energy centre and its chimneys, the median bridge, the terrace roof and shed, the office and laboratory sections, and the entrances. Taken together their articulation into a distinct head and body was clear.

So Coop Himmelblau applied 'playful deconstruction' of the elements, gave the energy centre its 'dancing chimneys', a 'median bridge' linking energy and production, a 'free-wing' formation to the shed roof and exploded-frame canopies to the entrances. They opened up the south corner too with a 'deconstructed' steel frame and glazing. They even put red 'combs' on the roof of the production shed on the grounds that since this was visible from the highway above, it would be seen as a fifth façade.

As Stein says, Coop Himmelblau analysed the programme, submitted it to an 'initial dissection – a process of functional distillation that owes an obvious debt to Frank O Gehry'. This led them to believe that there was little they could do to the original factory shed, hence their concentration on certain features such as the large, saw-toothed red canopy to the entrance with its support-

ing tension rods, and a folded-plate red screen passing under it somewhat like a staircase on its side, and the sloping glass walls with a huge, glazed canopy/cornice which replace the solid corner of the building.

As for the chimneys to the 'power centre', these are arranged as the 'frame' of a 'collapsing wigwam' with highly visible supporting struts and cables. That is to say, it could have been a wigwam if the chimneys were not of such different lengths. But they raise a fundamental 'deconstructivist' question: given that most chimneys are strictly vertical, is there any reason why these need not be? The answer is no! Since the wind changes direction frequently, there is no 'correct' direction for chimneys to take and these three chimneys at crazy angles are just as good, functionally, as any three vertical chimneys could have been.

Like Jean Tinguely before them, Coop Himmelblau are attacking the precision of the machine, its mind-numbing precisions and repetitions, its sheer mechanistic perfection. What is being 'deconstructed', literally, is the chilling precision of 'High-Tech'.

Deconstructed Skin Construction

This view is reinforced by one of the few examples so far of 'deconstructed skin' construction. For most frame-supported or suspended 'tents', and indeed most inflatables, have been strictly symmetrical, regular, and repetitive: one thinks of Michael Hopkins' Mound Stand at Lords Cricket Ground.

Ron Herron, survivor of Archigram from the 1960s, was faced

Morphosis, Sixth Street, Los Angeles

with an irregular space-to-be-roofed when Imagination took over two 19th-century school buildings in Store Street, London. Between them there was an irregular space, stepped and even tapered on plan with differences of level, openings across the gap which did not align, and so on. They wanted to roof it and Heron proposed a 'tent' in the design of which he could have ignored the irregularities, simply spanning across the different widths with a Hopkins-like entire regularity of rhythm. But whilst his five central bays are regular, Herron chose to respond to the irregular site conditions at the ends. The roof is supported on light bow-string arches with steel 'palm trees' held by rods rising from suspension cables.

From outside, as Welsh says (1989), it 'writhes and erupts, splurges and emerges' from the roof-tops whilst internally the light filters through the translucent white plastic. The 'sparkling' metal bridges criss-cross the space do so because the openings in the existing buildings demanded that they cross at 'deconstructionist' angles! All of this amounts to one of the most exciting 'deconstructed' spaces so far achieved.

This suggests that, again, what is being 'deconstructed' in terms of structures is nothing more nor less than the desiccated precision of High-Tech. Precision, of course, can be 'human'. It is, after all, a product of the human brain, but it can seem threatening, totalitarian, so there is a certain appeal in seeing it 'deconstructed'.

The Spread of Deconstruction
So those are the 'ground rules' as it were. The question remains as to whether 'deconstruction' in architecture is the preserve of a few: Tschumi and Eisenman; the practice of the whole MoMA group, including Coop Himmelblau, Gehry, Hadid, Libeskind and Koolhaas; a larger group still, including Benisch and Morphosis and SITE; or even a much more general 'style'.

Morphosis, for instance, have continued 'deconstructing' with houses in Santa Monica and Montecito, with their Was House, Comprehensive Cancer Centre, Leon Max Showrooms and Performing Arts Pavilion all for Los Angeles; their Chiba Golf Club and their Higashi Azabu Office Building (1989) for Tokyo; their project for the Wall and their American Library in Berlin. And Benisch too has continued with his banks for Frankfurt and Stuttgart.

Evidence for the wider spread of 'deconstruction', however, is presented by Architectural Record's Awards and Citations to, in 1989, Eisenman's Guardiola House; Morphosis' Crawford Residence in Montecito; Becket, Ellerbe's Schibsted Gruppen Headquarters in Oslo; the Interpretative Centre at Chattanooga, Tennessee by Hanrahan and Meyers; and the (rotating) Astronaut's Memorial by Holt, Hinshaw, Pfau and Jones.

Of course there have also been the large international competitions including, since the 'deconstructionist events' of 1988, the Alexandria Library, the Kansai Airport for Osaka, the Tokyo Forum and the National Library for Paris. To this one might add, on a more parochial level, the British Pavilion for Expo 92 in Seville.

Now that we have looked at some competition entries by Tschumi, Hadid and Koolhaas, let us look at some others.

British Pavilion, Seville Expo 92

Whilst Nick Grimshaw's winning scheme is 'deconstructed' only in the sense that, because of the extreme climate of Seville, the various elevations are treated differently, Allsop and Lyall's scheme is rather unique. It is as repetitive in plan and elevations as the most simple-minded of High-Tech but the section is worthy of Coop Himmelblau themselves in complexity and ingenuity with its 'banana' or bow-string columns, floor decks and roof trusses, tension cable and the helium-filled 'airship' which can be 'let out' through the roof to force air movement down into the building whilst also providing shade.

Bibliotheca Alexandria

Snøhetta's winning scheme for the Bibliotheca Alexandria matches Wigley's requirement for a 'deconstructivist' building – that a geometry be set up and then distorted – almost more clearly than any other since the New York Exhibition. For Snøhetta sets up a cylinder, actually the lowest segment of a cone, and then cuts it off in section with a diagonal roof descending to below ground level. What is more, he cuts it also in plan with a steel bridge spanning to the entrance.

Avci and Jurca's site plan looks like nothing compared to Derrida's 'seive' for the 'Choral Work' but the buildings within it have a thoroughly Rationalist regularity whilst Solomon's is another Arab Institute-like 'tooth'.

There are Coop Himmelblau 'whales' within Runo's scheme, hiding behind his 'veil' of corrosion-resistant steel whilst Pierre d'Avoine places fragmented geometric blocks – like large-scale Gehry – on a huge stepped plinth.

Tokyo Forum 1989

Several of the entrants, such as Richard Rogers, Cedric Price and Eco-Id presented projects which, in terms of programme, are literally 'deconstructed' – with auditoria and other elements separated out and given individual 'expression'. But in each case some unifying system is overlaid to counter the effects of this: a High-Tech frame in the case of Rogers; a uniformity of rectangular boxes in the case of Price; 'smother-by-planting' in the case of Eco-Id. Branson Coates surround a Greek theatre with Gaudí-esque auditoria (though Gaudí was a constructor) behind a 'deconstructed' screen and topped by 'five huge pneumatic canopies . . . like great tongues licking the Tokyo skyline.'

Viñoly's winning design has some 'deconstructive' elements: a Tschumi-in-Tokyo-like 'layering' of stages and auditoria ascending in size behind the street facade, a gap with bridges to the cigar-plan exhibition hall, and so on.

National Library, Paris

Arquitectonica's entry looks like a re-working of Jean Nouvel's Arab Institute with its tooth-like plan but the eight-storey reading room with its billowing glass wall (actually a segment of a cone) is as clear a reference as could be to the 'sail' of Zaha Hadid's office buildings for Berlin, not to mention her Tokyo Forum.

The effects of deconstruction on other architects can be seen in schemes such as Herzberger's where a vast rectangular atrium is surrounded by offices and covered by a High Tech vault. The stacks are pushed out of this atrium into two huge circular silos whilst the various library sections are housed within it as diagonal 'bars' much like Eisenman's for the Frankfurt Biocentrum.

There are certain Deconstructivist elements too in Grimshaw's scheme with his use of curves, diagonals and discontinuities in plan and, even more emphatically, in section.

In these competition entries, therefore, one can see hints, if no more, of 'deconstruction' spreading to work of other architects in their handling of the building programme, the overall form and the structure. One might include Predock's Fine Art Centre for Arizona State University at Tempe, Richard Rogers' for the Court of Human Rights in Strasbourg and Norman Foster's Heliport at Cannon Street Bridge in London.

Predock's Centre has a 'deconstructed' programme and therefore a 'deconstructed' site plan; so does Rogers's Court of Human Rights, given its glass walled entrance pavilion with towers, separate cylinders for the major public buildings and descending terraces of offices. What's more the cylinders have skewed tops; they are pure forms 'deconstructed' in the way which, for Wigley, was the essence of 'Deconstructivism'.

Foster's heliport of course is much more complex with a vast cantilevered 'pad' – Coop Himmelblau-like in section, and meandering walkways representing a Tschumi-like 'circuit'.

The significance of course is that Foster and Rogers have been the High Priests of British High Tech. If they have succumbed to 'deconstructed' forms then something significant may be happening. Although one doesn't wish to announce, as Farrelly did, the premature 'death' of a movement!

So what shall one conclude from all this? At a primitive level 'Deconstruction' may be a superficial affair, no more significant than cocking a snook at the 'pure' forms of the Modern movement. But deconstructing architectural texts, the theory of architecture and the programme for an actual building, may be more profound. Allied to the latter, the 'deconstruction' of structure may represent the death knell of that dismal Modernist idea that architecture consists of little more than circulation diagrams suspended over each other by a regular and visibly 'expressed' structure.

Onto-Theology

Derrida's attack on fundamental truths seems just as relevant to architecture as it does to philosophy. There is no 'one best way', no 'International Style', no 'roots' from which all architecture has grown. So there are no received truths – Classical, Modernist or other. To 'deconstruct' at all – programme, form or structure – is to demonstrate one's view that there are no absolutes in architecture, that attempts, such as Heidegger's, to find such absolutes are doomed to failure.

So, there is no Ontology of architecture and no Theology either! 'Deconstruction', of course, negates the idea of architectural 'gods'. The heroic figures of this, and of every other, century must be cut down to size. The 'Deconstructionist' can no longer worship Le Corbusier, Mies van der Rohe, Wright or even Suprematists such as Malevich or Constructivists such as Tatlin, the Vesnin Brothers and so on. Like Derrida with his many writer-victims, the 'Deconstructivist' architect will choose other people's heroes and treat them with a total lack of respect; 'deconstruct' them within their own terms of reference!

And in rejecting Theology with Derrida, of course, we deny the existence of God. So we would not expect any 'Deconstructionist' churches, nor have there been any, unless one counts Michelucci's Church on the Autostrada as a pioneer – the pioneer 'Deconstructivist' building.

Logocentrism

None of this means that we have to follow Derrida, Tschumi or Eisenman in their total rejection of meaning! Derrida's 'Logocentrism' was belief in the word as a single element within the 'sheer intelligibility' which is the divine Logos as a whole. As we saw he points out that we read one part of Saussure's, the signifier, within Plato's 'sensible' world and whilst the other, the signified, exists only in his 'intelligible' world.

But in Peircian terms there was only one kind of sign: the Symbol where such connection as there may be between 'signifier' and 'signified' has to be learned. And whether we like it or not, whether Derrida likes it or not, whether Tschumi and Eisenman like it or not, buildings signify in ways other than by symbolism, and these we have to learn. They may be likenesses, 'Icons' for each other, and they always 'indicate' by steps, entrances, corridors and so on how we may physically move about them.

So Derrida's strictures of Logocentrism apply only to Peirce's 'Symbols'. From this point of view all styles – Classical, Romanesque, Byzantine, Islamic, Gothic and so on – may share the problems of Saussure's 'learned' language. This may suggest an 'Architecture Degree Zero' analogous to Barthes's 'Writing Degree Zero': simple, geometric forms, with no 'surface' expression, although these too will contain their Indices and their Icons which will insist on bearing meanings to us.

The crucial point is meanings, rather than a single meaning – a fact which Derrida himself commends in his discussion on Post-Modernism (1980, 1986). He sees it as our attempt to recover from the Tower of Babel! The builders of the Tower sought political domination by imposing on the world their universal language and their universal architecture. Fortunately they failed and since then, according to Derrida, our aim should not have been to find another 'only and absolute' view but to seek a diversity of views. For if the Tower had been completed, it would have defined the 'one, true architecture'. There could have been no other architecture. The Tower's very incompleteness makes other architectures, not to mention the multiplicity of languages, possible. So, Derrida says (1986):

> Perhaps it is characteristic of postmodernism to take this failure into account. If modernism distinguishes itself by the striving for absolute domination, then postmodernism might be the realisation or the experience of its end, the end of its plan of domination. The postmodern could develop a new relationship with the divine which would no longer be manifest in the traditional shapes of the Greek, Christian or other deities, but would set the conditions for architectural thinking.

Visiocentrism

Just as Derrida saw language studies as 'everywhere and always' dominated by Phonocentrism: the 'privileging' of speech over writing, so architectural studies have been dominated, even more certainly, by the 'privileging' of vision over the other senses. Architecture has been seen as entirely a visual matter. I argued in *Design in Architecture* that seeing should be taken in context with the other senses: of hearing, touch and smell, of other less familiar senses such as those of heat and cold, of position and movement, and so on; not that there's been much sign of such sensory, Empirical thinking in most 'Deconstructionist' architecture, with honourable exceptions such as Tschumi's *promenade cinématique*, or Gehry's light shafts and framed views. Even these are visual but at least Gehry's concern is with the delight of light.

No, most 'Deconstructionist' architecture has been a matter of more abstract visual delight; of stunning visual effects especially in drawings and models. The other senses have had fairly short shrift in Deconstructionist thinking; indeed Eisenman, with his 'scaling', has tried to suppress *any* reference at all to the human beings for whom most buildings are designed in the first place. A true 'Deconstructionist' view in architecture surely would challenge the prevailing Visiocentrism to redress the balance between vision and the other senses, much as Derrida tries to redress the balance between speech which he sees as 'privileged' and writing which he sees as suppressed.

In 'Deconstruction', the crucial point is architectural thinking. Anything which stimulates that must be worthy of our attention and for all his complexities and contradictions, ambiguities and sheer incomprehensibilities, Derrida has succeeded in doing that. Otherwise there would have been no such journal as this!

REFERENCES

Aristotle, *Metaphysics*, trans 1927 by Tredennick, M A, 2 vols, Loeb Classical Library, Harvard University Press, Cambridge, Mass and Heinemann, London.

Auricoste, I and Tonka, H (1987) *Vaisseau de Pierres 2, Parc-Ville Villette*, Champ Vallon, Paris.

Barthes, R (1953) *Le Degré Zéro de l'écriture*, Editions du Seuil, Paris, trans 1967 by Lavers A and Smith, C, as *Writing Degree Zero*, Jonathan Cape, London.

Barthes, R (1970) *S/Z*, Editions du Seuil, Paris, trans 1974 by Miller, R as *S/Z*, Farrar, Straus and Giroux: Jonathan Cape, London.

Barthes, R (1957) *Mythologies*, Editions du Seuil, Paris, trans 1972 by Lavers, A, Jonathan Cape, London.

Cornford, F M (1937) *Plato's Cosmology: the Timaeus of Plato*, translated with a running commentary, Routledge and Kegan Paul, London.

Derrida, J (1962) *Introduction à 'L'Origine de la géometrie' de Husserl*, Presses Universitaires de France, trans (1978) Leavey, J P as *Edmund Husserl's Origin of Geometry: An Introduction/Jacques Derrida*, N Hays, Stony Brook, New York, 1989, edn consulted, University of Nebraska Press, Lincoln and London.

Derrida, J (1967A) *De la Grammatologie*, trans Spivak, G C as *Of Grammatology*, 1976 by Johns Hopkins University Press, Baltimore.

Derrida, J (1967B) *La Voix et le Phénomènone: introduction au problème du signe dans la phénoménologie de Husserl*, PUF, Paris, trans, 1973 as *Speech and Phenomena and other Essays on Husserl's Theory of Signs*, Northwestern University Press, Evanston.

Derrida, (1967C) *L'Ecriture et la Différence*, trans 1978, with Introduction and Additional Notes by Bass, Chicago University Press, Routledge and Kegan Paul, London.

Derrida, (1968A) 'Ousia and Grammé: Note on a Note from Being and Time' in *L'endurance de la pensée: Pour saluer Jean Beaufret*, Plon, Paris, reprinted in Derrida, *Marges: de la philosophie*.

Derrida, J (1968B) 'The Pit and the Pyramid: Introduction to Hegel's Semiology' Lecture at the *Collège de France* published (1971) in *Hegel et la pensée moderne*, PUF coll Epimethée and reprinted in Derrida, *Marges: de la philosophie*.

Derrida, J (1972) *La Dissémination*, Editions du Seuil, Paris, trans, 1981 by Johnson, B as *Dissemination*, University of Chicago Press, Athlone Press, London.

Derrida, J (1972) *Marges: de la Philosophie*, Minuit, Paris, trans 1982 by Bass, as *Margins of Philosophy* University of Chicago Press, Harvester Press, Hassocks.

Derrida, J (1972) *Positions, Entretiens avec Henri Ronge, Julia Kristeva, Jean-Louis Houdeline, Guy Scarpetta*, Minuit, Paris, trans 1981 by Bass, A as *Positions*, University of Chicago Press, Chicago, (1987) Athlone Press, London.

Derrida, J (1976) 'Fors: Les Mots Anglés N Abraham et M Torok' Preface to Abraham, N and Torok, M (1976) *Cryptonymie: Le Verbier de l'homme aux loups*, Flammarion, Paris, trans 1977 by Johnson B as 'Fors' in *The Georgia Review* 31, 1977.

Derrida, J (1985) 'Point de Folie – Maintenant Architecture' in Tschumi, B, *La Case Vide: La Villette*, reprinted in *AA Files* No 12, Summer 1986, Architectural Association, London.

Derrida, J (1986) 'Architetture ove il desiderio più abitare – Interview by Eva Meyer' in *Domus* No 671 April, 1986.

Derrida, J (1987A) 'Cinquante-deux aphorismes pour un avant-propos' in *Psyché* Derrida (1987A), Galilée, Paris, trans, Benjamin, A (1988a) as 'Fifty-Two Aphorisms for a Foreword' for Deconstruction, Academy Forum at the Tate, 28 March 1988, Academy Editions and Tate Gallery, London. Also published in *Deconstruction*, ed by A Papadakis, C Cooke and A Benjamin, 1989, Academy Editions, London and St Martin's Press, New York.

Derrida, J (1987B) 'Pourquoi Peter Eisenman écrit de si bons livres' in *Psyché*, Galilée, Paris, trans, 1988 as 'Why Peter Eisenman writes such good books' in *A+U* 1988/8.

Derrida, J (1987C) *De l'Esprit,* 1989 by Editions Galilée, Paris, trans Bennington, G and Bowley, R as *Of Spirit: Heidegger and the Question*, University of Chicago Press.

Derrida, J and others (1987C) *Mésure pour mésure: Architecture et Philosophie*, Cahiers du CCI, Centre Georges Pompidou, Paris.

Derrida, J (1988) Filmed interview with Norris, C for Deconstruction, Academy Forum at the Tate, and published in *Deconstruction*, 1989, Academy Editions.

Descartes, R (1637) *Discours sur la Méthode*, trans, 1960 by Wollaston, A as *Discourse on Method*, Penguin Books, Harmondsworth.

Descartes, R (1641) *Meditations,* trans, 1960 by Wollaston, A as *Meditations*, Penguin Books, Harmondsworth.

Eisenman, P and Derrida, J (1986) *Oeuvre Choral: Choral work* see Tschumi (1987), Auricoste, I and Tonka, H (1987), Derrida (1987B), Eisenman (1988A) and (1988B) '*Choral works: Parc de la Villette*' in *A+U* 1988/8, also Tschumi (1987) in Auricoste, I and Tonka, H (1987) and Derrida (1987B).

Eisenman, P (1980-81) 'Berlin Housing, West Berlin, 1982-86', in Eisenman, P (1988) and Graafland, A (1989).

Eisenman, P (1985) *Moving Arrows, Eros, and other Errors: An Architecture of Absence*, Third International Architectural Biennale: Venice, Italy 1985, Box 3, (1986) London, The Architectural Association, in Eisenman, P (1988) and Graafland, A (1989).

Eisenman P and Derrida J (1986-present) 'Choral Works/Parc de la Villette, Paris, France', in Eisenman, P (1988).

Eisenman, P (1988) 'Peter Eisenman,' *A+U,* August 1988.

Ellis, J M (1989) *Against Deconstruction*, Princeton, N J, Princeton University Press.

Foucault, M (1961) *Histoire de la Folie,* Plon, Paris, trans 1967 as *Madness and Civilization,* Tavistock Publications, London.

Foucault, M (1969) *Archaéologie de la savoir*, Gallimard, Paris, trans 1972 by Sheridan Smith, A M as *The Archaeology of Knowledge*, Tavistock Publications, London.

Graafland, A (Ed, 1989) *Recente projecten: Peter Eisenman: Recent projects*, CIP, Den Haag.

Heidegger M (1927) *Sein und Zeit* Max Niemeyer, Tubingen, trans 1962 by Macquarrie, J and Robinson, E as *Being and Time*, Basil Blackwell, Oxford.

Heidegger, M (1929) 'Was is Metaphysik?' Inaugural Lecture as Professor of Philosophy at Tübingen, trans by Hull, R F C and Crick, A as 'What is Metaphysics?' in Brock, W and others (1949) *Existence and Being by Martin Heidegger*, Vision Press, London.

Heidegger (1953) *Einführung in die Metaphysik Max Niemeyer*, Tübingen, trans 1959 by Manheim, R as *An Introduction to Metaphysics*, Yale University Press, Newhaven.

Heidegger, M (1955) 'Uber "Die Linie"' trans 1959 by Kluback, W and Wilde, J T as 'Concerning "The Line"' in *The Question of Being*, Vision Press, London.

Heidegger, M (1954) 'Bauen Wohnen Denken' in *Vorträge und Aufsätze*, Pfulklingen, Neske, trans 1971 by Hofstadter, A as 'Building, Dwelling, Thinking' in *Poetry, Language, Thought*, Harper and Row, New York.

Hirsch, E D (1983) 'Derrida's Axioms: Review of Culler, J' (1983) 'On Deconstruction' in *London Review of Books*, 31 July-3 August, 1983.

Husserl, E (1913-022) *Logische Untersuchungen*, trans 1970 by Findlay, J N as *Logical Investigations*, Routledge and Kegan Paul, London.

Husserl, E (1913) *Ideen au einer reinen Phänomenologie und phänomenologischen Philosophie*, trans 1931 by Boyce Gibson, W R as *Ideas: General Introduction to Pure Phenomenology*, Macmillan Publishing Co, New York and trans, Kertsten, F (1983) as *Ideas Pertaining to a Pure Phenomenology and to Phenomenological Psychology,* (2 Vols) Martinus Nijhoff, The Hague/Boston/Lancaster.

Husserl, E (1936) 'Der Ursprung der Geometrie als intentional-historisches Problem', trans Derrida, J (1974) in *L'Origine de la*

Géométrie, traduction et introduction par Jacques Derrida, Presses Universitaires de France, Paris, trans 1978 by Leavey J P as *Edmund Husserl's Origin of Geometry, An Introduction by Jacques Derrida*, 1979, University of Nebraska Press, Lincoln and London.

Internationalle Situationniste (1958) 'Définitions' in *Internationalle Situationiste,* No 1, June 1958, trans as 'Definitions' in Blazwick, I, and others *An endless adventure . . . an endless passion . . . an endless banquet,* ICA V, Verso, London.

Kant, I (1781) *Critique*, trans 1966 by Müllere, M as *Critique of Pure Reason*, edn consulted, Anchor Books, Doubleday & Co, New York.

Kipnis, J (1989) 'The Law of Ana- On Choral Works', in Graafland, A (1989).

Lévi-Strauss, C (1960) *Chaire d'Anthropologie sociale. Leçon inaugurale fait le 6 janvier 1960* par M Claude Lévi-Strauss, Professor Collège de France, Paris, trans 1967 by Paul, S O and Psaul, R A as *The Scope of Anthropology*, Jonathan Cape, London.

Plato, *The Republic,* trans with introduction and notes by Cornford, F M (1941) Oxford University Press.

Plato, *Phaedrus,* trans 1932 by Fowler, H A, Loeb Classical Library: Harvard University Press: Heinemann, London.

Rousseau, J J (1781) *Les Confessions*, trans 1953 by Cohen, J M as *Confessions,* Penguin Books, Harmondsworth.

Rousseau, J J (1751) *Essai sur l'Origine de Langage*, trans 1966 by Moran, J H as *On the Origin of Language*, New York.

Saussure, F de (1907-13) *Cours en Linguistique Générale*, trans 1960 by Baskin, W as *Course in General Linguistics*, Peter Owen, London.

Tschumi, B (1976) *Screenplays*.

Tschumi, B (1976) *Joyce's Garden*, theoretical project based on Joyce's *Finnegan's Wake*, exhibited at the Centre Pompidou, Paris, 1980.

Tschumi, B (1981) *The Manhattan Transcripts*, Academy Editions, London and St Martin's Press, New York.

Tschumi, B (1983) 'Illustrated Index: Themes from the "Manhattan Transcripts"' in *AA Files* No 4, July 1983, Architectural Association, London.

Tschumi, B (1984) 'Work in Progress in *L'Invention du Parc*' Editions Graphite, Paris.

Tschumi, B (1985) *La Case Vide*, twenty plates exploring future conceptual transformations and dislocations of the Villette project, with an essay on Bernard Tschumi by Jacques Derrida, an introduction by Anthony Vidler and an interview by Alvin Boyarsky, AA Folio VIII, Architectural Association, London.

Tschumi, B (1987) *Cinégramme Folie, le Parc de la Villette*, Champ-Vallon, Paris and Princeton University Press, Princeton, New Jersey.

Tschumi, B (1988) 'Parc de la Villette, Paris' in *Architectural Design*, Vol 58 3/4 1988.

Tschumi, B (1988) 'Notes towards a Theory of Deconstruction' in *Architecture and Urbanism* No 216, September 1988.

Vitruvius *De Architectura*, trans 1914 by Morgan, W H as *The Ten Books of Architecture*, Harvard University Press, Cambridge, Mass, reprinted (1969) Dover Publications, New York, also trans, Grainger, F (1934) as *Vitruvius on Architecture* Vols I and 11, Loeb Classical Library, Harvard University Press and Heinemann, London.

Zevi, B (1988) Letter to members of the *Cirque Internationale des Critiques d'Architecture*, August 15 1988.

AND THE FOLLOWING GENERAL REFERENCE WORKS:

Oxford English Dictionary.

Webster's Third New International Dictionary.

Encyclopaedia Brittanica.

Harrap's New Shorter French and English Dictionary.

Lewis, C T and Short, S (1879) *Latin Dictionary, founded on Andreu's Edition of Freund's Latin Dictionary*, revised and enlarged in great part, rewritten by Charlton T Lewis and Charles Short, Clarendon Press, Oxford.

Liddell, H G and Scott, S (1897) A *Greek/English Lexicon compiled by Henry George Liddell and Robert Scott*, new (9th) edition revised and augmented throughout by Sir Henry Stuart Jones with the assistance of Roderick McKenzie (1940), Clarendon Press, Oxford.